MULTILINGUAL ARTIFICIAL INTELLIGENCE

Multilingual Artificial Intelligence is a guide for non–computer science specialists and learners looking to explore the implementation of AI technologies to solve real-life problems involving language data.

Focusing on multilingual, multicultural, pre-trained large language models and their practical use through fine-tuning and prompt engineering, Wang and Smith demonstrate how to apply this new technology in areas such as information retrieval, semantic webs, and retrieval augmented generation, to improve both human productivity and machine intelligence. Finally, they discuss the human impact of language technologies in the cultural context, and provide an AI competence framework for users to design their own learning journey.

This innovative text is essential reading for all students, professionals, and researchers in language, linguistics, and related areas looking to understand how to integrate multilingual and multicultural artificial intelligence technology into their research and practice.

Peng Wang is an IT analyst and the chair of the Multilingual AI Track. She is the co-author of *Machine Learning in Translation*.

Pete Smith is Professor of Modern Languages at the University of Texas Arlington, where he also serves as Chief Analytics and Data Officer.

MULTILINGUAL ARTIFICIAL INTELLIGENCE

Peng Wang and Pete Smith

Routledge
Taylor & Francis Group

LONDON AND NEW YORK

Designed cover image: Getty Images | peterhowell

First published 2025
by Routledge
4 Park Square, Milton Park, Abingdon, Oxon OX14 4RN

and by Routledge
605 Third Avenue, New York, NY 10158

Routledge is an imprint of the Taylor & Francis Group, an informa business

British Library Cataloguing-in-Publication Data
A catalogue record for this book is available from the British Library

Library of Congress Cataloging-in-Publication Data
A catalog record has been requested for this book

ISBN: 978-1-032-74724-8 (hbk)
ISBN: 978-1-032-74722-4 (pbk)
ISBN: 978-1-003-47055-7 (ebk)

DOI: 10.4324/9781003470557

Typeset in Galliard
by codeMantra

CONTENTS

FIGURES

TABLES

PREFACE

Pete and I have been working to further research and educate students and others about multilingual and multicultural artificial intelligence (AI) for over a decade. However, we have consistently encountered challenges as a direct result of the limited curricular resources currently available for learners. This is particularly true for those who feel they do not have sufficient technical knowledge in this field.

As faculty members who come primarily from linguistics and communication backgrounds, with relevant technical skills, we aspire to reach a wider audience. Multilingual AI includes a variety of loosely connected techniques, used to process naturally occurring texts and achieve human-like processing in multilingual settings. To begin, as these techniques are typically organized and approached from a technical perspective, it is not surprising that AI has been primarily the domain of computer science. It stands to reason that there is often a steep learning curve for general users, including students who are our future linguists and language professionals.

With numerous generative pre-trained (GPT) models now available to the public, learners and general users can directly interact and experiment with AI tools and systems. These tools have become more accessible, helping people study, work, communicate, collaborate, and solve problems at a previously unseen scale involving language data. It is necessary to bring awareness of multilingual AI to a diverse audience, to readers and learners who will be able to use this technology in a responsible and ethical manner. With this book, our hope is to democratize and disseminate knowledge, as well as to develop skills and techniques in this ever-expanding and rapidly changing field.

This book contains three parts. The first two (from Chapters 1 to 7) were written by Peng Wang, focusing on the fundamentals of multilingual AI, as well as theories and implementations of Large Language Models. The last part (from Chapters 8 to 10), primarily on the topic of culture and multicultural AI, was penned by Pete Smith. We collaborated with each other throughout the process, regarding content consistency and linguistic style.

Our work was supported by Dr. Rachel Herwartz. In particular, all through Sections 7.3.2 to 7.3.4 in Chapter 7, Dr. Herwartz offered her pertinent and inspiring ideas to the authors. She also made her terminology platform available. In addition, Dr. Herwartz co-designed the case study in Section 7.3.4, with regard to the term definitions for LLM prompts.

While conceptualizing Chapters 1 to 7 of this manuscript, Megan Reid worked with Peng to improve her writing and define a logical flow of ideas. As a friend, Megan's support helped Peng motivate and pace her writing throughout this process.

As educators, we also wanted to add: writing a book-length manuscript has reminded us that teachers are also learners themselves. As we conceived of and wrote the book you now hold, we ourselves developed and sharpened our knowledge of the exciting field of multilingual AI. We are both also grateful for this process of authorship, growth, and change.

Thank you,

Peng Wang and Pete Smith

PART ONE

Fundamentals of multilingual artificial intelligence

1

MULTILINGUAL AI IN A MATHEMATICAL THEORY OF COMMUNICATION

1.1 Interdisciplinary collaboration: computational applications to multilingual natural language

Since civilization began between 4,000 and 3,000 BC, human beings have experienced a range of paradigm shifts. To begin, there was the agricultural revolution, followed by the industrial revolution, and now artificial intelligence (AI) has begun to impact everyday life. These seismic transitions are all closely related to the emergence of new tools and methodologies as well as their underlying theories. In February 1946, the first programmable general-purpose electronic digital computer, known as the Electronic Numerical Integrator and Computer (ENIAC), was produced (Freiberger & Swaine, 2024). At that time, not many people could have imagined how this new technology might disrupt life as they knew it. Further, digital computers allow a more practical, interdisciplinary collaboration between those who work with technology (such as scientists and mathematicians) and those who work primarily in human spaces (such as linguistics and other domain experts). In this sense, computers not only demonstrate a technological breakthrough, but they also allow domain experts to effectively explore their problem space as well as experiment with relevant computational methods to solve their problems.

One example of such interdisciplinary collaboration is the application of computational technology to multilingual communication, an exchange of information among members of various linguistic and cultural groups. By working together with these groups, technology experts successfully apply "a theoretically motivated range of computational techniques" to multilingual natural language, for example, to analyze and represent naturally occurring texts at different linguistic levels (Liddy, 2001, p. 1). The interdisciplinary interest and collaboration fostered the origin and development of some new disciplines, including natural language processing (NLP), which aims to make use of computational techniques to achieve humanlike language processing for a range of tasks or applications, for example, knowledge base question answering, speech recognition, and summary (Liddy, 2001, p. 1).

Regarding applications invented to solve real-life problems, the experiment of machine translation (MT) must be highlighted. It is not a coincidence that MT was unanimously

DOI: 10.4324/9781003470557-2

identified as the first substantial attempt for computers to solve non-numerical problems (Hutchins, 2004). Language is a natural area for computational and mathematical tools to demonstrate its power in synthesizing technological advantages and social influence. In March 1947, Warren Weaver wrote to Norbert Wiener, both of whom were mathematicians and scientists, expressing a desire "to design a computer which would translate" (Weaver, 1947; cited from Norman n.d.). His idea was soon implemented, when the IBM-Georgetown experiment demonstrated a Russian-English MT system in New York in 1954. It was the first computer-based application related to multilingual natural language (Hutchins, 2004). Since then, multilingual AI has undergone multiple major breakthroughs, from modularized models, to end-to-end artificial neural networks (ANNs), progressing to generative large language models (LLMs). Its emphases have been shifting from classical symbolic AI, or GOFAI ("Good old fashioned artificial intelligence"), to statistical as well as connectionist approaches, then to a holistic view which takes both symbolic AI and deep learning into consideration.

In its early development, multilingual AI tasks were primarily performed in the fields of science and engineering. This is not surprising, as the learning curves for computer science and engineering are relatively steep for linguists and other domain experts, who usually have a solid understanding of symbolic knowledge and intuitive recognition of the way the world works, rather than computational knowledge and skills. Since 2017, when the Transformer neural network architecture (Vaswani et al., 2017) was proposed, an increasing number of generative pre-trained (GPT) models such as OpenAI's ChatGPT have become widely accessible to the public, including domain experts in addition to the general users. In effect, it calls for and facilitates a more direct application of computational techniques to real-life problems, and thus raises requirements for all stakeholders concerning their cultural knowledge associated with these naturally occurring texts, as well as basic knowledge of multilingual AI tools and algorithms. On the one hand, this encourages use of major tools such as LLMs to linguists or social scientists, who were previously only tangentially engaged in model creation and use. On the other hand, it also allows computer scientists and engineers to step out of their comfort zone to take more linguistic and cultural factors into their development and deployment processes. Consequently, multiple roles have evolved and tend to integrate in multilingual AI technology development and application. For example, a developer can be both developing the tool and serving as a domain expert, who is also a user, and analyzes other users' needs like a researcher and asks other developers to develop these tools as a client.

This book aims to bridge the gap between various stakeholders in a multilingual communication process, who tend to study the same problem from different angles. By introducing basic concepts, algorithms, and applications of conventional as well as new, emerging technologies in multilingual artificial intelligence, the authors seek to find the common ground between these angles, which helps project participants effectively communicate with each other and facilitate interdisciplinary collaboration.

1.2 Artificial intelligence and cognition: deep learning and symbolic AI

Since McCarthy et al. (1955) coined the term artificial intelligence, it has been used as an umbrella term covering a broad field of science, encompassing not only computer science, but also psychology, philosophy, linguistics, and other areas. Consequently, as Wang and

Sawyer (2023, pp. 2–3) pointed out, many definitions of AI have emerged to highlight specific aspects, including computer science (Simon, 1995), intelligence (McCarthy, 2007; Nilson, 2009), and cultural elements (Gardner, 2003).

From a computational perspective, a definitive element of human-level artificial intelligence in deep learning lies in its generalization capabilities, that is, its ability to produce sensible answers in response to new inputs that it never encountered during training (LeCun et al., 2015, p. 437). Deep learning is "an approach to machine learning that involves training neural networks with many feed-forward layers on large datasets" (Garnelo & Shanahan, 2019, p. 17). Deep learning models in natural language applications are neural language models, which are used to convert a word symbol into a word vector (or word embedding) composed of learned semantic features in order to predict the next word in a sequence (Bengio et al., 2001, pp. 932–8). Once trained, intermediate processing layers between the input and output layers can be thought of as representations of the training data with multiple levels of abstraction (LeCun et al., 2015, pp. 440–1).

Before the introduction of neural language models, the standard approach to statistical modeling of language was based on counting frequencies of N-grams, that is, occurrences of short symbol sequences of length up to N. For example, the sentence "The cat is on the mat" can be divided into five short sequences, each of which consists of two words, that is, 'The cat', 'cat is', 'is on', 'on the', and 'the mat'. This is a bigram language model that examines the sentence in a two-word window. N-gram language models limit their generalization ability, as N-grams treat each word as an atomic unit, and thus cannot generalize across semantically related sequences of words. Conversely, neural language models associate each word with a vector of real valued features. Relationships between vector representations of words learned from text can be measured by mathematical calculations in a vector space. Semantically related words are closer to each other in that vector space (LeCun et al., 2015, p. 441). Chapter 4 will further elaborate on the inner workings of this generalization ability.

Unlike deep learning, symbolic artificial intelligence is an umbrella term to cover a wide range of AI areas that are based on high-level, human-readable symbolic representations of problems, logic, and searches (Garnelo & Shanahan, 2019). Focusing on the processing and manipulation of symbols or concepts, rather than numerical data, symbolic AI is deductive, top-down, and rule-based. It "works by carrying out a series of logic-like reasoning steps over language-like representations" (Garnelo & Shanahan, 2019, p. 17). Examples of symbolic AI include "expert systems based on production rules, automated reasoning and planning, theorem provers and verification" (Maruyama, 2020, p. 138). Natural language is a symbol system (Fodor, 1975), which is manipulable by rules based on the arbitrary shapes of words, that is, language-like representations. Such representations are typically propositional in character, asserting certain relations between certain objects and carrying out a series of logic-like reasoning steps according to a formally specified set of inference rules. Because of their language-like, propositional character, symbolic representations are amenable to human understanding (Garnelo & Shanahan, 2019, pp. 17–18). Consequently, human intelligence is more impactful in the symbolic paradigm with semantic interpretability (meaningfulness), which is one of the defining features of cognitivism (Harnad, 1994).

Unlike deep learning, intelligence in a symbolic paradigm of AI results from the manipulation of abstract compositional representations whose elements stand for objects and relations, which align with a hallmark of human intelligence, that is, the ability to re-use previously acquired experience as well as expertise, and transfer it to radically different challenges (Garnelo & Shanahan, 2019, p. 17). What really facilitates this transfer is the system's ability to extract explicit, formal rules that apply to both circumstances. For example, representations in symbolic AI conform to the principle of compositionality, that is, the denotation of a representation is a function of the denotation of its parts and the way those parts are combined. Thus, a symbolic AI system with compositionality has potential to create new combinations of objects and relations, similar to the way a child can imagine a rubber duck in a fish bowl even though he or she has probably never seen it in this specific context. However, it is entirely plausible that the child has encountered a rubber duck, a fish bowl, and even a rubber duck in a bathtub. In this example, a symbolic AI system demonstrates the ability to form abstractions and generalize beyond the system's past experience.

Overall, in both approaches, a system's ability to generalize can help distinguish between intelligent and non-intelligent technologies. For example, a typical Computer Assisted Translation (CAT) system, which aims to assist humans in their translating process by referring to previous work (i.e., translation memory) as well as extracting translatable strings for translators does not provide this generalization ability. In this sense, a CAT tool is not necessarily intelligent (Wang, 2024). Typically, a CAT environment is embedded with some AI features. For example, when a CAT system encounters a fuzzy translation memory (a sentence that is similar to a previous translation, but is not a 100% exact match with that translation), it refers to a second set of rules that follow these procedures: To begin, identify terminology that is different within the new sentence and the previous one. For example, if the translation memory includes the following sentence, "A cat is on the mat" and the new sentence to be translated is "A dog is on the mat," the word 'dog' is the new element. Second, refer to the system's term base to see if there is a term 'dog'. If so, replace the translation of 'dog' in the translation of the sentence in the translation memory. For example, the system first uses the French translation "Un chat est sur le tapis" in its translation memory, and then replaces the word 'chat' with 'chien' (French translation of the word 'dog'), according to its term base. As a result, the system generates the requested translation "Un chien est sur le tapis" for the source sentence "A dog is on the mat." Such an automatic combination of rules can be considered a type of rule-based generalization ability, when it 'translates', or rather, processes sentences that the system did not see previously. In many cases, human interventions are needed after automation as the abstracted rules and summary of logic-like reasoning steps cannot exhaust the list of patterns within all instances of natural language.

Note that in deep learning, semantic features of words are 'learned', that is, automatically discovered, by neural networks, rather than determined ahead of time by experts. Symbolic AI assumes that human knowledge representation is symbolic and that reasoning, language, planning and vision could be understood in terms of symbolic operations. Conversely, deep learning is based on neuron-like "subsymbolic" computations (e.g., Fukushima, 1980; Grossberg, 1976; Rosenblatt, 1958; see Lake et al., 2017, p. 7). As Harnad (1994) pointed out, the "language of thought" (Fodor, 1975) could be modeled in two forms: (1) the symbolic model of the mind, and (2) the model that conforms to deep learning, variously described as "neural networks," "parallel distributed processing," and "connectionism." In a symbolic model, the mind is "a symbol system and cognition is symbol manipulation." The possibility of generating complex output through symbol manipulation could be empirically simulated in the field of artificial intelligence (Harned, 1999). Conversely, the knowledge learned by neural networks in deep learning is distributed across the collection of units rather than localized as in most symbolic data structures (Lake et al., 2017, p. 7). Overall, deep learning and symbolic AI represent a distinction between the logic-inspired and the neural-network-inspired paradigms for cognition.

In addition, these two types of learning vary when it comes to their reliance on computation and data. As LeCun et al. (2015) pointed out, deep learning "requires very little engineering by hand, so it can easily take advantage of increases in the amount of available computation and data" (p. 436). Conversely, symbolic AI tends to be abstract, and often labor-intensive, lending itself to re-use in multiple tasks, which promotes data efficiency (Garnelo & Shannahan, 2019, p. 17).

To some degree, both symbolic AI and deep learning are mirroring two aspects of cognition, one is a symbolic, human-amenable paradigm, while the other one is statistical, and in the case of deep learning, subsymbolic. These two aspects represent deductive reasoning and inductive learning. Each of which "would be arguably the two fundamental wheels of the human mind" (Maruyama, 2020, pp. 129–30). In other words, both symbolic AI and deep learning are demonstrations of applying different types or aspects of human intelligence in a machine system.

Symbolic AI is usually considered classical artificial intelligence, which was "arguably the dominant approach until the late 1980s" (Garnelo & Shanahan, 2019, p. 17). Deep learning, in particular after 2017 when Vaswani et al. introduced a 'self-attention' mechanism that has been shown to be very effective in discovering relational structure in data, has achieved notable successes including commercially important applications such as OpenAI's ChatGPT. However, contemporary deep learning has a number of shortcomings, including (1) data inefficiency: Today's neural networks require large volumes of training data to be effective, while a human only needs to draw on limited amount of past experience; (2) poor generalization: Today's neural networks are prone to fail disastrously when exposed to data outside the distribution they were trained on, while a human is able to re-use previously acquired experience and expertise, to transfer it to radically different challenges; and (3) lack of interpretability: Today's neural networks are typically 'black boxes', with computations carried out by successive layers that rarely correspond to comprehensible reasoning steps (Garnelo & Shanahan, 2019, pp. 17–18).

Researchers have begun to look for ways to incorporate relevant ideas from symbolic AI in a deep learning framework. For example, Garnelo and Shanahan (2019) proposed reconciling deep learning with symbolic artificial intelligence. In particular, Garnelo and Shanahan (2019) focused on developing deep learning architectures capable of discovering objects and relations in raw data, and learning how to represent them in ways that are useful for downstream processing.

1.3 Multilingual artificial intelligence

In this book, the term multilingual artificial intelligence can refer to any intelligent computational technologies and algorithms as discussed in Section 1.2, including symbolic, deep learning, and integrated (both symbolic and deep learning) approaches to AI. Multilingual AI allows humans to lend their abstraction capabilities to machines or to interface with machine learning processes and leverage ML results in their daily communication processes. In particular, with the advent of large language models (LLMs), multilingual AI technologies have never been this accessible to the general public before. A range of user-friendly interfaces, such as chat and traditional graphic user interface (GUI), helps revolutionize human capabilities to effectively implement these technologies to solve real-life problems. Furthermore, a variety of LLMs aims to include a wider range of human languages, which weaves a more representative picture of humanity. For example, as a cross-lingual large language model, XLM-R is a transformer-based masked language model trained on one hundred languages, using more than two terabytes of filtered CommonCrawl data (Conneau et al., 2020). XLM-R will be further elaborated on in Chapter 4. Being such an impactful technology, multilingual AI provides individuals with new dimensions to their original thought patterns and cultural considerations, in addition to practical applications. As an indispensable part of cross-lingual communication, multilingual AI helps redefine the way the industry evolves on a daily basis. Specifically, some new features associated with relevant concepts in AI-driven multilingual communicative processes have surfaced or been highlighted:

1 Multilingual AI and thought

    a With the large scale of accessibility to multilingual AI technologies and their 'intelligence' features, it is important to include a dimension of how they impact and reshape humans' thought patterns. In this sense, tools are not only a form of technology, but more importantly, a theoretical framework for humans to structure their solutions as well as their underlying thoughts when solving problems.

    b In deep learning, underlying meaning in text is represented in multiple layers with real-valued vectors at different levels of abstraction. This provides a fresh lens for humans to process and understand meaning in mathematical terms. The results a deep learning model generates do not only provide functionality such as answering questions and translating text. Furthermore, the generated results allow observers to make inferences about how a mathematical approach to meaning differs from intuitive human creations. Such 'behavioral' observation provides a vehicle for people to understand the commonalities and differences between cognition and deep learning mechanisms.

2 A bigger picture of language

    a The concept of language has a broad definition in this book, including instances of natural language (human-generated language), synthetic or 'artificial' language (machine-generated language), as well as other language variants, such as computer programming language (an 'artificial' language for both machines (or compilers) and humans to read, execute and evaluate).

    b When natural language processing was first introduced as an academic discipline, it focused on 'naturally occurring texts' (Liddy, 2001, p. 1). In an age of generative AI (genAI), however, synthetic data is also used for deep learning purposes. Artificial language produced by genAI, for example, machine translation results, have started to play a more significant role in human communication.

    c With the rise of deep learning, multilingual AI applications are increasingly used to serve machines. For example, MT back translation is used to generate synthetic data to train a model in order to create more 'artificial' language instances. Yet the ultimate results, the generated 'non-natural' language data, is used for human communication. Considering the ultimate purpose of applying AI in multilingual communication, the primary aim is to serve human needs.

d As the term indicates, 'multilingual' means more than one language. This adds an extra layer of complexity to regular AI activities. A multilingual language model is typically trained on parallel data, although some models are based on unsupervised learning (e.g. unsupervised machine translation). For example, neural machine translation systems are trained on parallel corpora, which include many aligned source and target segments. As discussed in Section 1.2, neural MT can take advantage of available computation and data. Typically, there is a positive relationship between the amount of parallel data and neural MT performance. This correlation is ideal for high-resource languages, such as English, French, and Chinese. In these languages and language combinations (e.g., English to French, French to English), abundant resources are available, including parallel corpora, bi- or multilingual dictionaries, and translators or bilingual (multilingual) linguists. However, as Magueresse et al. (2020) pointed out, "most of today's NLP research focuses on 20 of the 7000 languages of the world, leaving the vast majority of languages understudied." These languages are often referred to as low-resource languages (LRLs), which lack useful training attributes such as supervised data, number of native speakers, or experts, etc. This book aims to address this problem, for example, by introducing cross-lingual language models such as XLM-R.

3 Multilingual AI and the industry

With the rise of AI, the industry for multilingual communication has been put under a spotlight and faces unprecedented challenges. ChatGPT, for example, aims to solve NLP tasks that conventional translators or localizers primarily focus on. Voices of 'human parity' or 'super human performance' machine translation have become louder, though as Poibeau pointed out, such terms are "misleading and do not bring much benefit to the evaluation process" (Poibeau, 2022). However, despite this debate, one thing is clear: the industry is redefining itself, from completing multilingual tasks, such as translation and data annotation, to using AI and other computational technologies to manage and control the whole process of communication across languages as well as cultures.

4 Attention to the role of culture

a The application of multilingual AI is also closely related to culture. Culture is intimately intertwined with language, its history and its pragmatic usage. The concept of culture lacks a widely agreed-upon definition, but can be thought of as a complex, integrated set of attitudes, beliefs, norms, and values.

b The way humans communicate, think and act in their daily lives is also embedded in a culture (or several cultures simultaneously). The communicative processes that will be explained and modeled here are one component in the larger social and cultural context of human interaction. Multilingual communication is by definition multicultural communication. And this cultural setting is a layer that is relatively unexplored from a computational standpoint. With recent advances in language modeling and machine intelligence, these questions of culture and computed culture are front and center for researchers and practitioners.

c There are long traditions of researching and quantifying culture and cultural elements, and more recently scholars both theoretical and applied have begun to consider the role of the multicultural in communication that is impacted by tools such as large language models.

1.4 Communication and multilingual AI: symbolic and mathematical views

From a holistic perspective, multilingual communication involves humans, deep learning, and symbolic AI. When multilingual AI is involved, the concept of communication is in a broader context, including data transformation across representation layers in deep learning, information exchange among humans, and human computer interaction. If there is a theoretical framework that can help explain the underlying patterns and scope of all these types of communication, the Shannon-Weaver communication model would be a strong candidate.

1.4.1 A mathematical theory of communication

Originally, this model was proposed by Claude Shannon in his paper (although some may refer to it as a technical report given its scientific complexies) "The Mathematical Theory of Communication" (1948). This paper focused on information transmission in digital communication. Later in 1949, another scientist, Warren Weaver, added an article entitled "Recent Contributions to the Mathematical Theory of Communication" to Shannon's original technical report, which provided a panoramic view of the field before entering more mathematical aspects. In his article, Weaver pointed out that some ideas in Shannon's model can be put into a broader application of the fundamental principles of communication theory (Shannon & Weaver, 1963, preface). Weaver emphasized that the word 'communication' was used "in a very broad sense to include all of the procedures by which one mind may affect another" and communication "would include the procedures by means of which one mechanism (say automatic equipment to track an airplane and to compute its probable future positions) affects another mechanism (say a guided missile chasing this airplane)" (Shannon & Weaver, 1963, p. 3). This definition includes two aspects, with the former focused on the social cultural aspect whereas the latter focused on the information (entity) aspect. Shannon's theoretical reflections with technical details on communication laid the foundation for modern information theory. Thus, Shannon is known as the "father of information theory" (Roberts, 2016).

In the mathematical theory of communication, an information source selects a desired message out of a set of possible messages, which may consist of written or spoken words, or of pictures, music, etc. in one language or culture. Messages are converted into signals, which are sent over the communication channel from the transmitter to the receiver, who may not share the same language or culture of the source. Weaver (1949) gave an example to further explain this communication process, "When I talk to you, my brain is the information source, yours the destination; my vocal system is the transmitter, and your ear and the associated eighth nerve is the receiver." He also pointed out, "... this word information in communication theory relates not so much to what you do say, as to what you could say." The analogy here indicates that both the information source and destination are sources to conduct cognitive activities, in terms of the potential to generate information, which in mathematics, is a variable rather than a constant. The cognitive processes in both the speaker's brain (information source) and the listener's brain (the destination) can be simulated by artificial intelligence, in a mathematical approach.

Figure 1.1 illustrates this communication process in offering an example of sending and receiving telegraphs. Throughout this process, the focus is on entities (e.g., information, message, signal, received signal, received message), transmission (noisy channel), data compression through encoder (transmitter), and data decompression through decoder (receiver).

As shown in Figure 1.1, a message in English can be encoded into Morse code by a transmitter, transmitted in a noisy channel (a telegraph wire), received, and decoded by a receiver from Morse code to human readable text. The fundamental task for this model is reliable communication in unreliable channels, that is, to make the received message as close to the original message as possible.

Figure 1.1 does not indicate how a message is generated from the information source, which relates to the social-cultural elements and humans' cognitive activities in a communicative process. Figure 1.2 includes these processes using a human spoken conversation as an example.

The process involved in producing a speech segment from source idea to text messages in the information source or the reversed process involved in understanding the transmitted message from text to idea in the destination could be further elaborated on. Figure 1.2 includes three communicative subprocesses: from information source to text message in natural language, from text on the sender side to text on the receiver side, and from received text to destination. The first and the last subprocesses are internal transmissions (within the communicator, e.g., the speaker or the listener) whereas the subprocess in the middle is external transmission (from one communicator to another).

Internal transmissions happen in a mechanism in the human brain, similar to neural language models, which are used to decode the idea to natural language on the sender side and to encode the natural language to an idea on the receiver side (See Wang & Sawyer,

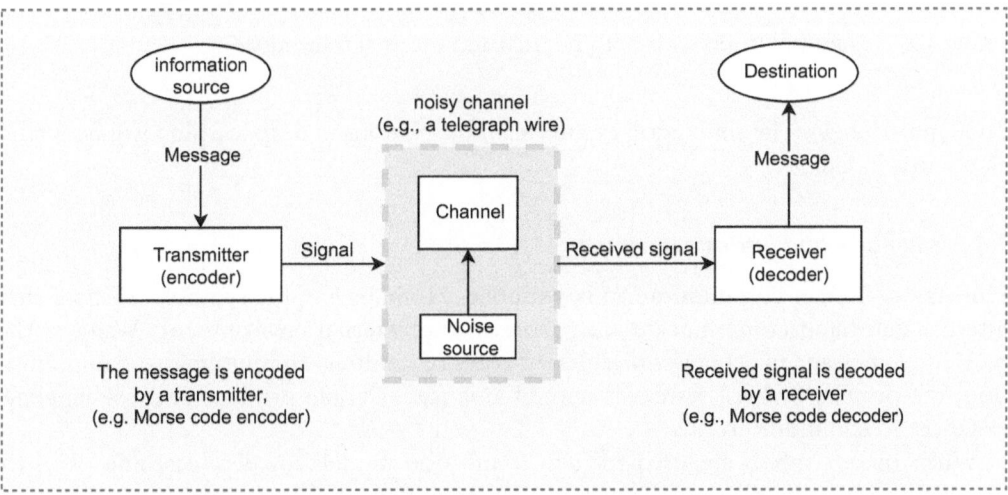

FIGURE 1.1   A mathematical theory of communication (adapted from Shannon, 1948).

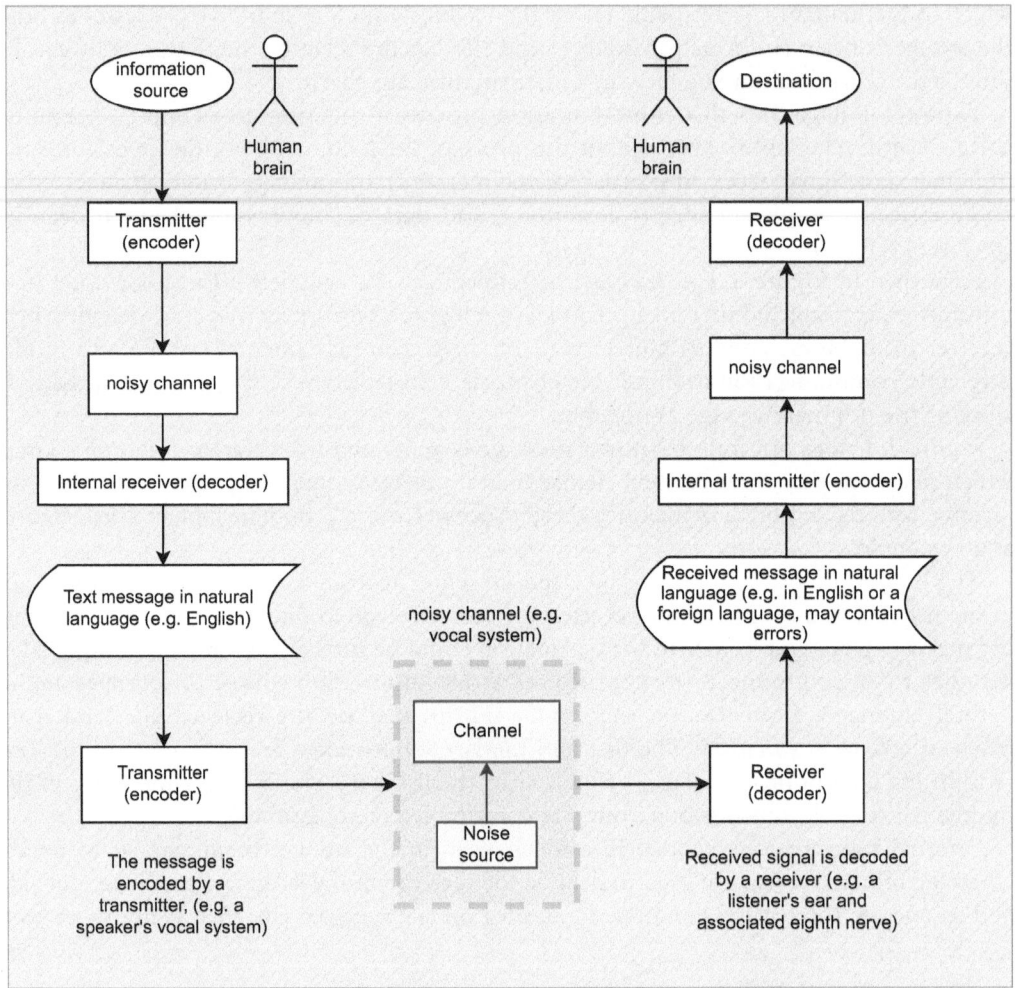

FIGURE 1.2 Communication with both internal and external transmissions.

2023, pp. 152–4). The simulation of internal transmissions in deep learning will be further elaborated in Chapter 4.

1.4.2 Symbols and intrinsic meaning

Human–to–human communication is symbolic. Humans employ symbols to share their internal states and communicate with those in the external environment (Wang, 2019, p. 273). A message may consist of different types of symbols. In multilingual communication, the primary symbol system is natural language. People produce and use language instances to communicate.

When these symbols are used to train foundation models for deep learning or in the fine-tuning stage for relevant downstream systems, they are represented in mathematical terms (vectors or embeddings). Computer programs form their own 'understanding' of text data based on word shape, and convert this 'understanding', to the best of their capabilities, back to symbols that make sense to humans. Harnad (1994) summarized fundamental features of a symbol system. It includes a set of arbitrary "physical tokens" that are manipulated on the basis of 'explicit rules'. A symbol system consists of both primitive atomic symbol tokens as well as 'rulefully combining' and recombining symbol-token strings. The entire system and all its parts, including the atomic tokens, the composite tokens, the syntactic manipulations both actual and possible, and the rules, are all 'semantically interpretable'.

If these symbols and corresponding manipulation are all based on word shape rather than meaning, everything the computer does, from receiving the input symbols, to manipulating them purely on the basis of their shape, and finally returning output symbols, does not mean the computer can understand the meaning as humans do. These symbols are systematically interpretable as having meaning, yet the interpretation is parasitic on the meanings in the mind of the interpreter, rather than intrinsic to the computer system that analyzes the symbols.

To address the problem of intrinsic meaning (or "intentionality"), also known as "the symbol grounding problem" (see Harnad, 1999; Searle, 1990), humans must be involved in a communication process. At each level of human–computer interaction, humans can use, amplify, evaluate, and correct machine generated results to accomplish their tasks, control risks, counter both intrinsic and extrinsic harms, as well as lead joint efforts by both humans and machines. Human–computer interfaces are significant control points to build multiculturalism throughout the entire process.

1.4.3   Noisy channels: a fundamental communication problem

Originally, the mathematical theory of communication was based on telecommunication practices, which primarily focused on how a message can be transmitted from one location to another or within one location yet transmitted at different times, e.g., a disk drive that stores a message (writes a binary digit) later needs to read out the stored binary digit. This theory allows individuals to use mathematical objects and formulas to quantify the information traveling over a noisy channel, for example, a telephone line (copper wire) over which two modems communicate digital information and the radio communication link from a spacecraft to the earth (MacKay, 2003, p. 3), or air that transmits sound waves from voice to the ear, or visual pathways that transmit nerve impulses from the optic nerve in the eye up to the visual processing center in our forebrain called the visual cortex (Gupta et al., 2022).

In each of the above cases, oftentimes there is some noise in these channels so the received message is not identical to the transmitted message. In order to achieve reliable communication over an unreliable channel, or noisy channel, Shannon proposed the addition of an encoder and a decoder to the communication system so it would be possible to detect and correct errors introduced by the channel (MacKay, 2003, pp. 3–5; see also Shannon, 1948; Lucky, 1967). Such an analogy applies to the basic architecture of deep learning.

In essence, reliable transmission of entity/information over a noisy channel is the fundamental problem of all communication processes. This problem applies to both social and mathematical aspects of communication. This is also the running theme of the book, which situates itself in the framework of the mathematical theory of communication, covering both human and machine aspects of multilingual AI. The power of the mathematical theory of communication lies in its ability to abstract, which is a technique to remove unnecessary details to reveal its underlying structure. As Henri Poincare stated, "Mathematics is the art of giving the same name to different things" (Verhulst, 2012). Abstraction allows people to define different mathematical objects[1] with the same structures or features no matter what specific use cases they are situated in. Without context in specific use, mathematical abstraction might seem to be independent of material reality. However, with the rise of machine or statistical learning, as well as the rapid increase of computing power and other supporting technologies (e.g. GPU and parallel computing), previously non-communicable human intuitions can be transmitted to machines with vectorization or other data processing techniques. Multilingual AI enables machines to process much more data and generate ML results that are intuitive enough for humans to interact with. For example, the 'meaning' of a sequence of words can be measured and quantified using Shannon's information theory, which focuses on the mathematical aspect.

From a social perspective, the existence of noisy channels is the primary problem of communication. In the three sub processes as shown in Figure 1.2, the noisy channels are associated with the mental language models when they convert text to idea or vice versa. In an external transmission, the noise may come from a crowded room in which a listener is unable to hear.

1.4.4 Deep learning and information theory

The main objective of a language model in deep learning, e.g., an Artificial Neural Network (ANN) model is to find a set of parameters that can produce labels that have a minimum distance from the labels produced by humans. This training objective can be quantified and measured through metrics such as the degree of randomness or entropy, when information is processed and transmitted between multiple layers of representations for the training data in neural language models. On the one hand, entropy is a fundamental concept of Shannon's mathematical theory of communication (1948); on the other, when the focus is on a mathematical representation of the conditions and parameters affecting the transmission and processing of information, it more accurately refers to information theory. In this context, information theory and communication theory overlap heavily with each other, with the latter focusing more on the detailed operation of particular devices in communication processes. (Markowsky, 2024).

The internal and the external transmissions form an analogy between the mental and neural language models in deep learning. As shown in Figure 1.2, the internal transmissions consist of a sub communication process within the information source, together with that in the destination. These two sub processes represent cognitive transmissions in human brains. Conversely, the external transmission from the information source to the destination occurs externally. It is conditioned by physical noises such as the sound of one's voice or a verbal speech pattern. However, the relationship between these two internal models is outside the scope of this project.

1.5 About this book

1.5.1 Target audience

For years, relevant disciplines associated with multilingual AI such as natural language processing (NLP) have been primarily the domain of computational linguists or computer scientists. With an increasing number of generative pre-trained (GPT) models available to the public, students and general users need to equip themselves with knowledge and skills in multilingual AI, e.g., NLP and natural language understanding (NLU). These new users bring a solid understanding of symbolic knowledge and physical realities of the world, which allow them to effectively understand problems that can be approached using AI techniques. Overall, it is possible for AI to do the heavy lifting for people in both the humanities and the sciences. For software developers, the focus of their work tends to shift from pure engineering to a larger picture that integrates both the sociocultural aspects of the problem space and applicable functionalities of technical solutions. The former sets conditions for the selection and evaluation of AI options, including those surrounding security, confidentiality, and quality assurance. Sociocultural considerations play a decisive role in AI deployment and implementation, as a business solution, rather than at an entertainment level.

This book considers a variety of aforementioned factors to entice a broader readership. Though the primary focus is the technical aspects of multilingual AI, it emphasizes a holistic, abstract angle. This approach allows the readership to integrate both human intuitive thinking and the capabilities of machines to function in multilingual communication. An approach such as this facilitates interdisciplinary collaboration among AI stakeholders, which is the key to leverage both human and machine power. Thus, the target audience for this book includes new as well as conventional users, such as domain experts, engineers, and computational linguists.

1.5.2 Characters

This book follows three primary characters.

To begin, it is necessary to address the imbalance between human and machine learning. In a production environment, it is not surprising that industry practitioners prioritize the productivity and quality of applicable AI techniques. This book, however, transcends industry boundaries. With the goal of building users' understanding of multilingual AI, this project advocates for continuous human learning as an effective method to address potential AI risks. A basic assumption of this book is as follows, given the scale of content that intelligent tools can produce, it only makes sense for humans to use machines to control machines. This includes both symbolic AI and deep learning approaches. It requires people to possess a basic AI competence in order to integrate their symbolic knowledge and AI capabilities.

Second, this book will help learners develop a systematic understanding of AI, so as to effectively manage various types of intelligent tools and human resources in a multilingual, multicultural context. In most cases, a single tool cannot solve a real-life problem. People need to design a plan that includes a set of tools for different circumstances, including symbolic AI, deep learning, as well as human intervention activities to maximize the value of human–computer collaboration. The wider accessibility of AI, while empowering people with AI technologies, has also pushed them to the forefront as coordinators, or project managers, utilizing the power of both humans and machines. While the old saying, "No man is an island", emphasizes the relationships between humans, in an era of artificial intelligence, the scope of that relationship has expanded to include both humans and machine agents.

Third, this book takes a practical, sociocultural approach to help individuals become familiar with and apply multilingual AI technologies. Before being put into practice, these technologies did not have any influence on the sociocultural environment. Only after they were leveraged to meet a certain sociocultural goal, were the effects of these tools recognized by society as a whole. These pages contain representative problems and adopt a design thinking approach to solve them. When it comes to deep learning models and systems, this book focuses on multilingual/cross-lingual large language models (LLMs), as well as using fine-tuning and prompt engineering to conduct downstream natural language tasks. Regarding symbolic AI, the book covers information retrieval, knowledge representation methods, and question-answering tasks.

1.5.3 *Structure of the book*

This book is divided into three parts. The first part, including Chapters 1 to 4, will introduce the fundamentals of multilingual AI, which contains two major paradigms, namely, symbolic AI and deep learning. Both mirror human cognition, with the former being symbolic and human-amenable, whereas the latter subsymbolic and mathematical. In essence, multilingual AI is a tool for humans, not only to improve their productivity, but also to reflect on their relationship with the machine world, as well as how they can map their reflections onto computer programs to achieve machine intelligence.

Such a perspective entails a holistic approach to communication, with humans being able to communicate their knowledge to machines, machines facilitating data transformation across representation layers in deep learning, as well as humans exchanging information in their daily lives. This theme runs through Chapter 1, which uses a mathematical theory of communication to model and explain all these types of communicative activities. Accordingly, linguistic data, including text corpora and lexical resources, serve as an interface to help both humans and machines to exchange information, recognize patterns, or gather insights. Specific data landscape will be discussed in detail in Chapter 2.

In a similar vein, techniques and methods involving both human and machine learning, are used to achieve human-level intelligence. While data annotation is an approach to transfer human knowledge to computer systems, machine learning uses both supervised and unsupervised learning to recognize patterns. In the case of natural language, while many tasks are called unsupervised, they actually refer to self-supervised learning, where the linguistic data provides the necessary supervision. These topics will be what Chapter 3 aims to cover.

Chapter 4 will examine the mapping of human cognition to computer programs from the perspective of meaning, which can also be represented in a symbolic or mathematical manner. Technically speaking, the former is a localist approach, considering each linguistic sign as an independent atomic unit, whereas the latter is distributional, spreading meaning across a range of features associated with a linguistic sign.

Part Two, including Chapters 5–7, will focus on large language models (LLMs) and their applications. Chapter 5 will dive into the algorithm of machine learning and deep learning, using information theory. While information theory defines the channel capacity to carry signals, machine learning is the other way around, focusing on extracting information from data. Starting from the raw input, deep learning comprises simple but non-linear modules, each of which transform the representation at one level into a representation at a higher, more abstract level. An LLM trained on a sufficiently large and diverse dataset is able to perform well across many domains and tasks. As a foundation model, an LLM can be leveraged in two major approaches (1) to be fine-tuned to do downstream tasks with a relatively small amount of data; and (2) to be prompted to do specific tasks with no data or a few shots of data. Chapters 6 and 7 will apply large language models in different areas. Specifically, Chapter 6 will focus on multilingual and cross-lingual information retrieval. Chapter 7 will discuss primary considerations when augmenting LLM performance with external knowledge.

The final three chapters consider the ongoing development of large language models as they are challenged by progressively more complex issues such as culture. Once scholars and users consider these models for linguistic forms they produce, the larger questions of culture arise: are current models representing the cultural attitudes, beliefs, experiences, and values appropriately aligned to the forms that generative models put out? This research is approached using long-standing scholarly models of culture and data collection on cultural themes, such as through the World Values Survey. And in asking about this cultural turn, we also consider how critical thinking and critical questions such as these can continue to be the focus of scholars, educators, and policy makers in the years ahead.

Note

1 Mitchelmore, M.C., White, P. (2012). Abstraction in Mathematics Learning. In: Seel, N.M. (eds) Encyclopedia of the Sciences of Learning. Springer, Boston, MA. https://doi.org/10.1007/978-1-4419-1428-6_516

2

DATA LANDSCAPE FOR MULTILINGUAL AI

2.1 Aspects of linguistic data

Linguistic data is evidence that people communicate. If individuals have no intentions of sharing their thoughts and feelings or soliciting responses from others, there is no need to verbalize their internal state in this way. Using and generating languages in everyday communication, humans can engage with each other, as well as other entities, such as computer systems. As a carrier and a tool for communication, data is significant in connecting individual, internal, cognitive states with external, behavioral, and observable outcomes of the physical world.

A communicative approach to multilingual AI considers data, in particular, linguistic data, as an interface for communication. This applies not only in a data analytics cycle for human–computer interactions, but also in real-life human–to–human communication processes. For example, a reader (in a written communication process) or a listener (in a spoken communication process) cannot read another person's mind. However, they can get connected with that person's thought through the linguistic symbols produced. Form and meaning of language are like two sides of the same coin, with form as an interface, or starting point, for a communicator to further interact with the meaning the other communicator intends.

To create multilingual artificial intelligence that is on par with the human mind, linguistic data serves as both the access point and raw materials for computer programs to play with. Generally speaking, an AI-related process can be organized in two ways: around its workflow actions (what is happening) or around its data (what is being manipulated). In a business scenario, a workflow leads to an organization's daily operations, starting with understanding of the problem space, and further deconstructing the context into subproblems that can be aligned with one or a set of technological tools. Chapter 3 will examine basic techniques in multilingual AI. Chapters 6 and 7 will approach relevant techniques from the perspectives of information retrieval and knowledge representations. These techniques help narrow down the problem space. For example, in feature extraction,

DOI: 10.4324/9781003470557-3

as a representation of data, a feature "contains only the information that is relevant for the problem at hand" (Manolescu, 1998, p. 2).

While the workflow approach prioritizes human understanding and learning, it is intertwined with data. Every business operation generates data. In particular, a well-designed workflow contains operations that are necessary not only to cultivate relevant data, but also facilitate machine learning on the fly, that is, the system learns while running and interacting with humans. Following a data-oriented stream, products at each stage of a data flow can be consumed by both humans and machines, with corresponding formats. For example, in deep learning, data is transformed from the input layer to the output layer via an artificial neural network. While both humans and machines are able to understand and process data representations in the input (entry) and output (exit) layers, those between these two layers are hidden, which may only be accessible by computer systems. These hidden layers are composed of sub-symbolic vectors. Chapter 5 will further elaborate on different levels of abstractions in deep learning. When it comes to data mining, the results of data analytics, in the form of linguistic symbols, are primarily used by humans. Chapter 4 will elaborate on both the symbolic and sub-symbolic forms of data; in terms of meaning interpretation. Section 4.3 of Chapter 1 points out the fundamental problem of reliable transmission of the entity/information over a noisy channel is the running theme of the book. To further scrutinize this idea, what is being transmitted is data, which is the actual handler of this transmission activity.

Language represents facts about the world as well as peoples' conceptualizations of or reflections on these facts. Data builds a connection between the objective world and humans' internal cognition. Any type of representation includes two aspects: both an interpretation of the objects it represents and an object that must be interpreted (Sebastian-Coleman, 2013). This process involves two-way communication. From internal cognition to outside facts, or vice versa. When the connection between the objects and human reflections is established, data becomes meaningful to people. That connection is where the meaning lies. Oftentimes, people create different ways of representing the same concepts or objects, which generates complexities of the data-interpretation relationship. Every meaning, or connection, is situated in a certain context. Context can be thought of as data's representational systems; such a system includes a common vocabulary and a set of relationships between these components.

With the rapid change in technology and the increase of technological capacity, the scope of data continues to expand as well. People's understanding of what data is and how to use data also changes. Today people can capture a much wider variety of information electronically. Objects that were not previously thought of as data are added, for example, videos, pictures, sound recordings, and documents. On the other hand, data is not limited to information that has been digitized. Information captured on paper, for example, is also data, considering data-related principles apply to both digital and non-digital data, equally.

As a result, the boundaries between data, information, and knowledge become blurry. In information theory, for example, data is understood as information that has been stored in digital form. Thus, some relevant terms in the space of data as well as other aspects such as data typology, organization, and functionality (that is, what sort of operations or principles can be applied to that data), must be addressed first. To this objective, understanding the data landscape for multilingual AI is fundamental.

2.2 Data, information, and knowledge

Overall, the concept of data emphasizes its role in representing facts about the world. These facts are collected and can be analyzed to generate insights (see also Wang & Sawyer, 2023, pp. 131–2). Data is one of the most valuable assets in machine learning and must be maintained and protected by humans. For example, data custodians are responsible for using their data in an ethical way and protecting the privacy, confidentiality, and security of personal identifiable information (PII), such as a person's name, date of birth, and phone number.

In information theory, the data in computers, or digital communications, consists of a sequence of bits (MacKay, 2003, cited from Dave, 2006, p. 34). Transmitting data and its associated message or meaning is the reason why communication is needed. As the father of modern information theory, Claude Shannon pointed out, the "fundamental problem of communication is that of reproducing at one point either exactly or approximately a message selected at another point" (Shannon & Weaver, 1963, p. 31). Shannon further clarified the definition of 'message'. He argued that messages frequently have meaning, referring to or being correlated "according to some system with certain physical or conceptual entities." From this perspective, the key to communication is how to transmit data in a way that communication channels can effectively accommodate; and as MacKay (2003, p. 3) pointed out, how to communicate perfectly over imperfect communication channels.

From the engineering perspective, data can be measured in bits. A bit is the smallest unit of measurement in computer memory. Other sizes of the measurements include bytes (one byte equals 8 bits), kilobytes (MB, 1 MB equals 1,024 bytes), megabytes (GB, 1 GB equals 1,024 kilobytes), terabytes (TB, 1 TB equals 1,024 gigabytes), and other higher units based on bytes. Bit refers to "binary digits." A bit can be a 1 or a 0 (See Lobur, 2018, Chapter 1).

In a mathematical approach, communication includes both the semantic and engineering aspects. On the one hand, Shannon argued that "the semantic aspects of communication are irrelevant to the engineering aspects" (Shannon & Weaver, 1964, p. 31). On the other hand, Weaver pointed out in his comments that the above Shannon statement "does not mean that the engineering aspects are necessarily irrelevant to the semantic aspects" (Shannon & Weaver, 1964, p. 8). Both of them emphasized that the real significant feature of communication is the potential of making choices, or in Shannon's words, "that the actual message is one selected from a set of possible messages" (Shannon & Weaver, 1964, p. 31). This means even though specific engineering operations are independent of the semantic aspects of communication, these engineering tasks may help investigate how meaning is transmitted in a communication process.

The possibility of choices, as well as their associated meanings, produces information. Weaver summarized this concept, saying "information in communication theory relates not so much to what you *do* say, as to what you *could* say," and "information is a measure of one's freedom of choice when one selects a message" (Shannon & Weaver, 1964, pp. 8–9). In this context, the amount of information can be measured by the logarithm of the number of available choices. Specifically, the concept and methodology of 'entropy' is introduced. Entropy is related to "missing information," that is, "the number of alternatives which remain possible to a physical system after all the macroscopically observable information concerning it has been recorded" (Shannon & Weaver, 1964, p. 3). This topic will be further discussed in Chapter 6 concerning multilingual information retrieval and extraction.

In multilingual communication practices and for the general public, information refers to the facts (data) that are systematically presented in a given context. That is to say, information is a combination of context and data. It contains refined data filtered through a specific context. Context provides guidance to organize, structure, and process raw data, making the data compiled in a meaningful context relevant and useful to the person or entity according to their purposes or business goals. From the technical operation perspective, a dashboard is a typical information management tool. It is used to visually track and represent key performance indicators (KPIs), evaluation metrics, and data structure.

The above general understanding of information aligns with both Shannon and Weaver's arguments concerning the relationship between the engineering and semantic aspects of communication. In particular, the concept of entropy completely depends on combinations of binary selections in a hierarchical system. It measures the degree of randomness, or of "shuffledness" in a context. The calculation can completely ignore the meaning of each selection. Yet the result of the calculation can contribute to the understanding of the meaning of communication. For example, through mathematical calculations or communication engineering techniques, people can predict the most probable and logical selection, without even understanding the meaning of these options in a way humans understand. This is why machine learning, which is primarily an engineering aspect, is applicable in a semantic, social-cultural context.

Interestingly, information can be further personalized or internalized to knowledge. Knowledge consists of useful information for an individual. It represents a person's awareness and understanding of a specific topic, and thus relates to that person's cognitive state in terms of his or her individual experience and cognitive processing competence. In this sense, knowledge is a combination of information, experience, and cognition. In many cases, there is a lot of common ground of knowledge for a group of individuals.

Finally, statistical information and information in the eyes of the general public are both related and different. To begin with, statistical information is based on mathematical methods. When these methods are applied to data, statistical information is generated, for example, means, totals, ratios, percentiles, frequency distributions, and parameter estimates. When these statistics are instantiated in a social cultural context by an individual, his or her interpretation becomes information, which can be further internalized as knowledge for that individual. From the mathematical perspective, data have meaning and value, but they are difficult to identify. Statistical methods are a way of summarizing the data so that the meaning becomes clear.

2.3 Data in human and machine learning lifecycle process

As pointed out in Section 1.2, the definitive element of artificial intelligence (AI) lies in its generalization capabilities, rather than simply referring to automation, or task repetition. AI is programmed to learn (and evolve) from the inputs, that is, data, it receives. This results in the system making decisions on its own. While AI describes the capabilities of computer systems, machine learning (ML) focuses on the learning process that AI uses to train computer systems to complete a task, just like human learning processes. From the computer programming perspective, machine learning is "an established and frequently used technique in industry and academia" (Studer et al., 2021, p. 392). Unlike conventional programs that provide a set of instructions for computers to execute, ML programs the recipe and style for *learning*. For example, in supervised ML, the program accepts the instructions to learn by comparing input data (questions) and reference data, or label (answers). In unsupervised ML, the program receives instructions to learn or make inferences through input data and mathematical calculations. The key to this entire process is twofold: data and instructional guidelines concerning how to learn. The ability to learn means an entity can develop its models to gain new and additional knowledge. Prior to the techniques of machine learning, this ability had been only limited to humans and other living organisms.

2.3.1 Data movement in machine learning, data mining, and text mining

ML technology centers around data, including both the inputs an ML model is trained on, and the outputs an ML model produces, as well as other relevant data, such as testing data to evaluate the quality of an ML model. The digital transformation trends and explosion of data have greatly increased engineering capabilities to process data. The advances in many application areas of machine learning, as well as its implementations in multilingual AI, are largely due to the fact that people now have sufficient data and enough computing power to train ML models robustly.

For a long time, the machine learning community lacked a standard process model to represent data movement in a machine learning lifecycle. As a result, many projects resorted to alternative models that were closely related to ML. One of the frequently borrowed industry standards for machine learning lifecycle processes is the Cross-Industry Standard Process model for Data Mining (CRISP-DM) (Studer et al., 2021, pp. 392–3). According to the CRISP-DM model, the lifecycle of a data mining project consists of six phases, namely, business understanding, data understanding, data preparation, modeling, evaluation, and deployment. This model emphasizes the cyclical, or iterative nature of data mining. That is, data mining is not over once a solution is deployed. Rather, the lessons learned during the deployment phase in the previous cycle may lead to new and often more focused business questions, and thus begin another round of cycle with a deeper business understanding. The sequence of the phases is not rigid. Though there are frequent dependencies between some phases, it does not mean a phase can only be conducted after another phase is performed. For example, instead of moving to the deployment phase after evaluation, the project can go back to business understanding for a new cycle. A shorter cycle ending at the evaluation phase continues until the evaluation results are good enough for deployment (see Chapman et al., 1999).

The flexibility of the CRISP-DM model provides a reference for organizations to customize their specific data mining frameworks. For example, Statistics Canada (Statistics Canada, 2021) proposed a data journey model for government agencies to follow. This model includes four steps in a typical data journey: Step 1- define problem space, find and gather data; Step 2- explore, clean, and describe data; Step 3- analyze data and develop model; and Step 4- tell the story learned from the model. The data journey is supported by a foundation of stewardship, metadata, standards, and quality.

It is not surprising to see the introduction of such models as CRISP-DM to ML considering the interrelationship between data mining and machine learning. Data mining is "the automatic or semiautomatic process of finding implicit, previously unknown, and potentially useful knowledge in collections of electronically stored data" (Žižka et al., 2019, p. 3). This definition indicates that although it is widely considered a computational methodology with specific techniques, data mining is a process of discovering knowledge for humans, or internalizing and restructuring the new information or insights that have recently surfaced. For humans, a data mining process facilitates learning. This perspective determines the fact that data mining finishes a cycle of learning once knowledge is extracted from data. Conversely, machine learning focuses on facilitating learning for machines. Thus it emphasizes ML model development, deployment, along with continuous model monitoring and maintenance.

Another concept that is relevant to multilingual artificial intelligence is text mining. Text is a special data type, and a highlighted investigation area for multilingual AI. Text mining can be loosely categorized as one type of data mining. According to Feldman and Sanger (2007; cited from Žižka et al., 2019, p. 1), text mining refers to "a knowledge-intensive process in which a user interacts with a collection of documents by using analytic tools in order to identify and explore interesting patterns." Specifically, text mining uses two analytics approaches to find knowledge, usually in a large number of texts: the statistical or machine learning approach and the linguistic or symbolic approach. These two approaches represent how a text mining process leverages both human and machine intelligence. This is consistent with the two types of basic communication means or mechanisms, as mentioned in Chapter 1. The symbolic approach comprises linguistic symbols and symbolic rules (e.g. grammar, vocabulary, and semantics), whereas the statistical approach is based on numeric systems, including binary, decimal and hexadecimal numbers, as well as associated mathematical objects and operations.

2.3.2   *Human and machine learning lifecycle processes*

As Studer et al. (2021) pointed out, lifecycle process models for data mining such as CRISP-DM do not "cover the application scenario of ML models inferring real-time decisions over a long period of time" (p. 393). In machine learning, a model must be adaptable to a changing environment to avoid degradation of the model's performance over time. Thus, ML lifecycle models such as the Cross-Industry Standard Process model for the development of Machine Learning applications with Quality assurance methodology (CRISP-ML(Q)) (Studer et al., 2021) added a mandatory step, monitoring and maintenance, after the deployment phase (pp. 394–5). In addition, CRISP-ML(Q) merges business understanding and data understanding into a single phase, namely, business and data understanding. This is reasonable as these two activities are strongly intertwined: on the one hand, business objectives can be derived or changed based on available data; and on the other, data can be collected based on specific business goals. Overall, the CRISP-ML(Q) model is grounded on industrial data mining experience, with special considerations concerning the ML model adaptation to changing environments. It is regarded as most suitable for industrial projects among related process models.

The upper half of Figure 2.1 (located below) illustrates the CRISP-ML(Q) machine learning lifecycle, which aims for machines to continuously learn. This process centering around data can also be examined from a human perspective, that is, through the lens of how humans can learn new knowledge (in data mining and text mining) by interacting with each phase of this model. The lower half of Figure 2.1 (located below) depicts data flow for the purposes of human learning. For each data-driven ML project, human activities begin with identifying the problem space, collecting data, then moving to data preparation as well as contributing to the ML model development through customization or adaptation. Generally speaking, customization represents traditional machine learning, involving two separate processes: training and prediction. Conversely, adaptive machine learning merges these two processes into one, performing data collection, grouping, and analysis, while also learning from it (*The Difference Between Adaptive ML and Traditional ML*, 2021). For example, adaptive machine translation relies on user feedback, including corrections to previous translations, terminology, and style guides, as well as ratings concerning the quality of the translations, to improve real-time performance and results (Moslem et al., 2023). These activities align with the first three phases in an ML lifecycle. Data preparation (Phase 2) aims to feed machine-readable data into the system. The following phase, model customization and adaptation (Phase 3), includes both using data in modeling and generating new data. Human learning lifecycle merges evaluation and deployment in an ML lifecycle into one phase. This phase is related to presenting data output in a way that the readership is able to understand, operate, evaluate, and provide feedback regarding possible improvement. Data output intuitive to humans can provide a new starting point from which it is possible to further understand business and data, prepare data, as well as customize models and enable these models to adapt to changes. From a communicative perspective, the data movement, as shown in both cycles, indicates information flow in communication. During this process, data is transmitted from one point to another, with the value of potential information measured by the possibility of

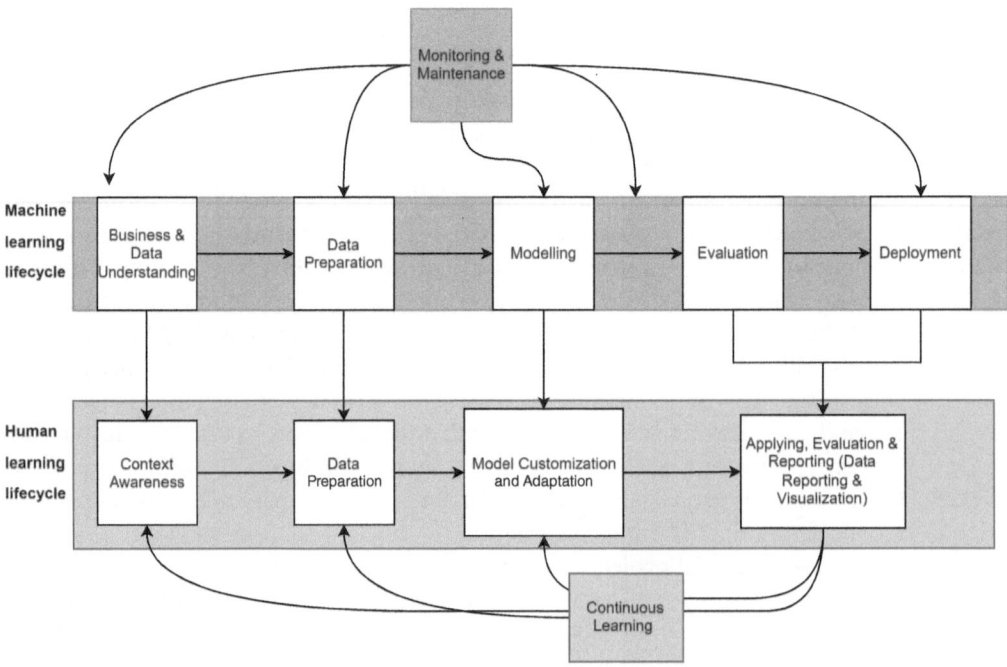

FIGURE 2.1   Human and Machine Learning Lifecycle Processes.

what could be accomplished, or in Weaver's term, there is "... freedom of choice when one selects a message" (Shannon & Weaver, 1964, pp. 8–9).

The primary purpose of this book is to facilitate and empower human learning through the use of machine learning technologies and AI capabilities. Following this theme, the initial data pipeline and flow of information focus on the outcomes of machine learning model development, rather than the internal process as a whole. After all, the ML outcomes or generated results are real, tangible, and observable for humans to access, use, evaluate, and control within their mental model development cycle. Most people will not be involved in a machine learning model development process, although they increasingly interface with ML products. The role of data in each stage of the ML process is the secondary line of thought and will be examined only when necessary. For example, to achieve effective understanding of the system outcomes as well as evaluating their quality, it is important to examine the process. However, it should be noted that this task requires special technical knowledge and skills to take it on. Overall, human and machine learning cycles are both intertwined and interdependent. Such a relationship will be further elaborated upon in the following chapters with concrete examples.

2.4   Exploratory data analysis

Both lifecycles require an understanding of business and data, or context awareness. The word context is used, as both business situations and data associated considerations are part of the larger data-driven process. In practice, during these phases, Exploratory Data Analysis (EDA) techniques are typically adopted. EDA performs initial data investigation by means of statistical and often visualization techniques (*What Is Exploratory Data Analysis?*, n.d.).

In data-driven processes, raw data is refined for the purposes of pattern recognition through relevant stages of EDA, including data understanding, such as initial data collection, description, and quality evaluation, as well as data preparation, such as data selection, cleaning, construction, integration, and formatting. To conduct these activities, one must be able to understand data from a statistical perspective.

2.4.1   Statistical data types

To begin, certain statistical measurements only apply for specific data types. In addition, some machine learning methods set conditions for data types. For example, generally speaking, decision trees, one of the ML algorithms, allows binary data, whereas simple linear regression requires decimal data. Thus, to conduct any ML or data analytics project, a user must understand data types and its relevant measurements.

From a statistical perspective, data generally falls into two basic categories: categorical and numerical data. Further, categorical data includes two subtypes, namely, nominal and ordinal, whereas numerical data can be further classified into discrete or continuous data[1] (Figure 2.2).

Categorical data represent characteristics of objects, or values within a variable. These values are more like labels, representing mutually exclusive categories or classes. For example, the languages spoken by a multilingual individual could be French, English, German, and Spanish. In this case, the concept of language is a variable in mathematics. There are four

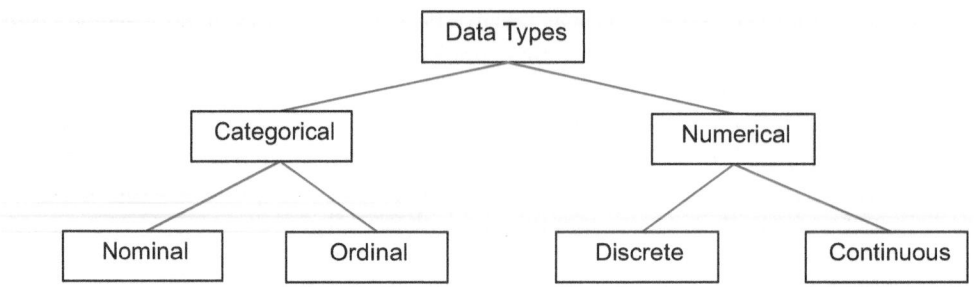

FIGURE 2.2 An illustration of data type categories.

values in this variable: (1) French, (2) English, (3) German, and (4) Spanish. Each value represents a class or category. Even when a number is assigned to each language, for example, French is 1 and Spanish is 4, these numbers do not have real values in mathematics. That is to say, these options are not related in mathematical terms, for example, French is not bigger in number than English. In this case, the values are nominal data that cannot be ordered or ranked in a meaningful way. Conversely, when further context is provided, the data type might change. For example, this individual can rank these values based on how fluently he or she can speak various languages. In this case, these options are related to each other in terms of the individual proficiency levels of this person. Thus the values of language can be classified as ordinals. As defined in the Cambridge dictionary, the term ordinal refers to "a number such as 1st, 2nd, 3rd, 4th, that shows the position of something in a list of things." Ordinals have an inherent rank order based on common sense and logic (see also Bhandari, 2020). Text data is typically considered nominal if no additional context is required.

Both nominal and ordinal data can be analyzed, summarized, and visualized. Typically, such statistical methods, as the mode (an item in a set of numbers that appears the most often) and count (the frequencies of each category in a dataset) can be applied to these two data types. Nominal data can be visualized using pie charts and bar graphs. For example, if there are a group of individuals who speak different languages, by counting the number of individuals who speak each language or determining the value that appears most, investigators can uncover what language is spoken by the greatest number of people. Ordinal data can be described using percentiles, medians, as well as other methods.

Numerical data, also called quantitative data, can be either discrete or continuous. Discrete data contains separate values. For example, instead of taking all possible numbers from 0 to 1, it can only take 0 and 1. Conversely, continuous data takes an infinite number of values on the continuum, such as 0.01 and 0.9999. Discrete data can be only counted, rather than measured. In real life, discrete data is widely used. For example, the number of cows on a farm, or the number of computers in a house, can only be represented in whole numbers, not discounting a special context. Usually, people do not count 2.3 cows. Continuous data, on the other hand, primarily represents measurements, rather than counts. For example, a person's weight in pounds can be any number between 0 and a maximum weight number. Most statistical methods can be used to describe continuous data. For example, by examining the mean and standard deviation of each feature in a dataset, a researcher can identify the central tendency and variation of the values within the dataset for the feature. Likewise, the minimum and maximum values of continuous data can help identify the range of a certain feature. To visualize continuous data, a histogram (which shows the number of observations that fall within each smaller range) or a boxplot (which describes how values in a dataset are spread out) can be used.

Here, it is worth noting that numbers are not necessarily decimals. In machine learning, binary numbers are widely used. Decimals can be converted to binary numbers. For example, a basket contains 3 apples, 10 oranges, and 11 pears. These numbers represent discrete numerical data. The categories of fruit in the basket can be represented by three decimals: apple -1, orange -2, and pear -3. These three numbers can be converted to a two-digit binary number, which is expressed in the base-2 numerical system. In this system, number 1_{10} (the subscript 10 represents a base-10 numerical system, *i.e.*, decimal system) can be translated into $(0\ 1)_2$ (the subscript 2 represents a base-2 numerical system, *i.e.*, binary system) for the apple category, number 2_{10} into $(1\ 0)_2$ for orange and number 3_{10} into $(1\ 1)_2$ for pear.

2.4.2 Data preparation

As a matter of fact, the conversion between different numerical systems is part of data pre-processing and feature engineering in Exploratory Data Analysis (EDA). In practice, EDA involves a set of possible activities, including data integration, analysis, cleaning, transformation, and dimension reduction. Each activity has a particular purpose. For example, data cleaning aims to improve the effectiveness of analysis by removing or correcting data that is incomplete, incorrect, duplicated, or improperly formatted. Pre-processing can help data scientists focus on the most relevant data variables or features for analysis, as well as speed up the computation process.

Though generally considered technical in nature, data-driven processes and their associated activities need to be considered in a social cultural context. This also applies to the data pre-processing and feature engineering processes. For example, a data scientist can leverage his, her, or someone else's domain knowledge to create meaningful information from raw data, by selecting and transforming existing variables.

For example, in the dataset about fire incidents to which the Toronto Fire Service (TFS) responds, there are 43 features (City of Toronto, 2017; Werner, 2015). A feature represents an individual measurable property or characteristic of a phenomenon (*Feature (Machine Learning)*, n.d.). Domain knowledge and business goals help data scientists narrow down the features, based on their research questions. Some variables do not have predictive power to determine the dependent variable they aim to investigate. Some features include missing values, which will negatively impact the modeling. In many cases, depending on the question, at least over half of the features will be removed during the data preparation stage.

Table 2.1 is a case study for translator management. There are four translators in this table, as well as fields (columns) to describe translator price quotes, including the name of a translator (Translator Name), how many words they can translate each day (Daily Word Count), the rate of translation per word (Rate), and the domain in which they specialize. The column 'Daily Word Count' can be further classified in three categories (category 1: 3000–3500, category 2: 3501–4000, category 3: 4001–4500) and the column 'Rate' into three categories (0.10 < category 1 <= 0.15, 0.15 < category 1 <= 0.20). The last two rows show data types and whether or not data transformation, or feature engineering, has occurred.

TABLE 2.1 An example of data types and feature engineering for values of translator price quotes

Translator no.	Translator Name	Daily word count	Daily word categories	Rate (USD/Word)	Rate categories	Specialized domain	Specialized domain in binary numbers
1	John	3,000	1	0.2	2	medical	1_2
2	Emily	4,000	2	0.15	1	marketing	10_2
3	Erik	4,200	3	0.13	1	legal	11_2
4	Tom	3,500	1	0.18	2	financial	100_2
Data Types	Nominal	Continuous	Ordinal	Continuous	Ordinal	Nominal	Binary*
Feature Engineering	Raw data	Raw data	New feature	Raw data	New feature	Raw data	New feature

Remarks: * Binary variables can only take on two values, such as 0 and 1 or True and False or Male and Female. For the purpose of analysis, these variables can be considered either continuous or categorical. The numbers in this column have a subscription of 2, meaning these numbers are base 2 numbers.

2.4.3 Feature extraction

During the feature engineering process, raw data is transformed to new features. There is a deviation between these two forms of data. When it comes to feature extraction, the degree of deviation can be more significant. In this process, the original input variables are transformed into some new space "where, it is hoped, the pattern recognition problem will be easier to solve" (Bishop, 2006, p. 2) and this preprocessing stage is sometimes called feature extraction. For example, in many cases, image data cannot be used for direct analysis. Thus, researchers extract the redness value, or a description of the shape of an object in the image, to represent this type of data. Though there is a difference between raw data (image) and the extracted data (redness value or description), at least some information can demonstrate the relationship between this dataset. Even though the entities might vary greatly in such factors as data values, types, and formats, the relationships among them in these systems mirror each other in terms of the possibility of what could be accomplished, or the potential information embedded in these two systems. That is the foundation explaining how the transformed space can parallel or be comparable with the original space.

In Natural Language Processing, feature extraction techniques are widely used. Typical examples include Principal Component Analysis (PCA), Bag of Words (BoW), and Term Frequency-Inverse Document Frequency (TF-IDF). BoW is an effective technique where the words, which can be considered features, used in a text, can be extracted and classified by their usage frequency. Each document can be represented by a vector of word counts. Machine learning algorithms use this word count as an input vector (*What Is Feature Extraction? Feature Extraction Techniques Explained*, n.d.).

2.4.4 The purpose of analysis

Data typology is a useful tool in machine learning, in particular, on the operational levels of data analytics. However, it must be noted that none of the classification systems for data are exhaustive, nor could they describe all attributes of real data, which can be interpreted from different angles depending on situational context (see Velleman & Wilkinson, 1993). For example, based on individual perspective, a person can draw different conclusions concerning the type of image data, as well as the level of measurement. Similar to words as a linguistic representation, images can refer to nominal data, as a visual representation of some objects. Conversely, digital images can be measured in an array of numbers (for example, RGB color values are measured in terms of values of red, green, and blue light sources), which makes them a source of continuous data. As a general practice, rather than focusing on determining these data types for their own sake, it is important to put this question into the appropriate context. What specific function does a certain data type of classification framework play in a particular project? For example, data sources fed into a machine learning system will be turned into numerical data at some point, through feature extraction, using Word2Vec. This will be examined in Chapter 4. In this case, RGB values are typically used to represent image data. Of note, for other analytic tasks, such as image classification through captions, the image data is represented in word form, which is nominal data.

The purpose of analysis is shaped through both the engineering and social–cultural contexts. For example, the way a question is framed in a specific communicative situation leads to different conclusions regarding data types. A person's weight can be quantitative, continuous data. Yet if the question is "what is the number of pounds you have gained over the holidays," the answer is meant to be a discrete number, e.g., 3, 5 or 10, rather than 3.2, 5.5, or 10.1. That is to say, data analytics is not just a technical problem, but one that is situated in a social cultural context. Such context information sets conditions for us to conduct such tasks as Exploratory Data Analysis (EDA) and feature extraction.

From the engineering perspective, the purpose of analysis must be examined through feasible data analytics and machine learning methods. For example, classification and regression are machine learning tasks. While classification aims to predict a categorical value, what regression aims to is a numerical value. In practice, to use machine learning & data analytics tools such as RapidMiner (RapidMiner, n.d.) and Weka (Waikato Environment for Knowledge Analysis, see Gordon, n.d.), a user must be able to identify data types to determine which method is going to be applied while using these tools.

Overall, data literacy, the ability to understand, manage, and communicate data as meaningful information, is significant for any data-related tasks. This ability is the foundation for stakeholders to identify the purpose of analysis from both the social–cultural and engineering perspectives.

2.5 Linguistic data

The analytical part of multilingual AI could involve all types of data. As shown in Table 2.1, in a translation vendor management process, different data types discussed in Section 4 might apply, just like other types of machine learning tasks. However, one particular data type stands out in multilingual AI, that is, linguistic data, which, in general situations, can be considered nominal data, as shown in Figure 2.1. From a language perspective, multilingual AI data can be divided into linguistic data and non-linguistic data (e.g., audio data, image data). Linguistic data is usually the first access point for most researchers and users to perform a multilingual AI task.

From an engineering perspective, there are two types of language data that a linguistically motivated programming task (a task performed by computers to solve linguistic problems) handles: texts and words. Language can be either natural language or non-natural (artificial) language. In this case, 'natural language' means "a language that is used for everyday communication by humans" (Bird et al., 2009, Preface), which includes both spoken and written scenarios as well as multiple languages such as English, Hindi, or Portuguese. The opposite of natural language is artificial languages, such as programming languages, mathematical notations, and controlled languages. A recent trend regarding artificial language is the increasing usage of synthetic language data, which is generated by a particular language model, e.g., machine translation systems, ChatGPT, or chatbot, rather than by humans in communication.

2.5.1 Text corpora and lexical resources

A primary tool to organize linguistic data is through corpus, which is a large collection of authentic texts that have been gathered in electronic form according to a specific set of criteria (Bowker & Pearson, 2002, p. 9; see also Biber et al., 1998, p. 12). As this definition indicates, corpus includes natural texts, that is, authentic text generated by humans in communication. Corpus is gathered in electronic form and organized according to a specific set of criteria. From linguistic and social–cultural perspectives, these criteria must ensure the sampled or selected texts to be representative and balanced with respect to particular problems to be investigated. A corpus can be representative in terms of subject matters, or domains, for example, all texts are on politics (political domain), or reflecting a specific language style, e.g., informal or formal, or demonstrating a writer's language proficiency levels, e.g., second language learners' writing samples. If a corpus aims to investigate how genres impact language styles, it must cover a balanced type of genres such as newspaper articles, literary fiction, spoken speech, legal document, etc.

In multilingual communication, translation-driven corpora are significant for both researchers and practitioners to examine how corpora and corpus linguistics techniques have been used in translation descriptive research (Zanettin, 2013, pp. 20–1). Translation-driven corpora include linguistic data in a specific context that can be used by both humans and machines. For example, multilingual linguistic data is used to improve the productivity and effectiveness of both human translators and automatic translation systems (Wang & Sawyer, 2023). Specifically, the data allows human translators to refer to previous translations (translation memory) or a machine translation system to improve their overall performances.

Corpus can be further annotated. This refers to "a single set of data annotated with the same specification" (Pustejovsky & Stubbs, 2012, Chapter 1). Annotation marks the structural, contextual, and content information of a corpus. This will allow a computer to filter relevant datasets to address real-world problems. It is an effective tool for humans to communicate their intentions to programs, as well as manage corpora and query datasets.

This book focuses on the engineering aspects of corpus, which are linguistically motivated. After all, the ultimate goal of every multilingual AI technique and methodology in this book is to solve problems in multilingual communication. How can linguistic data be manipulated and analyzed by computer programs in a variety of ways to investigate a particular problem in communication? In this sense, there are two fundamental data types: lexicons and texts. Derived from this typology, corpus can also be classified as lexicon corpus (lexical resources) and text corpus. Though in a human communication process, these two types of corpora look similar, as all text comprises a certain number of words and punctuations. In multilingual AI, however, they have fundamental differences in terms of database structure, annotation, and functionality.

2.5.1.1   Lexical resources

Lexical resources can be represented using a record structure, with a key plus one or more fields or attributes. Table 2.2 is an example of a record structure. In terms of database structure, there are two lexical entries, corpus (1) and corpus (2). Though they share the same form, their attributes or characteristics are different. Each attribute is summarized in one column of the table. As shown in Table 2.2, these two entries have the same values for some columns (Word forms, and Part of speech), yet vary in other columns (Definition, and Chinese translation).

For example, WordNet (Fellbaum, 1998; Princeton, n.d.) is a large lexical corpus of English. In this corpus, nouns, verbs, adjectives, and adverbs are grouped into unordered sets of cognitive synonyms, also known as 'synsets'. Each synset expresses a distinct concept and they are interrelated by means of conceptual-semantic and lexical relations. The resulting network consists of meaningfully related words and concepts. The WordNet 2.1 database includes a total of 155,327 unique words and 117, 597 synsets (Princeton, n.d.). The lexical resources are organized in a record structure. In the dataset of words, for example, a word form element contains attribute-value pairs indicating the state of semantic tagging associated with that word form, the syntactic category, and semantic tag information. When a sense is assigned, several attribute-value pairs representing the semantic tag are added to a word form element. An attribute represents one characteristic, or dimension, of a word form. For example, the link verb 'be' is used as an abstract base form (lemma) for concrete word forms, such as 'is', 'was', 'are', 'were', and 'be' (here 'be' is used as both the base and the value it represents). In this case, the lemma attribute indicates the base form of a concept. Both the base form and its associated values are stored in the WordNet database. From another perspective, the lemma is a form of

TABLE 2.2 Record structure of lexical resources

Lexical entry number	Key (Lemma or head word)	Word forms	Definition	Part of speech	Chinese translation
1	corpus	corpora	a collection of written or spoken material stored on a computer and used to find out how language is used (*Cambridge Dictionary*, n.d.)	Noun	语料库 (*Cambridge Dictionary*, n.d.)
2	corpus	corpora	a body or the main part of an organ (*Cambridge Dictionary*, n.d.)	Noun	尸体 (*Cambridge Dictionary*, n.d.)

metadata, or rather, a name, or a label, for an abstract concept representing a group of values. The introduction of the lemma concept allows researchers to consider different forms of a word as the same idea.

Using such programming languages as Python, a user can extract information from the WordNet package in Natural Language Toolkit (NLTK). For example, to find words with similar meaning as 'motorcar', a user can identify the synset of 'motorcar'. The program will return 'car.n.01' for the word 'motorcar'. In effect, the WordNet package includes more than one synset for 'car': "[Synset('car.n.01'), Synset('car.n.02'), Synset('car.n.03'), Synset('car.n.04'), Synset('cable_car.n.01')]." The result is in the format that Python returns. The label 'car.n.01' refers to the first noun meaning of car. Having five synsets, the word 'car' is ambiguous. The system can print the lemma names of these synsets: (1) ['car', 'auto', 'automobile', 'machine', 'motorcar'], (2) ['car', 'railcar', 'railway_car', 'railroad_car'], (3) ['car', 'gondola'], (4) ['car', 'elevator_car'], and (5) ['cable_car', 'car']. As shown in the lemma names, 'motorcar' is included in the first synset. This is how the program is able to identify that the meaning of 'motorcar' is only related to that synset. In addition, a user can perform other activities to retrieve information, including printing out the definition of this shared meaning, giving examples of this meaning, and finding hyponyms (a word whose meaning includes a group of other words, cited from Cambridge Dictionary, n.d.) for a word. For example, 'car.n.01' is defined as "a motor vehicle with four wheels; usually propelled by an internal combustion engine," and an example of this word use in a sentence is "he needs a car to get to work" (Bird et al., 2009, pp. 67–73).

Lexical resources are useful both as a standalone product and when applied to different types of Natural Language Processing tasks. For example, as "a series of manually compiled electronic dictionaries," WordNet covers most English nouns, adjectives, verbs, and adverbs in various domains (Morato et al., 2004). This lexical corpus in and of itself provides essential information about synonyms and semantic relationships between lemmas and word forms. As a lexical resource, WordNet is useful for people when looking up meanings of relevant words. Furthermore, based on the WordNet structure, there have been efforts to develop multilingual databases for several other languages. For example, EuroWordNet aims to create similar wordnets for other languages of Europe, such as Dutch, Italian, and Spanish (Green et al., 2001; Hirst, 1999; Vossen, 1998).

Second, lexical resources can be applied to other natural language tasks. For example, WordNet is widely used for disambiguation, semantic distances, document structuring, and categorization (Morato et al., 2004). Other lexical resources such as wordlist corpora are useful to filter corpora. A wordlist corpus includes nothing more than wordlists (Bird et al., 2009, p. 60). In a task to process natural languages, some common words (e.g., 'the', 'a', and 'an') might be of little value when investigating a specific problem (e.g., the topic of a document). These words are used in a variety of texts and thus their presence often does not tell how one text is different from another. These words, also called "stop words," are usually filtered out before the linguistic data is sent for further processing (*Dropping Common Terms: Stop Words*, n.d.). The concept and methodology of "stop words" allow researchers to apply multilingual AI techniques when addressing real-life problems. In an example given by Bird et al. (2009, pp. 60–1), through the use of a program function to determine what fraction of words in a text are not included in a "stop words" list, over a quarter of the words within the text are automatically filtered out.

2.5.1.2 *Text corpus*

In the above example, featuring "stop words," two different kinds of corpus or data types are used: a lexical resource and a text corpus. At the most abstract level, text corpora are different from lexicons. While lexical resources use the attribute-value, unordered structure for each entry (see Table 2.1), a text is a representation of a real or fictional speech event, and the time-course of that event carries over into the text itself (Bird et al., 2009, p. 411). A text contains a sequence of linguistic units (such as words and punctuation marks), which include both the units themselves as well as their order. To some degree, meaning is more relevant to the order than the units themselves.That is to say, meaning, which differentiates usages within the same group of lexicons, exists not in the linguistic units, but in the temporal relationship between words in a text. In this sense, a text is an instantiation of selecting and ordering concrete lexical resources from a system of language. This positional information, or the temporal relationship between linguistic units in a text, does not inherently exist in lexical resources (see Wang & Sawyer, 2023, p. 23).

In linguistics, the lexicon of a natural language is an instantiation of linguistic 'signs'. As Ferdinand de Saussure pointed out in his *Cours de linguistique général* (2005 [1916]), a sign is a combination of both the signifier, such as word form, and the signified, such as meaning of the word form (or French, *signifiant* and *signifié*). A linguistic sign, including the signifier, the signified, the bond between the two, and the sign as a whole, is arbitrary (Ruthrof, 2010, p. 157). In other words, there is no inherent reason why a signifier is linked to a signified; in order to make sense of a sign, one can only examine how this sign relates to other signs in the same system (Saussure, 1966; cited from Wang & Sawyer, 2023, p. 21). In terms of describing the relationship between signs, mathematical concepts and methods can function effectively. For example, specific relationships between words in a text could be measured using numerical systems, such as indexes for the positional information, as well as the presentation patterns for linguistic units in a text (e.g. the frequency of their occurrences). This is the fundamental reason why statistical information for a text, retrieved through multilingual AI techniques, enables 'understanding' of the text. Statistical measurements of a text are not the same as those for individual, non-temporal lexicons.

In Natural Language Processing (NLP), a text is processed as a list of words, along with their associated positional information. For example, a sentence "Call me Ishmael." in a text is represented in Python as "sent1 = ['Call', 'me', 'Ishmael', '.']." The way a text is stored like this allows a computer program to query some relevant information about the sentence. For example, a user can ask about the length of the above sentence by entering the prompt of "len(sent1)." The system will return 4. The order of occurrence in the list of words, that is a text, must be marked. The number that represents the position of a word, in a text, is the item's index (Bird, 2009, p. 12). For example, the third item in 'sent1' is 'Ishmael'.

Specifically, there are a range of statistical indicators that describe the internal structure of a text. For example, statistics about word types in a text can be used as a measure of the lexical richness of the text. A word type is "the form or spelling of the word independently of its specific occurrences in a text" (Bird et al., 2009, p. 8). Each occurrence of this word type can be considered a token. Here, a token is "the technical name for a sequence of characters that we want to treat as a group" (Bird et al., 2009, p. 7). In this case, a token is a word. For example, in a text about a UN resolution of biodiversity conservation (the English version of a resolution adopted by the General Assembly on 16 April 2021, Symbol A/RES/75/271), there are 568 unique words (word types) and 1,976 word tokens[2] based on the calculation of AntConc, a corpus analysis toolkit for concordancing and text analysis (Laurence, n.d.). This information describes the vocabulary size and provides some clues about the lexical density of this text. Further, statistics about frequency distributions of a particular word, such as counting how often a word occurs in a text, and computing what percentage of the text is taken up by a specific word, can be used to identify the topic and genre of the text. As shown in Figure 2.3, except for some words that commonly appear in every document, which could be included in a list of 'stop words', the word with the highest frequency is 'biodiversity'. Thus this document is most probably related to the topics of biodiversity and climate change.

Figure 2.4 describes basic statistical information about the word type 'biodiversity'. As shown in this figure, there are 28 occurrences of 'biodiversity' in this text. The summary even visualized a dispersion plot of 'biodiversity' which appears in the text. In the plot at the bottom right of Figure 2.4, each stripe represents an instance of a word, while each row represents the entire text. This positional information concerning the location of the word 'biodiversity' in a text, helps analysts understand how this word is used in context. For example, 'biodiversity' appears most frequently in the beginning of the text, a possible assumption being to introduce it as a topic. The word is evenly distributed in the second half of the text as a repeating concept within this document. Such analysis, based on statistics, must be accompanied by qualitative examination, which occurs when reviewing sentences that include this word, in context.

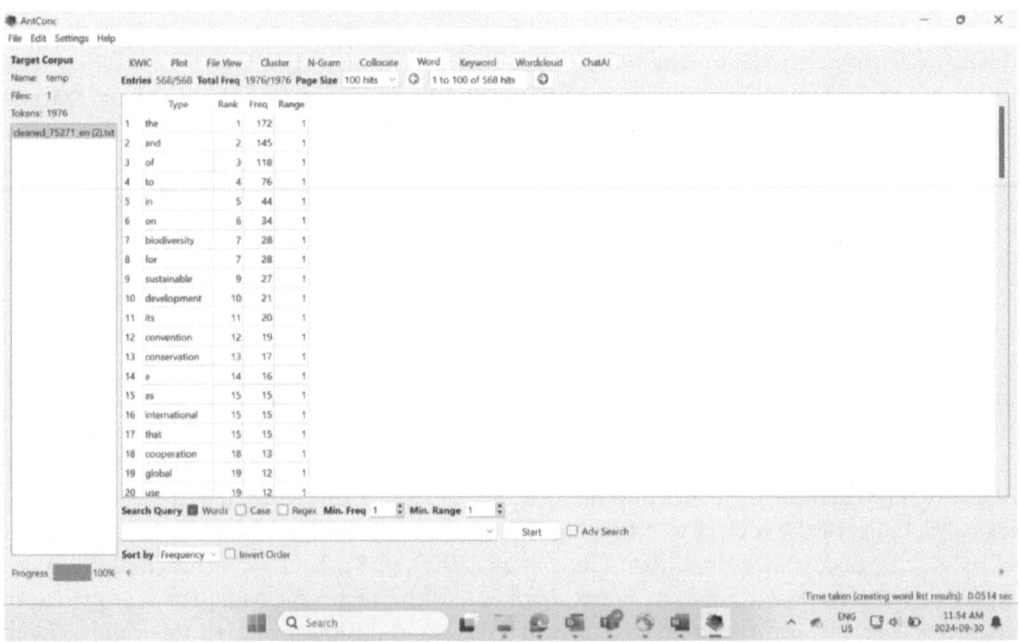

FIGURE 2.3 Frequency distributions of words in document A/RES/75/271.

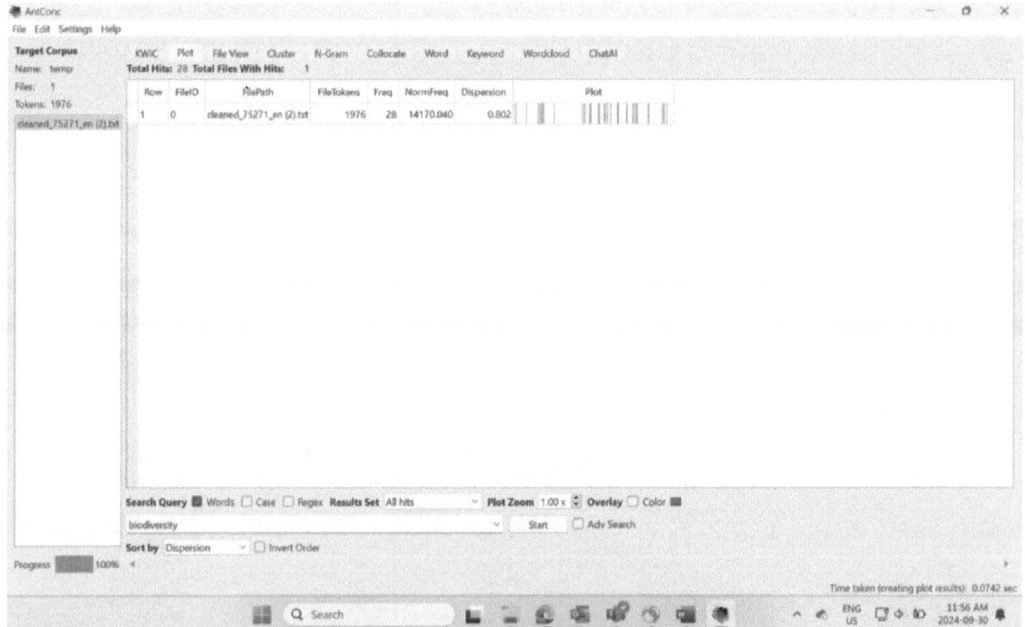

FIGURE 2.4   The dispersion plot for the word type 'biodiversity'.

The internal structure is also presented through the temporal relationship between tokens. Further statistical information can be extracted by calculating the frequencies of certain words appearing before and after 'biodiversity' (see Figure 2.5). For example, Wang and Sawyer (2023, pp. 61–3) used distances between words in a vector space to indicate their meaning relations. This will be discussed in greater detail in Chapter 4.

2.5.2 Hybrid corpora: a case study

Most corpora include a combination of both lexicon and text corpus. For example, the Natural Language Toolkit (NLTK) is a suite of libraries and programs written in the Python programming language, for symbolic and statistical natural language processing (NLTK, n.d.). In the NLTK, there is a TIMIT corpus, which was the first annotated speech database developed by a consortium including Texas Instruments and MIT (thus the name TIMIT). This corpus has a clear organization, both for its lexical resources and text corpus.

Regarding the text corpus, TIMIT has a balanced selection of genres, sources, dialects, and speakers. Originally, TIMIT was a speech corpus. However, its transcriptions and associated data are text, which can be processed using conventional NLP processing packages such as NLTK. This is an example to illustrate the extended scope of text corpus.

The NLTK includes a sample from the TIMIT corpus. This sample includes speeches by 16 speakers from eight different dialectic regions. Specifically, TIMIT includes a total 160 recordings of sentences (ten recordings per speaker). The recording is transcribed to a total of 130 sentences (ten sentences per speaker). Among the 16 speakers from eight different dialectic regions, there are one male and one female from each distinct region.

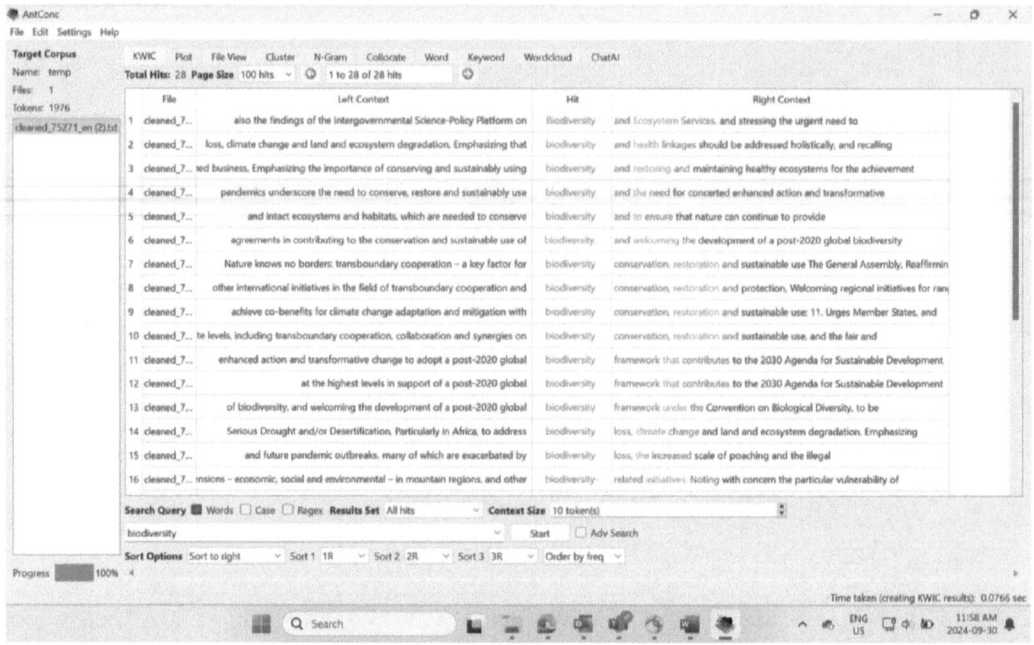

FIGURE 2.5 Collocation of the word type 'biodiversity'.

In addition, TIMIT includes a lexicon that provides the canonical pronunciation of every word, which helps describe what a speech processing system would have to do in producing or recognizing speech in a specific dialect. Finally, TIMIT includes demographic data about the speakers. The introduction of speaker demographics allows researchers to incorporate additional independent variables, such as speakers' vocal, social, and gender information, when investigating dialect variation in the data collected. The demographic data for each speaker is managed in key-value structure without a temporal relationship among data points, for example:

[SpeakerInfo(id='VMH0', sex='F', dr='1', use='TRN', recdate='03/11/86', birth-date='01/08/60', ht='5\'05''', race='WHT', edu='BS', comments='BEST NEW ENG-LAND ACCENT SO FAR')]

In this sense, the demographic speaker data is an instance of lexicon corpus or a lexicon data type (see Bird et al., 2009, pp. 407–12).

2.5.3 Multilingual corpora

According to Schmidt and Worner (2012, p. xi), the term 'multilingual corpus' refers to "any systematic collection of empirical language data which enables linguists to carry out analyses of multilingual individuals, multilingual societies or multilingual communication." Schmidt and Worner (2012) also pointed out that a multilingual corpus need not necessarily contain texts in more than one language. If a text or speech is produced by a multilingual speaker in a multilingual communicative setting, for example, the monolingual data can also be considered multilingual, since this data also describes some characteristics of multilingualism. Such a consideration is based on "a consequence of how a corpus is designed, documented and used" (p. xi).

However, the working definition for the concept of multilingual corpora, in this book, is primarily related to the analytical and engineering aspects of Natural Language Processing. Based on the discussions from Sections 5.1.1 to 5.1.3, multilingual corpora refer to lexical resources and/or text corpora in more than one language. From the perspective of data collection, management, and retrieval; the characteristic of being multilingual adds a layer of complexity, concerning how linguistic data in one language is related in other languages. There could be a variety of reasons why certain lexicons and texts in multiple languages can be organized as a set of corpora to address particular multilingual problems. In Natural Language Processing and translation studies, one typical example is parallel corpora, which includes both the source texts/speeches (the original texts to be translated) and the target texts/speeches (translated texts/speeches of the source text). The source and target texts are aligned based on equivalence of meaning at various linguistic levels, including words, phrases, sentences, paragraphs, and documents. Translation memory is an example of a parallel corpus, comprising a number of translation units. Each translation unit consists of a segment (which typically refers to a sentence) of the source text and its corresponding translation. For the purposes of multilingual communication, two or more (sub)corpora can also be paired on the basis of other shared features, such as textual similarity or subject matter areas. The combination of such corpora being compared is usually called comparable corpora. For example, to compare linguistic features of texts in different languages regarding the same topic, texts about this topic in one language are aligned with texts about the same topic in another language. These two corpora are comparable, as they share the same topic (Wang & Sawyer, 2023, pp. 132–5). In this context, parallel corpus is a specific type of comparison, with the shared feature as equivalent meaning between the source and target segments.

The complexity layer and alignment principles apply to lexicons. For example, multilingual terminology management systems are effective tools to store and manage concepts as well as their relevant word forms, in different languages. If the set of terms are aligned based on meaning, the terminology management system can host parallel lexical corpora. Otherwise, when they are aligned based on other comparable criteria, such as topics, genres, and disciplines, the system can host comparable lexical corpora.

2.5.4 Synthetic text corpora

Data is essential for machine learning. The advances in many application areas of multilingual AI, are largely due to the fact that people now have sufficient data and enough computing power to train ML models robustly. Large text corpora are available for language modeling such as machine translation for some language combinations. However, the quality of performance of these language models varies due to a range of factors. For example, Bang et al. (2023) performed 7 natural language tasks across a set of languages with mixed resource levels, including English, Chinese, French, Indonesian, Korean, Japanese, Sundanese, and Buginese, using ChatGPT. Results show that ChatGPT achieved relatively strong performances in high- and medium-resource languages such as English and Chinese. For low-resource languages such as Japanese and Sundanese, however, ChatGPT had difficulties understanding these languages. Furthermore, many classes of artificial intelligence models that interact with the outside world, such as question answering, require "custom datasets that capture both the full scope of desired behavior in addition to the possible variation in human language" (Marzoev et al., 2020). When such a dataset is only limited to authentic language examples as well as natural language annotation, it will be both expensive and time-consuming, if such a goal is achievable at all.

One technique to address this problem is using synthetic data, which is generated by computer systems, rather than humans in real-life communication. This book will focus on synthetic text corpora, as texts are the most frequently used data type or corpus category for machine learning, in multilingual communication. Theoretically speaking, the categorization of lexical resources and text corpus in natural language seems to be equally applicable to synthetic linguistic data. However, the so-called 'synthetic lexical resources' may cause confusion regarding how to define the concept of 'synthetic'. Synthetic products are made from artificial substances, often copying a natural product (*SYNTHETIC | English Meaning—Cambridge Dictionary*, n.d.). In a text corpus, the characteristic that describes the synthetic or artificial feature is the order or temporal relationship between linguistic signs. That is to say, text generated by computer systems could have its specific ordering of linguistic signs, compared to human creations. For lexicons, however, the re-ordering of letters to create a new word, would be too radical as data for machine learning purposes. Computer programs can generate groups of lexicons. For example, automatic terminology extraction programs can extract specialized terms from a text, based on certain algorithms. Such a production might be the same as or different from a list of lexicons manually collected by humans from the same text. Regarding what to include in the list, computer programs use their own recipes. Yet the substances, that is, the lexical units included in the list, are composed of natural languages. There may be debate in the future as to whether machines will create new word forms or concepts. Yet, this is outside the scope of this book. At least for now, humans have not given machines the ability to create words. Thus, synthetic linguistic data in this book, primarily refers to text corpora.

There are no engineering restrictions in terms of which natural language methods and techniques can be applied to synthetic data. That is to say, without further annotated information, computer programs consider natural and synthetic data the same. Synthetic linguistic data is useful in helping to address issues such as data imbalance (e.g., in domain vs. out of domain), data privacy concerns, and data quality, in a machine learning process.

When the scope of linguistic data is extended to include synthetic data, the criteria to evaluate the quality of data must include considerations from computational and machine learning perspectives, in addition to judgments made by humans. For example, for parallel corpora used for machine translation system development, one significant metric to evaluate the data quality is whether there is system performance improvement after applying the data, taking into consideration both authentic and synthetic text corpora. Conversely, researchers can also evaluate the data quality by asking human reviewers to examine whether or not the translation is accurate. There may be discrepancies in the aforementioned two evaluation methods. At times, a parallel corpus, which is concluded to be low quality by a human evaluator, might be able to improve the machine translation system, or vice versa. There are many reasons behind these discrepancies. For example, often human evaluation cannot cover all segments in a dataset, and sampling cannot accurately represent the quality of the dataset as a whole. From a machine learning perspective, using the system outcomes, rather than directly examining the data, to evaluate quality is widely used to great effect. To some degree, judgment concerning data accuracy or quality at a certain segment level that is intuitive for humans to process (e.g., sentences and paragraphs), is similar to an internal examination within data. On the other hand, evaluating data quality from the overall results the system generates, parallels an external examination, regarding the influence of data. When the machine generated outcomes make sense to humans, it is evidence that the language model is optimized to align with commonly held perspectives.

Notes

1 There are other frameworks for data typology. From a data analytics perspective, one common typology includes four analytic data types: Nominal/Categorical, Ordinal, Ratio, and Interval Data (Foxwell, 2020, Chapter 2; Gatzeva, n.d.). In this framework, nominal is also called categorical. Nominal data "measures are used to capture qualitative attributes that have no size or extent characteristics"; and ordinal data is a special case of nominal/categorical data, "where there is an implied quantitative difference among the categories but not so specific as to allow for mathematical comparison" (Foxwell, 2020, Chapter 2). Ratio data typically measures quantities that have a possibility of being zero (none), with interval data as a special case of ratio data. However, ratio calculations are not interpretable since there is no absolute zero quantity defined (Foxwell, 2020, Chapter 2). Gatzeva (n.d.) pointed out that all data can be divided into two categories: discrete and continuous, and nominal and ordinal variables can be considered as discrete and interval/ratio variables as continuous.
2 The original documents in the United Nations Official Document System are available in .PDF and .Doc formats. The Word version was downloaded and converted to plain text format (UTF-8). There is a minor discrepancy between AntConc's automatic calculation results and the manual calculation based on the PDF or Word versions.

3

BASIC TECHNIQUES TO ACHIEVE ARTIFICIAL INTELLIGENCE

3.1 Deep learning and symbolic artificial intelligence

Since the term was proposed in 1955 (McCarthy et al., 1955), artificial intelligence (AI) has been used as an umbrella term covering a broad scientific field encompassing not only computer science but also psychology, philosophy, linguistics, and other areas (Wang & Sawyer, 2023, pp. 2–3). The diversity of subject areas included in AI indicates this concept is a much broader term that covers not only the computational processes through which a machine can be made to simulate features of intelligence, but also the outcomes generated by these processes that interact with humans in multilingual communication.

A unique characteristic of human-level artificial intelligence refers to machine's capability to generalize, that is, its ability to produce sensible answers on new inputs that it has never encountered during training (LeCun et al., 2015, p. 437) or in its past experience based on which it forms abstractions (Garnelo & Shanahan, 2019). The former, which is usually based on large volumes of data, is statistical in nature, whereas the latter, which is often based on past human experiences that can be digitized, stored and managed by computer programs, is symbolic. Symbolic AI was dominant for much of the 20th century. However, much of the current progress in AI has come from recent advances in the application of a particular paradigm of the statistical approach, namely, a connectionist paradigm in deep learning (Garnelo & Shanahan, 2019, p. 17). Connectionism refers to an approach to neural-network-based cognitive modeling, which encompasses the recent deep learning movement in artificial intelligence (Kiefer, 2019).

Deep learning is a sub field of machine learning, characterized by neural network-style models with multiple layers of representation (Lake et al., 2017, p. 1). As LeCun et al. (2015) point out, conventional machine-learning techniques were limited in their ability to process natural data in their raw form (p. 436). Deep learning architecture with multiple processing layers, however, allows computational models to learn representations of data using multiple levels of abstraction (LeCun et al., 2015, p. 436). That is to say, data is transformed from the raw material that is intuitive to humans, to a form

DOI: 10.4324/9781003470557-4

that is more easily understood and used with mathematical operations. This process is also referred to as representation learning, which allows a machine to be fed with raw data and to automatically discover the representations needed for detection or classification. An inductive learning-based statistical AI is primarily driven by data (LeCun et al., 2015, p. 436). Before the introduction of neural network-style language models, for example, the standard approach to statistical modeling of language was based on counting frequencies of occurrences of short symbol sequences of length up to N, that is, n-gram, rather than distributed representation (LeCun et al., 2015, p. 441). However, deep learning methods contain the process to transform raw input into a higher, slightly more abstract level, and consequently include multiple levels of representations (LeCun et al., 2015, p. 436).

A symbolic AI, "works by carrying out a series of logic-like reasoning steps over language-like representations" (Garnelo & Shanahan, 2019, p. 17). Symbolic representations tend to be high-level and abstract, which involves more complex human thought or reflections on physical or concrete language symbols. and are amenable to human understanding as a result of their language-like, propositional character (Garnelo & Shanahan, 2019, pp. 17–18). For many people, these symbolic representations are intuitive. Furthermore, abstract rules based on symbolic representations could be hard-wired into a computer system to execute human instructions directly.

To some degree, symbolic and statistical AI are mirroring the symbolic and statistical paradigms of cognition, representing deductive reasoning and inductive learning aspects, which "would be arguably the two fundamental wheels of the human mind" (Maruyama, 2020, pp. 129–30). Humans use both logical reasoning and statistical inference to make various judgments, and in many cases, it is hard to tell which part of human cognition is essentially symbolic or statistical. In other words, both symbolic and statistical AI are demonstrations of applying different types of human intelligence in a machine system. Currently, the research community aims to map such dualism of logic and statistics existing in the human mind, onto AI system design. For example, some researchers advocate an integrated AI approach, that is, the integration of symbolic and statistical AI, due to the limitations of deep learning (CDRS, 2019; Garnelo & Shanahan, 2019; Maruyama, 2020). This book will not cover AI paradigm development from a computer science perspective. Rather, it will focus on the application aspects of using both symbolic and statistical AI, in particular, deep learning, to achieve business goals.

As an example of multilingual communication, machine translation includes various paradigms and each of them adopts a specific approach to AI. Rule-based machine translation is primarily symbolic AI, whereas neural machine translation is based on deep learning. It should be noted that rule-based and neural MT differ in terms of their reliance on data. Furthermore, they vary concerning the degree of interference from human intelligence as well as when and where it occurs. Deep learning requires little engineering by hand and thus could easily take advantage of increases in the amount of available computation and data (LeCun et al., 2015, p. 436). Conversely, symbolic representations tend to be high-level and abstract, lending themselves to re-use in multiple tasks, which promotes data efficiency (Garnelo & Shannahan, 2019, p. 17). In both cases, linguistic data is a starting point from which one can approach AI. This is particularly true in the case of deep learning.

3.2 Linguistic data: an open base for communication between human and machine systems

Wang and Sawyer (2023, pp. 76–8) compared human's conceptual reflection and machine's mathematical representation of meaning, or 'interlingua', which represents an ideal level of understanding (see Vauquois, 1968, p. 335). In his memorandum, Warren Weaver made an analogy for the communication between these two systems to process meaning:

> Think, by analogy, of individuals living in a series of tall closed towers, all erected over a common foundation. When they try to communicate with one another, they shout back and forth, each from his own closed tower. It is difficult to make the sound penetrate even the nearest towers, and communication proceeds very poorly indeed. But, when an individual goes down his tower, he finds himself in a great open basement, common to all the towers. Here he establishes easy and useful communication with the persons who have also descended from their towers.
>
> *(cited in Hutchins, 1999, p. 6)*

According to this analogy, every language system, while providing intricate structures, in addition to socio-cultural elements, that help people navigate their thoughts, also limit human communication. Separate linguistic systems are like 'closed towers' or silos. The complexity and intertwinedness of each system is contained within itself. Attempting to force its own structure on the other system during communication will not permit the voice to be heard from within the other tower. However, this method of communication has long been established. Such a reflection tends to be more apparent to non-socio-cultural, linguistic professionals, such as mathematicians and computer scientists. Thus, it is not surprising when Jelinek, an NLP researcher who was accustomed to thinking from a programming perspective, pointed out this communication problem in his famous quote, "Every time I fire a linguist, the performance of the speech recognizer goes up" (Hirschberg, 1998). From the mathematical perspective, the ideal starting point to communicate 'ideas' between these two systems lies at the bottom of the tower, that is, in the 'open basement' with minimum amounts of interference from internal structures in both systems. In multilingual AI, one of the key elements for the 'great open basement' is linguistic data, which are "common to all the towers." This means linguistic data, in particular, text corpora as discussed in Section 5.1.2 of Chapter 2, can be captured, observed, and analyzed by both humans and machines.

The focus on linguistic data, instead of human summarized rules about language, such as syntax, semantics, and pragmatics, is fundamental for deep learning (DL). Typically, results generated by DL systems are supposed to align with human reflections on language, the abstraction of which is linguistic systems, visualized as 'closed towers' in Weaver's analogy. In return, the outputs from the machine system could facilitate advanced human–computer interaction within or between each respective 'closed tower'. By way of an example, it is possible for individuals to 'talk' with the ChatGPT with its generated language. This is a demonstration that neither perspective is an absolute solution for multilingual communication. Using linguistic systems (symbolic approach) or starting from the 'great open basement' (deep learning) must work in tandem according to context and business requirements.

However, humans and machines process and 'understand' the linguistic data according to their own systems, varying from one another in both the elements and relationship between them. In order to train a machine to reach a performance level that aligns with human behavior and potential cognition, the primary question to ask is how humans can communicate their understanding of linguistic data to computer systems.

3.3   Enhancing data quality through annotation

By default, text corpora in themselves deliver information about human intention, or meaning, through the choice of tokens as well as the temporal relationship between them, which is the foundation for a language model to predict the next potential word. Every example of language in use contains a signature of human creation. As long as 'authentic' linguistic data is leveraged in a model development and optimization process, human intervention is inescapable. When humans speak or write in their native languages, the resulting text or speech typically makes sense to others who speak the same language. It is the concepts (meaning) as well as the forms (words and the relationship between them) that comply with the communicators' thoughts. 'Authentic' linguistic data, as human creation, is the starting point for the 'great open basement' when communicating ideas to computer programs.

However, the primary purpose of a naturally occurring text is not for computers to 'learn', but for humans to communicate. Thus, the signatures in natural language texts are often taken for granted, when individuals focus on communicating, rather than discovering hidden characteristics unique to humans. For special purposes when computers process and 'understand' text, annotation is often performed. This adds an extra layer of human intervention to the linguistic data. According to Pustejovsky and Stubbs (2012), annotation, also known as tagging in practice, "refers to the process of adding metadata information to the text in order to augment a computer's capability to perform Natural Language Processing (NLP)" (p. ix). In machine learning, adding metadata (i.e. data about data) to natural language text, provides additional information and context to data at multiple levels. For example, the Texas Instruments and MIT (TIMIT) corpus, as discussed in Section 5.2 of Chapter 2, contains two layers of annotation, at the phonetic and orthographic levels. Annotation, as well as associated metadata schemas, helps ML models understand relevant cases and capture 'interesting' information from raw data. To annotate a text corpus or lexical resources, an annotator often has a deeper understanding of the data, domain-specific knowledge, and analytical skills, in order to make informed judgments to provide meaningful annotations. Such knowledge can be represented in a way that computers can absorb. Chapter 7 will discuss these knowledge representation methods in detail.

Annotation can also play a significant role in data creation, management, and queries. Metadata about the datasets, such as their quality, size, and sources, could differentiate characteristics of corpora using these factors. Annotation regarding the content of the data, e.g., part of speech (POS), named entity, and machine translation post-editing errors, could provide query capabilities. This allows users to focus on a combination of extracted information and a fast, on-the-fly creation of new datasets for advanced data analysis tasks. These may lead to discovery of new information or insights for humans to incorporate as knowledge (see Staar et al., 2020, p. 2).

In corpus linguistics, annotation reflects key features of corpus design. Based on specific goals, a corpus may be annotated according to different frameworks. In general, annotation can be conducted at various linguistic levels, including morphological, syntactic, and discourse levels. The *Longman Grammar of Spoken and Written English* (Biber et al., 1999) is based on a 40 million-word Longman Spoken and Written English corpus (LSWE). This corpus includes four core registers, namely, conversation (BrE only), fiction (AmE and BrE), news (BrE), and academic prose (AmE and BrE). The annotation allows researchers to narrow down specific relevant datasets in the tagged corpus for automated computer analysis.

In many cases, in particular, during the early stages of machine learning, annotation is often done manually, by human experts. The annotators are considered knowledgeable external supervisors, who understand these examples in the training set. These experts also design annotation schemas for organized annotation activities before they annotate. In doing so, they standardize the metadata that is used to communicate human ideas to computer systems. Annotation as well as its schema reflect human considerations as to the effective use of computer techniques to achieve certain purposes.

Yet the human annotation process is usually time- and cost-consuming. To avoid this bottleneck, automatic annotation algorithms are potentially developed through both rule-based and machine learning approaches. It is worth noting that relatively 'simplistic' human reflections on linguistic information could be extremely difficult for computer programs to absorb, in a way that aligns with human perception. This is particularly true prior to the point when neural-based automatic annotation systems are sufficiently trained.

3.4 Basic machine learning approaches

Annotation enhances data quality by assigning meaningful tags to raw data. Another important concept in machine learning is labeling, which focuses on adding informative labels to unlabeled data. In machine learning, each instance of data is considered a vector, which can be considered a list of numbers. These vectors can be applied in regression analysis. For example, linear regression aims to model the relationship between two variables, e.g., independent variable 'x' and dependent variable 'y'. Generally speaking, there are two basic approaches for computer systems to 'learn' from or recognize patterns within data: supervised learning and unsupervised learning. In supervised learning, an example, or a particular instance of data, is labeled. A labeled example includes both feature(s) and the label, which can be expressed as follows:

Labeled examples: {features, label}: (x, y)

In the above expression, there are two variables: (1) the input variable, or a 'feature', which is the 'x' variable in simple linear regression, and (2) the output variable, or a 'label', which is the 'y' variable in simple linear regression. The learning objective is to predict the 'y' variable that most closely aligns with human creation/judgment given the same conditions. A simple machine learning project might use a single feature, while a more sophisticated machine learning project could use many more features (Google Developers, 2024). In both cases, feature values represent an object's characteristics and are typically presented to the computer system in the form of a vector, specifically, an input feature vector.

An unlabeled example contains features, or input feature vector, without a label. The notation for this relationship within the unlabeled dataset is shown as follows:

unlabeled examples: {features,?}: (x,?)

Regression analysis is often used to estimate the statistical relationship between a dependent variable ('y' variable, or label) and one or more independent variables ('x' variable, or feature vector). The data category of the 'y' variable can help differentiate specific forms of regression analysis. Simple linear regression, for example, is used to model the statistical relationship between two continuous variables, that is, to estimate how 'y' changes as 'x' changes. Conversely, a classification model predicts discrete values. Logistic regression is used to predict the categorical dependent variable using a given set of independent variables. This statistical relationship is described by fitting a line to the observed data. Simple linear regression uses a straight line, whereas logistic regression models use a curved line to describe the relationship between 'x' and 'y' variables.

In a typical supervised learning model development process, there are two major phases: (1) training, which enables the model to gradually learn the relationships between features and label by showing the model labeled examples, and (2) inference, which applies the trained model created in the training phase to unlabeled examples, in order to make useful predictions, often represented by the symbol 'y'' or 'ŷ' (see Google Developers, 2022). When evaluating the performance of a model, labels, usually added by humans, serve as a ground truth or a reference, from which to determine whether the model classification or predictions are correct.

For example, sentiment analysis, also known as opinion mining, is a classification task widely used in NLP. This technique determines people's attitudes toward a certain topic through the classification of the polarity in their utterances—whether the expressed opinion is positive, negative, or neutral (Satapathy et al., 2017; cited from Xiao & Li, 2023, p. 105). Sentiment analysis is one area of artificial intelligence, in which computer systems make human-like decisions concerning people's attitudes based on information gathered from text data. When training a sentiment analysis model, the model 'learns' the relationship between each data point and its associated label (e.g., positive, negative, or neutral). During the inference phase, the trained model created in the earlier phase, was applied to unlabeled examples, in order to make useful predictions. These unlabeled examples are supposed to be data points that the system has never seen before. To evaluate the model performance, it is necessary to compare the predicted value ('ŷ') with the real value of each data point. Suppose the model is $y = 2x + 3$. Data points for the predicted value ('ŷ') fall on the line. Actual value of the data point can be on or around the line, depending on the strength of the statistical relationship.

Unsupervised learning relies on unlabeled data, aiming to identify intrinsic correlations and patterns within, rather than externally imposing correlations from annotated datasets (IBM, 2023). This method of learning does not measure results against any pre-known 'ground truths', that is, human's judgments about the data, as indicated in labels. For example, in e-commerce, a recommendation system can be developed using an unsupervised association model, which could predict which products are frequently purchased together. The utility of the model is not derived from replicating human predictions, but from discovering correlations not apparent to human observers (IBM, 2023).

In the case of natural language, while many tasks are called unsupervised, they actually refer to a variant of unsupervised learning, namely, self-supervised learning, where the data provides the supervision. Using this approach, the 'correct' predictions, or the 'ground truth' can be inferred from data that is not explicitly labeled. That is to say, self-supervised learning learns a function from pairs of inputs and outputs within the input text. In other words, output data is also part of the input text. As discussed in Section 2, by default, 'authentic' linguistic data possesses signatures of humans and entails their intention and intervention in the text. The text or speech produced in real-life communication has the 'ground truth' in its word choice and positional information. Given the intrinsic relationships among words within the input text data, weak annotation information can be extracted, serving as automatically generated labels, or output data, rather than having annotators manually label the text. In so doing, self-supervised models can independently learn semantic feature representations of data, which can be further used in other downstream tasks (Synced, 2019).

Word embedding, which will be discussed in Chapter 4, adopts a self supervised learning approach. For example, word2vec, an algorithm to produce word embeddings (see Mikolov et al., 2013a), is a self-supervised learning where training labels are present in the original text. Text clustering tasks aim to categorize documents according to their semantic similarity, without using 'supervision' or manually assigned labels. This is another example of self-supervised learning, or the self-training approach (Hadifar et al., 2019).

In both supervised and unsupervised learning, the computer system, or the learning agent, are provided with a set of training examples. Each example is a description of a situation either with or without a specification (i.e., a label) of the correct action the system should take in that situation. Supervised learning aims to train the agent to extrapolate, or generalize, its responses to act correctly in situations not present in the training set. Unsupervised learning, without being provided examples of correct behavior, aims to find structure hidden in collections of unlabeled data. From the situation-reaction perspective, a third machine learning approach, alongside supervised learning and unsupervised learning (including self-supervised programs), namely, reinforcement learning, is proposed. In this type of learning, an agent's primary problem is trying to maximize a reward signal instead of trying to find a hidden structure. Reinforcement learning problems involve discovering how to map situations to actions so as to maximize a numerical reward signal (Sutton & Barto, 2014, pp. 2–4).

OpenAI's InstructGPT is an application of reinforcement learning. There are three steps in the InstructGPT method: (1) supervised fine-tuning (SFT), (2) reward model (RM) training, and (3) reinforcement learning via proximal policy optimization (PPO) on this reward model. Specifically, reinforcement learning from human feedback (RLHF) is used to fine-tune GPT-3 to follow a broad class of written instructions (Ouyang et al., 2022).

According to computational scientist, Yann LeCun, who introduced his "cake analogy" in 2016: "If intelligence is a cake, the bulk of the cake is unsupervised learning, the icing on the cake is supervised learning, and the cherry on the cake is reinforcement learning (RL)." LeCun updated his cake recipe later at the 2019 International Solid-State Circuits Conference (ISSCC) in San Francisco, replacing "unsupervised learning" with "self-supervised learning" (SSL). In practice, sometimes people use these two terms interchangeably. However, in his keynote slides at the 2019 ISSCC, Yann LeCun declared that it is necessary to disambiguate self-supervised learning from truly unsupervised learning (see Synced, 2019). The name (and formal concept) may have its origins in a 2007 paper by Raina, et al, entitled "Self-taught learning: Transfer learning from unlabeled data" in *Proceedings of the 24th international conference on machine learning* held on 20 June 2007.

According to LeCun's cake analogy, unsupervised learning, in particular, self-supervised learning, is the most significant part in multilingual AI. This has been echoed by the recent development of deep learning models as well as their applications. For example, to solve multilingual problems, more research has emerged exploring unsupervised/self-supervised models. These models include unsupervised neural machine translation (Artetxe et al., 2018), unsupervised cross-lingual Part-of-Speech tagging (Eskander et al., 2020) and pre-training of large language models such as Bidirectional Encoder Representations from Transformers (BERT) developed by Google and XLM-R developed by FacebookAI.

3.5 Using multilingual AI technologies to solve business problems

A unique characteristic of human-level artificial intelligence refers to a machine's capability to generalize, that is, its ability to produce sensible answers based on new inputs that were not encountered during training (LeCun et al., 2015, p. 437) or in its past experience based on which it forms abstractions (Garnelo & Shanahan, 2019). Such technologies, in particular, applications based on deep learning, rely more on the amount of available computation and data (LeCun et al., 2015, p. 436) than conventional linguistic rules and contextual information. Following this line of thought, multilingual AI technologies can be classified as intelligent and non-intelligent tools.

3.5.1 *Intelligent and non-intelligent tools*

To begin, intelligent technologies can be categorized based on two major paradigms for artificial intelligence, that is, symbolic and statistical approaches to AI. In multilingual communication, in addition to AI, non-intelligent tools without this generalization ability are also widely used. For example, a typical computer assisted translation (CAT) system, which aims to assist humans in their translating process by making use of previous translations (translation memory) as well as extracting and segmenting translatable strings for translators, is primarily non-intelligent. In a translation project, CAT could work separately to assist human translators so as to improve productivity. A machine translation system could also be plugged in a CAT system. In this case, an intelligent tool (i.e., a machine translator) translates and the translating results are curated and managed by CAT, a non-intelligent tool. As discussed in Section 1, the machine translation system could be rule based, which adopts a symbolic approach to AI, or neural based, which is based on deep learning.

As Garnelo and Shanahan (2019, p. 17) point out, in the recent transition wave, the connectionist paradigm to AI is increasing. This is not surprising considering the application of deep learning as an effective way to address the historical issues of labor shortages, or rather, labor shortages for new, emerging tasks that many people are not prepared for nor capable of doing when the tasks require human efforts. When new technologies come out, oftentimes the general public is not aware of the relationship between these technologies and their daily work. For example, AI technology can help extract information from text corpora, including automatically extracting terms from text. By examining a list of extracted terms, an analyst could describe some linguistic features, such as what words or phrases stand out, based on the algorithm at play. Such analysis provides information about the text type. In many cases, such qualitative analysis is limited to linguists, rather than more general users, such as Subject Matter Experts (SMEs) and business analysts. However, if such linguistic analysis can be further synthesized by machine learning, or artificial intelligence, to a level that makes sense to these general users, the multilingual AI techniques and processing results will be widely applicable. These users can immediately apply results to address their real-life problems. That is to say, machine learning can make the tools more accessible to the general public and play a more active role in the process of transferring data to information, and ultimately knowledge. As discussed in Section 2 of Chapter 2, the transfer of knowledge also depends on an individual's cognitive state. In short, the concept of 'multilingual AI' in this book includes intelligent tools as well as non-intelligent ones that support the implementation of intelligent functionalities.

3.5.2 Aligning human problems with functional technologies

It is worth noting that relatively 'simplistic' human reflections on linguistic information may be extremely difficult for computer programs to absorb, in a way that aligns with human perception. A problem that is intuitive to humans will probably differ from natural language tasks for which a technology is designed. Oftentimes such a problem must be analyzed from a machine perspective and broken down into multiple sub tasks to align with relevant functions of specific technologies, including both intelligent and non-intelligent tools. Symbolic AI often accompanies the data-driven deep learning processes, for example, as a quality evaluation and control measure. Likewise, machine learning could be embedded in a symbolic AI process. For example, conventional quality estimation methods include both hand-crafted feature engineering and machine learning processes.

That is to say, humans can easily obtain a basic understanding of a document by classifying it as a particular pre-defined, known category. If this person has some knowledge regarding what a medical document is, he or she would be able to identify if a new document belongs to the medical category or not. If this task is delegated to computer systems, this can be a typical text classification problem, which aims to achieve the goal to automatically assign natural language texts to predefined categories based on their content (Rahman et al., 2010). As a classifier task, one way of achieving this goal is to use supervised learning, training the model against texts that have been manually classified as labeled data. Another way to tackle this task is to use the concept of association rule of data mining. Association rule mining techniques are used to derive feature sets from pre-classified text documents. Then Naïve Bayes classifier is used on these extracted features for final classification. Naïve Bayes classifier is a probabilistic approach for learning to classify text (Lewis, 1992). It includes a set of supervised learning algorithms. Each word position in a document is defined as an attribute and the value of that attribute is the word found in that position. As a result, the problem of identifying text categories is divided into feature extraction tasks and machine learning tasks (See Rahman et al., 2010).

As Table 3.1 shows, multiple AI-related technologies and machine learning methodologies are adopted in this text classification problem. First, data is collected from multiple resources, e.g., electronic books, web scraping, and local documents. To build a text corpus from a website, it is important to remove HTML tags and only leave plain text as the

TABLE 3.1 Problem breakdown and corresponding technologies

Problem: text classification

No.	Problem breakdown	Corresponding technologies	Technology approach
1	Acquire a set of example documents as the training set	Data acquisition	Web scraping techniques, such as BeautifulSoup Python library
2	Preprocess the text documents by parsing and removing stop words	Data preparation	NLP techniques such as NLTK
3	Collect frequently occurring words from each document	Association rule mining	Machine learning
4	Apply association mining method	Association rule mining	Machine learning
5	Classify new documents using Naïve Bayes classifier	Naïve Bayes	Machine learning

component of the corpus. There are a number of Python libraries that can extract plain text from a website. For example, BeautifulSoup is a Python library for pulling data out of HTML and XML files (*Beautiful Soup 4.12.0 Documentation*, n.d.). To prepare data, multiple NLP techniques could be used, e.g., sentence or word segmentation, tokenization, and stop word removal. To prepare for association rule mining, frequently occurring words are typically collected from each document. In this case, each document is treated as a transaction and the set of frequently occurring words are viewed as a set of items in the transaction. Then the association mining method (Frank, 2000; cited from Rahman et al., 2010) is applied to discover sets of associated words in the documents. These sets of associated words act as features. Finally, the Naïve Bayes approach is used to classify the document. In this case, derived feature sets are used, rather than the original raw data.

Humans could usually obtain a higher level of understanding after browsing this document in addition to text categories. On the computer side, this involves more natural language tasks, for example, text retrieval, which retrieve texts in a particular text category that is required by a user through their queries, and text understanding, which transforms text in some way such as producing summaries, answering questions, or extracting data (Rahman et al., 2010).

4

SYMBOLIC MEANING AND VECTOR SEMANTICS

4.1 Symbolic approach to meaning

If a computer program aims to understand or process natural language to a significant degree, the first task it must accomplish is to represent meanings of words within its own system. Oftentimes this process involves conversion between symbolic and non-symbolic representations. Although the conversion may not be 100% accurate initially, it is hoped that the accuracy continues to increase through model optimization. As discussed in Section 1.4.3 of Chapter 1, there are two fundamental approaches for a computer program with Natural Language Understanding (NLU) capabilities to represent meaning: one is localist, symbolic, considering each linguistic sign an independent atomic unit; the other is distributional, sub symbolic, spreading meaning across a range of features associated with a linguistic sign. This section will explore these two approaches from the lexical perspective.

4.1.1 Structuralism: the Saussurean linguistic model

In modern linguistics and semiotics, a sign is a combination of meaning and form. According to the Swiss linguist Ferdinand de Saussure (b. 1857–d. 1913), acknowledged as the founder of modern linguistics and semiology (Joseph, 2023), a sign is the unified whole including both the signifier (form) and signified (meaning), or in French, *signifiant* and *signifié*. The sign is arbitrary, meaning there is no inherent reason why a signifier is linked to the signified. Such arbitrary symbolism is particularly obvious in a multilingual and multicultural environment. For example, to express the meaning or concept of 'tree', in French the signifier is 'arbre', in Spanish 'árbol' and in Chinese '树', and the selection of each signifier to represent the concept is arbitrary (see Wang & Sawyer, 2023).

Saussure proposed a linguistic model that is based on structuralism. In this model, language is comprised of a system of signs and signification. The meaning of a sign is not referential. As Jane Caplan summarized, Saussure claimed that meaning is

> the product not of reference to things exterior to it, but of a system of difference internal to language as a code...these emphasize the arbitrariness of any system of signification,

DOI: 10.4324/9781003470557-5

and to detach it from external reference, whether to the past or to the real, as the guarantee of its meaning or truth.

(1989, p. 271; see also Neilson, 2019, p. 108)

That is to say, the Saussurean linguistic model prioritizes the system of signs and sign relations within a language system, rather than simply focusing on individual signs and how they refer to actual physical objects (see also Chandler, 2017; Wang & Sawyer, 2023). This is well summarized by Firth's famous quote, "you shall know a word by the company it keeps" (1957). This book prioritizes linguistic models based on structuralism, which opens a new dimension for scientists to approach meaning through the internal structure of language, before linking signs to the physical world. It is the detachment of these two processes that makes the modern linguistic theory applicable in the development of multilingual artificial intelligence. The way in which a human begins to process language in initial stages to process meaning, even subconsciously, is often simulated by computer programs.

4.1.2 Symbols and conventions

Language is a system of symbols, in particular, it is a 'symbolic' sign system. Symbolism reflects one form of relationship between a signifier and the signified (Chandler, 2017, p. 38). From this perspective, the term 'symbol' is defined as "a sign which refers to the object that it denotes by virtue of a law, usually an association of general ideas," which causes the symbol to be interpreted as referring to that object (Peirce, 1931–58, vol. 2, p. 249). In other words, symbols are interpreted according to 'a rule' or 'a habitual connection' (Peirce, 1931–58, vol. 2, p. 292, 297, 369; cited from Chandler, 2002, pp. 38–9). These rules must be agreed upon and learned by a society as a whole. These social symbols are often used to communicate something (Chandler, 2017, pp. 40–6). Otherwise, it is not necessary for these symbols to be converted from ideas or thoughts to concrete symbolic forms. To some degree, the English verb 'to mean' or the noun phrase 'the speaker's meaning' in an oral communication process relates it either to communicative intentions or to understanding and interpretation (Lyons, 1995, p. 42). The latter is typically guided by the former, and thus is also related to intentionality.

Peirce further pointed out that "The symbol is connected with its object by virtue of the idea of the symbol-using mind, without which no such connection would exist" (1931–58, vol. 2, p. 299). In summary, the concept of a linguistic symbol is referential, which is conducted by a 'symbol-using mind'. The connection between signs and symbols is created through cognitive activities, which are bound by social conventions, for the purposes of communication. For example, the three letters of the word 'man' are not in the least like a man, nor is the sound with which they are associated. However, when people use and understand it as 'man' following conventions or rules, it is a symbol to indicate the relationship between the signifier and the object (1931–58, vol. 4, p. 447; see also Chandler, 2002, p. 39). Adding symbolic dimension to the concept of a sign is useful in terms of knowledge of semantic meanings organized in non-referential structures, as well as allowing individuals to make external connections when communicating with each other according to societal rules and conventions.

The fundamental characteristics of a linguistic symbol mirror those of a non-linguistic symbol. Both types of symbols have no immanent or inherent symbolic value but can represent and organize abstract concepts (see also Chandler, 2002, p. 75). That is to say, they are useful tools to represent human knowledge of meaning or reasoning, although they do not necessarily provide symbolic value. For example, as another arbitrary symbolism like language, mathematics is a system with mathematical symbols as well as their relations. In mathematics, the signified elements are indisputable concepts; mathematical symbols do not need to refer to objects in an external world (Langer, 1951, p. 28). Rather, they represent mathematical objects, which are de facto concepts. With these, one can carry out deductive reasoning as well as mathematical proofs. However, when mathematical symbols enter human communication, they go beyond tools for humans to organize their conceptual ideas. They function like linguistic symbols, providing similar symbolic values for people to communicate in a particular context.

4.2 Symbolic word representation

The idea of symbols and structuralism allows human intelligence to be directly and conveniently projected onto computer programming, to generate artificial intelligence. Before the 1990s, the problem of representing meaning in computer systems had typically been addressed using list-based symbolic structures (Sutcliffe, 1991, p. 279). These structures, also known as linguistic knowledge bases (KBs), offer one traditional symbolic approach to semantic meaning. There are different approaches to represent knowledge of the semantic meaning of words, in a computer system. This is often referred to as 'word representation' in multilingual AI.

4.2.1 Representation built on linguistic knowledge bases

WordNet, for example, illustrates a typical symbolic approach in action. WordNet is a structured large lexical database of English symbols developed by Princeton University. The main vehicle through which words are structured in WordNet is based on synonyms. For instance, 'car' and 'automobile' are close in relation. Cognitive synonyms are grouped into unordered sets, which are called 'synsets' in WordNet (Fellbaum, 2005). Synonym-based structures enable WordNet to be a useful tool for computers to process the meaning of natural language.

In practice, the common ground that multiple synonymous words denote is typically referred to as the same concept. Words with the same concepts are interchangeable in a variety of contexts. Each synset includes words that are interlinked by means of conceptual-semantic and lexical relations. Along a similar vein, a synset can be related to other groups of cognitive synonyms based on their specific conceptual-semantic and lexical aspects.

Linguistic KB-based approach for word representation relies significantly on linguistic analysis and the data it uses are lexical resources as discussed in Section 2.5.1 in Chapter 2. The source knowledge of semantics in this type of word representation comes from introspective reasoning. Typically, researchers reflect on the relationship between words and construct a network to represent these relationships, which are the source of word semantics. In addition to the KB-based approach, representation for a word can also be built from the context the word resides in, as structuralism suggests. There are two conventional ways to realize this goal, namely, one-hot word representation and corpus-based word representation.

4.2.2 One-hot word representation

One-hot word representation is the most straightforward symbolic method for words and phrases. This representation builds a one-to-one relationship between a linguistic symbol and a fixed-length binary vector. It maps each word to an index of vocabulary, which is denoted as 'V'. A vocabulary includes a list of all the unique words or word types in a given corpus. The size of the vocabulary can be denoted as $|V|$. This vocabulary includes a finite set of unique words, that is, $V = \{w^1, w^2, \ldots w^{|V|}\}$. Suppose a corpus consists of one sentence, "Today is a cold, cold, wet day." There are six unique or distinct words in this corpus (The word 'cold' appears twice). This vocabulary is mapped on to a $|V|$-dimensional vector W.[i] Each dimension corresponds to a direction characteristic of a unique word. One-hot representation represents a word in the vocabulary, where only the dimension characteristic of this word has a value of 1, whereas all other dimensions have a value of 0.

Table 4.1 illustrates one-hot representations for each word in the above corpus. As shown in this table, each word is represented as a vector. For example, one-hot representation for 'today' is [1 0 0 0 0 0], which is different from the representation for 'day' [0 0 0 0 0 1]. However, the vector representations do not contain any syntactic or semantic information. From this representation model, one cannot tell whether 'today' is closer in meaning to the word 'day', when compared with the word 'is' ([0 1 0 0 0 0]).

One-hot representation is the foundation of bag-of-words models (Hu et al., 2023, p. 33). The one-hot word representation can be extended to represent a sentence based on the bag-of-words hypothesis. Bag-of-words model represents sentences as a multiset of its words while ignoring the order (Hu et al., 2023, p. 83). Although there is no internal semantic structure in the one-hot representation and bag-of-words model, they play a significant role in converting linguistic symbols to mathematical symbols (vectors), to facilitate computer processing. This transition allows computer systems to further convert them to real-value vectors in distributed representations, which will be discussed in Section 4.3.

4.2.3 Corpus-based word representation

Compared with the one-hot approach, the source of semantics of corpus-based word representation comes from corpora. That is, the meaning of a word depends on the statistical

TABLE 4.1 One-hot representations for the example corpus

	Today (w^1)	is (w^2)	a (w^3)	cold (w^4)	wet (w^5)	day (w^6)
Today (dimension 1)	1	0	0	0	0	0
is (dimension 2)	0	1	0	0	0	0
a (dimension 3)	0	0	1	0	0	0
cold (dimension 4)	0	0	0	1	0	0
wet (dimension 5)	0	0	0	0	1	0
day (dimension 6)	0	0	0	0	0	1

features of this word in a corpus. The corpus-based approach uses the bag-of-words hypothesis to conduct analysis. According to this hypothesis, some fundamental semantics can be captured if a document is considered a bag of words, in which the order of words is ignored. The frequencies of the words in the bag offers some semantic information about a document or text data. Suppose a corpus contains two documents, each of which contains one sentence:

Document 1: Today is a cold, cold, wet day.
Document 2: Yesterday was a warm, warm, dry day.

Table 4.2 illustrates frequencies for each word in these two documents, which offers statistics for vectorization. In this table, there are nine words in the bag: 'Today', 'Yesterday', 'is', 'was', 'a', 'cold', 'warm', 'wet', 'day'. In each cell, the number is the count of frequency of that word. For example, 'cold' appears twice in document one, whereas it does not appear in document two. In this way, a document is represented by a row vector. Document one's vector is $[1, 0, 1, 0, 1, 2, 0, 1, 1]$ and document two's is $[0, 1, 0, 1, 1, 0, 2, 1, 1]$. Each column represents the occurrence of a word in these two documents. The statistics for each word symbol tells some semantic features of these two documents. For example, 'cold' appears twice in document one and 'warm' appears twice in document two. Intuitively, these two words are the most outstanding differences between these two documents. One can naturally paraphrase this difference as the first document highlights the 'cold' feature of weather, whereas the second document highlights the 'warm' feature.

Such intuitions can be measured using machine learning methods such as Term Frequency Inverse Document Frequency (TF-IDF). Equation 4.1 defines a common way to calculate TF-IDF (Salton & Buckley, 1988).

$$tf - idf\left(t_i, d_j\right) = \text{count}\left(t_i, d_j\right) \times \log \frac{|\text{corpus}|}{\text{count.doc}\left(t_i, \text{corpus}\right)} \qquad \text{(Equation 4.1)}$$

In Equation 4.1, $\text{count}(t_i, d_j)$ refers to the frequency of term t_i (the i-th word) in a document d_j (the j-th document) in a corpus. Term frequency (tf) represents the number of times a word appears in a document. In the second part of the right-hand equation, the numerator $|\text{corpus}|$ refers to the number of documents in the corpus. The denominator $\text{count.doc}(t_i, \text{corpus})$ refers to the number of documents in the corpus that contain the term t_i.

For example, TF for 'cold' in document one is 2 and in document two is 0; TF for 'warm' in document two is 0 and in document two is 2. Inverse Document Frequency (IDF) for both words ('cold' and 'warm') is the same. Out of a total of two documents in a corpus, each word is included in one document. Thus, $\text{count.doc}(t_i, \text{corpus})$ is $\log \frac{2}{1} = 0.301$.

TABLE 4.2 Document representations based on bag-of-words

	Word frequency								
Bags-of-words	Today	Yesterday	is	was	a	cold	warm	wet	day
Document 1	1	0	1	0	1	2	0	1	1
Document 2	0	1	0	1	1	0	2	1	1

For the word 'cold', tf in document one is 2. Thus tf-idf for 'cold' in document one is $2 \times 0.301 = 0.601$. Conversely, tf for 'cold' in document two is 0 and tf-idf is 0. This means the word 'cold' is more outstanding in document one than document two.

4.2.4 Problems of symbolic word representation

In a symbolic approach, each word is considered a discrete symbol that contains a semantic meaning. An approach such as this is developed favorably for cognition. The concept of a 'symbol' is primarily a vehicle for humans to better understand the world and communicate with one another. However, this approach is not the best choice for computers. To begin, the linguistic KB-based approach involves a great amount of human effort in terms of both summarizing lexical semantic features and aligning these features with computer algorithms. To some degree, this approach originates in human intelligence and strives to instruct machines to execute this intelligence in a computer system, which does not necessarily work the same way as humans.

For example, as a large lexical database, WordNet organizes English nouns, verbs, adjectives, and adverbs into sets of synonyms, based on human reflections and reasoning synonym sets, or synsets, demonstrate semantic relations among words within a synset as well as among different synsets. The structured database facilitates functionalities to extract information based on meaning, rather than form, such as alphabetics. WordNet combines traditional lexicographic information and computing capabilities (Miller, 1995): the former is an example of human intelligence, whereas the latter demonstrates what humans can make machines do, depending on how humans materialize their intelligence, as well as the strength of the design. However, such a capability is not machine intelligence, as it is handcrafted externally, rather than learned from data within a computer system. Thus, though intuitive and interpretable, such an approach does not fully utilize machines' learning abilities.

The other two types of symbolic approaches convert symbols to vectors as a way to represent words. One hot representation uses binary numbers for elements within a vector and corpus-based word representation uses text statistics. These two approaches offer limited functionality to capture sufficient semantic information due to the issues associated with high dimensionality. In the corpus illustrated by Table 4.1, there is only one sentence. If a corpus includes 10,000 unique words, then the vector size for that corpus is 10,000. If one hot word representation is used, each word must be represented in a vector that includes values of 9,999 entries of 0 and only 1 dimension with a value of 1. That is the reason behind the one 'hot' name, as there is only one element in the vector with a value of "1." Computers require both large storage capacities and significant computing power to work on these high-dimensional representations. Furthermore, as most entries of a vector are zeros, also known as the data sparsity issue, the computation is less meaningful even though it costs a huge amount of computing power. The results for computing similarities between different words are often not significant enough for computers to tell the differences between these words.

4.3 Distributed word representation

Word representation aims to build a computational model of meaning. Such models can be roughly divided into two broad classes: localist and distributed (Ralph, 1998, p. 339). The three conventional symbolic models discussed in Section 4.2, adopt localist architectures to model word meaning. In the localist approach, each word is represented by one single unit or entity in a computer system, which can be a node in a synset of WordNet, or a binary number (0 or 1) in one hot encoding, or a decimal number that signifies the outstanding quality of a word in a corpus.

Conversely, distributed models do not use this one-to-one correspondence. In distributed representations, each lexical item is encoded as a pattern of activation across a number of elements, each of which can be utilized as a component of many different representations (Ralph, 1998, pp. 339–40).

4.3.1 Distributed vs. localist representations

Distributed representations are often associated with connectionism, which is an approach to the study of human cognition that utilizes mathematical models. These models are also known as connectionist networks or artificial neural networks, which are usually presented as highly interconnected, neuron-like processing units (*Connectionism*, n.d.). Within a connectionist distributed representation, abstract knowledge materializes as a pattern of activation across many processing units. This is a breakthrough of human understanding of their internal cognitive state, not only from a theoretical perspective, but more importantly, through practical simulations in computer systems. Again, as Ralph (1998) pointed out, in artificial neural networks, each processing unit contributes to representations of multiple words, rather than only one word or object (Bowers, 2009, p. 220; cited from Dawson, 2020).

Such an architecture also explains why distributed representations are not interpretable to a large extent. The units or entities this type of modeling operate on are not symbols, but parts of the symbols, or 'sub symbols'. The task of dividing symbols into pieces or dimensions is delegated to machines, primarily following computational and mathematical rules, rather than human intuitive reasoning. As the dimensions and units involved (or 'neurons') in this task increase exponentially, the inner workings of distributing meaning across units become impossible for humans to trace manually, as well as to explain how such a result is generated based on reasoning.

This chapter focuses on neural network-based, or connectionist distributed representations. As discussed in Section 3.1 of Chapter 3, the connectionist approach to neural-network-based cognitive modeling, encompasses the recent deep learning movement in artificial intelligence (Kiefer, 2019).

Furthermore, the differentiation between localist and distributed representations depends on the level of natural language analysis. For example, Term Frequency Inverse Document Frequency (TF-IDF) uses one number to refer to the outstanding quality of a word in a corpus. This is a one-to-one correspondence on the word level. On the document level, however, each document can be represented by TF-IDF numbers for all unique words in this document. In this sense, the vector to represent the document is distributed representation.

Finally, it should be noted that 'distributed representation' is different from 'distributional representation' or 'distributional hypothesis' (Harris, 1954). The former describes the form of representation, in the same vein as symbolic representation. The latter, however, indicates the source of semantics. As discussed in Section 4.2.3, the corpus-based approach is based on the distributional hypothesis, which can be considered "a simplified version of the classic structuralist hypothesis" (Gastaldi & Pellissier, 2021). According to this hypothesis, the meaning of a word is described by its companions, using contextual information (see also Wang & Sawyer, 2023; Firth, 1957).

4.3.2 The word space model

The word space model is a corpus-based method for inducing distributed semantic representations for a large number of words. When Schutze (1992, pp. 895–902) proposed this model, he emphasized using lexical occurrence statistics to automatically generate such a representation. In a word space model, the meaning of a word is spread across feature vectors. As Schutze (1992, p. 896) pointed out, the features are used to represent words, but cannot be interpreted on their own. Schutze (1992) argued that "Vector similarity is the only information present in Word Space: semantically related words are close, unrelated words are distant" (p. 896). It is important to note that the emphasis in the word space model is on semantic similarity, rather than decomposition into interpretable features.

A word space is multidimensional. In this space, each word has its own individual representation. Schutze (1992, p. 896) argued that a space with high dimensionality is likely to capture more of the complexity of semantic relatedness present in natural language. The primary goal of this space is not to cluster words into classes, as any clustering introduces artificial boundaries (Schutze, 1992, p. 897). Though this paper was published in 1992, its focus on semantic relatedness measured in real values, as well as the idea of projecting representations in an n-dimensional space, is significant for research and applications in this field. As Sahlgren (2006, p. 17) pointed out, among many computational models to generate a word space, such as Word2Vec (Mikolov et al., 2013) and Bidirectional Encoder Representations from Transformers (BERT) (Devlin et al., 2019), the underlying theories and assumptions are all based on semantic similarity or relatedness.

4.3.3 Vector space

Word space is an example of vector space application. In linear algebra, a vector space consists of a set of vectors and a field which contains scalars as its elements. Scalars are usually considered to be real numbers. In this space, two operations can be conducted: (1) vector addition, which produces a third vector that also belong to this vector space; and (2) scalar multiplication, which produces a new vector that belong to this vector space by taking a scalar in this field and a vector in the space. That is to say, in a vector space, vectors can be added collectively and multiplied, or 'scaled', by numbers (*Vector Space- Definition, Axioms, Properties and Examples*, n.d.).

In mathematics and physics, a vector is an object that has both a magnitude (size) and a direction. Geometrically, a vector can be pictured as a directed line segment, whose length is the magnitude of the vector and with an arrow indicating the direction (*An Introduction to Vectors*, n.d.). In Natural Language Processing and Understanding, as- *The Measurement of Meaning* (Osgood et al., 1957) argued, a sign "is represented as a point in an n-dimensional space" and "the sign has projections onto each of the dimensions" (p. 28). That is to say, when the meaning of a word is defined as a point in space, each dimension carries part of the overall meaning. Suppose there is a word in a five-dimensional space.

The location of this word is described as a vector [0.135, 0.352, 1.582, 3.891, –8.832]. In the list of numbers within the vector, each number indicates the value in one dimension for this word, or one aspect of the word's meaning.

4.4 Semantic embeddings

Vectorization is an effective way to measure the meaning. Such an approach prioritizes language in use, which is often collected and organized in corpora. The first step of vectorization of natural language is to convert symbolic words to numbers.

4.4.1 Sparse vectors

One way to achieve this goal is through statistics about linguistic distribution. As Zellig Harris (1954) pointed out, if A and B have almost identical environments except that they are in different sentences, A and B are synonyms, for example, 'oculist' and 'eye-doctor'; if A and B have some environments in common and some not, for example, 'oculist' and 'lawyer', they have different meanings (p. 157). Harris (1954) reinforced that "the amount of meaning difference corresponds roughly to the amount of difference in their environments" (p. 157).

Some methods to measure meaning were derived from this distributional hypothesis. For example, term-term matrix, also known as word-word matrix or term-context matrix, converts words in a corpus to vectors according to co-occurrence statistics. This method uses the number of instances of one word co-occurring with other words in the context in the training corpus, to create a vector. For example, in the training corpus, the word 'conservation' co-occurs four times with 'biodiversity', eight times with 'sustainable', but never occurs with 'global'. These three words, 'biodiversity', 'sustainable', and 'global' can be considered three dimensions of the vector for the word 'conservation', which is [4, 8, 0] (see Wang & Sawyer, 2023, pp. 61–4).

As discussed in Section 4.3.4, word representations using a symbolic approach to vectorization have high dimensionality and data sparsity issues. In this approach, each dimension corresponds to a unique word (or word type) in the vocabulary. If a corpus contains a huge amount of unique words, the size of the vector could be very large with values of most dimensions being zeros. Thus, dense vectors are often used to further extract features from the original corpus to reduce dimensionality, which helps ease the sparsity issue.

4.4.2 Dense vectors

Unlike sparse, long vectors, dense vectors are short, with the number of dimensions ranging from 50 to 1,000, rather than the much larger vocabulary size. These vectors "are dense: instead of vector entries being sparse, mostly-zero counts or functions of counts, the values will be real value numbers that can be negative" (Jurafsky & Martin, 2020, p. 112).

Dense vectors entail feature extraction (Wang & Sawyer, 2023, p. 64). Such feature extraction usually applies additional mathematical techniques above and beyond using frequencies of words or word context (co-occurrence). In processes such as these, computer programs are more autonomous, when compared to feature extractions conducted by humans. For example, the concept of 'father' includes multiple facets, such as 'man' and 'parent'. In a linguistic KB-based approach, one can consider each of these facets, or 'sub-concepts', as dimensions, which are both intuitive and interpretable.

However, features extracted through an autonomous process oftentimes are not interpretable using human intuition. Each dimension refers to an 'artificial' feature machines have learned from the training data, rather than pre-defined by humans. For example, if a vector for the concept of 'father' [0.135, 0.352, 1.582, 3.891, -8.832], one can not directly align a number in this vector with a symbolic feature such as a word. The value of 0.135 does not necessarily mean 'man'. Though not interpretable, the whole vector contributes to the meaning of the word.

Furthermore, these vectors can be added collectively and multiplied. For example, word-2vec is a technique to learn word embeddings using shallow neural networks. Based on this technique, the male/female relationship is automatically learned. With induced vector representations, king – man + woman results in a vector very close to queen (Mikolov et al., 2013b, p. 746).

Such mathematical operations allow dense vectors to go beyond human intuition. Methods such as word2vec offer a new dimension of thinking as to what is meant by a word and how the meaning of a word is related to other words semantically (Wang & Sawyer, 2023, p. 59).

Dense vectors are often called embeddings, as the meaning is embedded in a vector space. Generally, embeddings are "vectors for representing words as a point in a multidimensional semantic space that is derived from the distributions of word neighbors, although the term is sometimes applied more specifically to dense vectors like word2vec" (see Jurafsky & Martin, 2020, p. 100; cited from Wang & Sawyer, 2023, p. 58). Most modern multilingual AI algorithms use embeddings as the representation of word meaning.

4.4.3 Case study: using word2vec to generate word embeddings

Word2vec (the coined word originates from the phrase "word to vector") uses shallow neural networks to learn word embeddings (see Mikolov, Chen, Corrado, and Dean, 2013a). Instead of counting how often each word occurs near a target word, like the term-term matrix solution, word2vec trains a classifier on a binary prediction task, which aims to identify whether a word is likely to show up near the target word or not (see Wang & Sawyer, 2023, pp. 65–7). As a binary classifier, the algorithm can decide whether an input, represented by a vector of numbers, belongs to some specific class.

Word2vec adopts self supervised learning, which includes both input features and labels. As Section 3.4 of Chapter 3 suggests, the training labels used by the word2vec model are present in the original text. That is to say, the same word in the training data can be both features and labels. Word2vec's classification algorithm is based on a linear predictor function. Such a function includes a set of coefficients and independent variables, whose value is used to predict the outcome of a dependent variable (Makhoul, 1975). In a training process, the system aims to find the optimal coefficients or weights to make the outcome produced by the model as close as possible to the labels provided in the training data.

In word2vec, what is more relevant to embeddings is not the values the prediction model produces, but rather the resulting learned classifier weights, when the model is optimal. At this optimal state, the distance between the predicted outcomes and labels in the training data are minimal. These weights or coefficients are sources of embeddings that represent word meaning.

There are two model architectures for word2vec, namely, the Continuous Bag-of-Words (CBOW) model and the Continuous Skip-gram (Skip-gram) model. In the CBOW architecture, the system is provided with the context of the word and its task is to predict the word. The contextual range before and after the word can be pre-determined by developers. For example, there can be two words before and after a given word. In the Skip-gram model, however, the system is given this word, but needs to predict the surrounding words (Mikolov, Chen, Corrado, and Dean, 2013).

Embeddings implicitly learned through the input-layer weights of the word2vec model have been found to be surprisingly good at capturing syntactic and semantic regularities in language (Mikolov, Yih, & Zweig, 2013, pp. 746–51). Vector representation of words produced by word2vec allows simple algebraic operations to be performed. For example, to find a word that is similar to small in the same sense as biggest is similar to big, one can compute vector X = vector("biggest") –vector("big") + vector("small"). Then, by searching in the vector space for the word closest to X, measured by cosine distance, using it as the answer to the question (the input question words during this search were discarded). When the word vectors are well trained, it is possible to find the correct answer (word 'smallest') using this method (Mikolov, Yih, & Zweig, 2013, pp. 746–51).

Wang and Sawyer (2023) used a UN corpus to customize a word2vec model in 2021. Specifically, the authors adopted the Gensim word2vec model to generate word embeddings. The vector size set in this model is 100. With the generated word embeddings, the system can identify semantic features of certain words. For example, the result returned from the model's call to compare the similarity between 'biodiversity' and 'document' is –0.1630206. This example illustrates that these two words are not close in meaning. Conversely, the similarity score between 'resolution' and 'assembly' is 0.12890144, suggesting these two words are positively related. There are other useful results generated from customized learning. For example, the system can show the top five words that are associated with 'biodiversity' and 'cooperation'. These terms are 'initiatives', 'strategic', 'importance', 'people', and 'stakeholders' (Wang & Sawyer, 2023, pp. 61–7). Though this process is autonomous and not instructed by humans, the results are significantly aligned with those of human analysis.

PART TWO

Large language models

Theories and applications

5

MULTILINGUAL LARGE LANGUAGE MODELS, FINE-TUNING, AND PROMPT ENGINEERING

5.1 Machine learning

In Section 2.2 of Chapter 2, the concepts of data and information were defined and differentiated. To begin, data represents facts about the world. Information, however, refers to the facts (data) that are systematically presented in a given context. In other words, information contains refined data filtered through a specific context, which can be both physical and cognitive. When people describe a piece of information as irrelevant or redundant, this judgment is based on their individual understanding.

5.1.1 Information in communication

If a person wants to find out whether it is raining outside, the answer that it is 23 degrees celsius is a fact but does not help answer the question. Thus, it is not relevant information for the person who seeks the answer. When an individual aims to answer this question, the way in which they filter data is a process of choice, depending on the context. The question and the answer, each involve the same message, even though these pathways require different approaches. The problem of choice regarding the message from the questioning individual and the respondent is the key when communicating with each other. As Section 2.2 pointed out, a most significant feature of communication is the potential of making choices. The possibility of choices, as well as their associated meanings, produces information, and can be used to measure information. To echo Shannon and Weaver (1963), "information is a measure of one's freedom of choice" (pp. 8–9) when selecting a message.

The transmission of data and the flow of information centering around the same message, as well as their associated meanings, are significant reasons illustrating why communication is necessary. As Shannon and Weaver (1963) described, the "fundamental problem of communication is that of reproducing at one point either exactly or approximately a message selected at another point" (p. 31). Specifically, the information transmitted over a noisy channel is the fundamental problem of all communication processes (see Section 1.4.3 of Chapter 1).

DOI: 10.4324/9781003470557-7

5.1.2 *The noisy channel model*

Here, the center of the problem is the noisy channel, which is a blocker of a communication process and allows a range of options to be considered. To address this challenge, the noisy channel model provides a probabilistic framework to conceptualize natural language processes when handling uncertainty in communication, including machine translation, spell checker, question answering, and speech recognition. In this framework, language production and understanding are a communication process over a 'noisy channel'. The noise in this channel can be actual noise in a room in oral communication. In multilingual communication events, the noise can be a language barrier, for example, the speaker speaks English, but the listener can only understand French. The objective of this model is to recover the original message (the intended meaning), which is considered distorted or "corrupted" by noise, based on the observed, noisy output.

Situations that require passing messages from one point in communication to another vary, including asking questions to seek answers, translating source texts to target texts, and summarizing a full text with a short summary. These situations constitute the fundamental relationships between information at one point and that reproduced at another point in natural language tasks. In statistical machine translation, for example, the noisy channel model assumes that a source sentence is a noisy version of a target sentence. The model entails a channel model probability that operates in the reverse direction as well as a language model probability (Yee et al., 2019, p. 5696).

This model can be illustrated using information theory. To begin, the information source produces a text message written in natural language, say in English, which is denoted as e. This message is encoded by the transmitter, using an encoding system, e.g., Morse code. Through the noisy channel, in this case, a telegraph wire, the signal (encoded message) was transmitted to the receiver, which decodes the signal from Morse code to a text message written in natural language, which is denoted as f. This received message can be in English or in another language.

The problem is that given the final message f, how the original message e can be reconstructed. This reconstructed message is also the predicted message from the source, which is denoted as $\hat{e}$. Due to the noise in the channel, the final decoded message may contain errors. That is to say, e and $\hat{e}$ are often not identical. The goal of the encoder and decoder is to find a message of $\hat{e}$ that maximizes the probability of f given e (see equation 5.1). Whatever message that satisfies these conditions would be the best hypothesis for the original message e.

$$\hat{e} = \mathrm{argmax}_e \, p \, (e \mid f) \qquad\qquad \text{(Equation 5.1)}$$

According to Equation 5.1, the estimate $\hat{e}$ equals an argmax[1] operation over the original message e, meaning the objective is to find a message e which maximizes the total value of the equation $p(e|f)$, p of e given f. To facilitate reliable communication over an unreliable channel, an encoder (transmitter) and a decoder (receiver) are added to the communication system, to detect and correct errors introduced by the channel. If there is an error-free transmitter and an error-free receiver, e and $\hat{e}$ must be identical.

Based on the available resources, there are three components to work on: a collection of the original information, a collection of the received information, and some possible factors that might cause errors in transmission. Accordingly, three model can be constructed: (1) by examining the dataset of the original information in natural language, for example, the English message, one can construct a language model for the source message, p (e); (2) similarly, by examining a dataset of the decoded information, one can construct a language model for the received message in the target language, which can be English or a foreign language, p (f); and (3) if some insights as to what causes errors in transmission can be leveraged, one can construct a probabilistic model of the channel, p $(f|e)$, p of f given e.

As none of these models are included in Equation 5.1, Bayes's Theorem (Equation 5.2) for conditional probabilities (Bayes & Price, 1763) is used.

$$p(e \mid f) = \frac{p(f \mid e) \; p(e)}{p(f)} \qquad \text{(Equation 5.2: Bayes's Theorem)}$$

Bayes' Theorem defines a posterior probability $p(e \mid f)$, that is, the updated probability of an event occurring after taking into consideration new information, in terms of the three component distributions modeled from the available resources, namely, language models $p(e)$ and $p(f)$ as well as the channel model $p(f \mid e)$. If Equation 5.2 is plugged in Equation 5.1, Equation 5.1 will be redefined with these models (Equation 5.3).

$$\hat{e} = \text{argmax}_e \; \frac{p(f \mid e) \; p(e)}{p(f)} \qquad \text{(Equation 5.3)}$$

The denominator of the fraction in Equation 5.3 is $p(f)$, which only depends on f. It will not affect the argmax operation over the English message e, that is, an instance of e that maximizes the total value of the equation $\frac{p(f \mid e) \; p(e)}{p(f)}$. The equation is simplified by removing the denominator. Thus Equation 5.1 was finally redefined as:

$$\hat{e} = \text{argmax}_e \; p(f \mid e) \; p(e) \qquad \text{(Equation 5.4)}$$

In Equation 5.4, the estimate source information $\hat{e}$ is only defined by the channel model $p(f \mid e)$ and the English model $p(e)$. In a statistical machine translation model, the channel model $p(f \mid e)$ is the translation (or equivalence) model and $p(e)$ is the language model for the target language.

In machine learning, oftentimes the model performance can be controlled by manipulating the encoder and decoder. As long as the behavior of the two events e and f can be observed, a person can use the noisy channel equation to find what types of encoders and decoders produce the best estimate of e.

5.1.3 Machine learning and information theory

One significant contribution of Shannon's mathematical theory of communication is its abstraction power. This theory allows mathematical symbols and operations, such as 1s and 0s, to be applied to both human communication in daily lives and data transmission from one point to another. A mathematical approach to the quantification, transmission, and processing of information is the foundation of modern information theory. According to Murphy (2012), information theory

> is concerned with representing data in a compact fashion (a task known as data compression or source coding), as well as with transmitting and storing it in a way that is robust to errors (a task known as error correction or channel coding).
>
> *(p. v)*

In essence, machine learning and information theory are two sides of the same coin (MacKay, 2003, p. v.). On the one hand, information theory defines the channel capacity to carry signals (information as opposed to noise) whereas machine learning is the other way around, focusing on extracting information from data. For example, Shannon's noisy channel coding theorem (1948) describes the maximum possible efficiency of error-correcting methods versus levels of noise interference and data corruption, whereas a rule-based machine learning method, association rules, aims to discover interesting relations between items in large databases. To some degree, the success of a machine learning algorithm depends on how much 'interesting' information (as opposed to noise) has been captured from the original data.

5.1.4 Representation learning

Strictly speaking, the 'interesting' information captured from data is in the form of features. A feature is a representation of the data, which "contains only the information that is relevant for the problem at hand" (Manolescu, 1998, p. 2). The process of extracting (new) features from existing ones, or raw data is called feature extraction. This topic will be further discussed in Chapter 6.

The choice of features greatly impacted the performance of machine learning methods (see Bengio et al., 2012, p. 1). As discussed in Chapter 2, natural language data in its raw format, as symbols that are intended for human understanding and served as the basis for machine intelligence, can be considered an entry to a machine world. Within this world, to unleash machine power, a fundamental task that must be completed is to convert the raw text data into a format that can be processed by machine learning algorithms.

Conventional machine learning techniques usually require careful engineering and considerable domain expertise to design a feature extractor. This process is called feature engineering, which focuses on the design of preprocessing pipelines and data transformations. To make machine learning more effective, feature engineering takes advantage of human knowledge to address the weaknesses of current learning algorithms. However, this approach is labor-intensive and cannot extract and organize the discriminative information from the data (Bengio et al., 2012, p. 1).

Alternatively, a system can automatically learn features from raw data. This means the system will be intelligent enough to understand the world around us. In other words, the system "can learn to identify and disentangle the underlying explanatory factors hidden in the observed milieu of low-level sensory data" (Bengio et al., 2012, p. 1). Such a process is representation learning, or feature learning. It refers to learning transformations of the data that make it easier to extract useful information when building classifiers or other predictors (Bengio et al., 2012, p. 1). Representation learning is data-driven. It allows a machine to discover representations needed for detecting or classifying patterns in the raw data on its own.

5.2   Artificial Neural Network (ANN)

There are various ways for a machine to learn features. This book will focus on neural network-based approaches. Word embeddings, as discussed in Chapter 4, is based on learning a distributed representation for each word. Word2vec, for example, uses a shallow artificial neural network. Conversely, deep learning contains multiple non-linear transformations of the data, "with the goal of yielding more abstract—and ultimately more useful representations" (Bengio et al., 2012, p. 1). Starting from the raw input, such as text data, deep learning comprises simple but non-linear modules, each of which transform the representation at one level into a representation at a higher, more abstract level. Theoretically, the higher the layers of representation from the raw input, the more relevant the information is, in terms of how the learning objectives are achieved. As LeCun et al. (2015) pointed out, deep learning is "obtained by composing simple but non-linear modules that each transform the representation at one level (starting with the raw input) into a representation at a higher, slightly more abstract level" (p. 436).

5.2.1   Perceptron

The building block for an artificial neural network is perceptron. A perceptron, also known as McCulloch–Pitts neuron, is a supervised learning algorithm. Figure 5.1 illustrates its architecture. A perceptron starts with an input layer, which is a single layer of neurons $(x^1, x^2 \dots x^m)$. Usually, there is an additional input, known as bias, which acts as a constant offset. By applying weights $(w_1, w_2 \dots w_m)$ to these neurons, the perceptron produces an output, through an activation function. Note that there are no hidden layers between the input and output in the perceptron.

Weights $(w_1, w_2 \dots w_m)$ connecting features are adjustable. As a result of weight adjustments, the impact of individual inputs is scaled. The nonlinear activation function is based

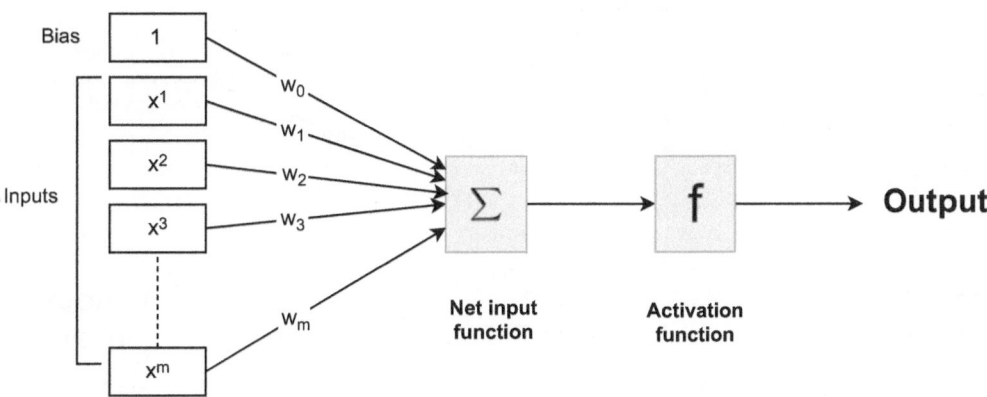

FIGURE 5.1   Perceptron algorithm.

on the weighted sum of inputs. If the sum is above some threshold, the neuron "fires" a signal, otherwise it does not. Thus, there are two options (classes), "yes or no," or "0 or 1," or other labels, meaning the neuron is activated or not activated.

5.2.2 Multilayer perceptron (MLP)

A single perceptron is limited in its functionality. It divides the classes of inputs and outputs with a straight line, thus cannot solve any function that is not linearly separable. To overcome this limitation, multiple perceptrons are stacked together. Such models are referred to as multilayer perceptrons (MLP) or simple neural networks. An MLP refers to a type of artificial neural network (ANN) that consists of multiple layers of interconnected nodes (neurons) organized in a feedforward manner, meaning the data representation activities move from the input to the output, layer by layer, without recurrent activities. Unlike perceptron, an MLP typically has one or more hidden layers between the input and output. Each hidden layer applies an activation function to the weighted sum of its inputs. The MLP model can learn complex non-linear relationships in the data and make predictions based on those learned patterns. Figure 5.2 illustrates the algorithm of an MLP.

In perceptrons, the input units are directly connected to the output units. In this case, it is relatively easy to find learning rules that iteratively adjust the relative strengths of the connections so as to progressively reduce the cost error (see Minsky & Papert, 1969). The input connections are fixed by hand. The representations of the data are not learned but determined by the input vector. The goal of weight adjustments is to find a modification rule appropriate for a particular task domain.

However, MLPs can include one or more hidden layers between the input and output. In this case, learning becomes "more interesting but difficult," as the actual and desired states of these hidden units are not specified by the task (Rumelhart et al., 1986, p. 533). To achieve the desired input-output behavior, the learning procedure must decide under what circumstances the hidden units should be active (Rumelhart et al., 1986, p. 533).

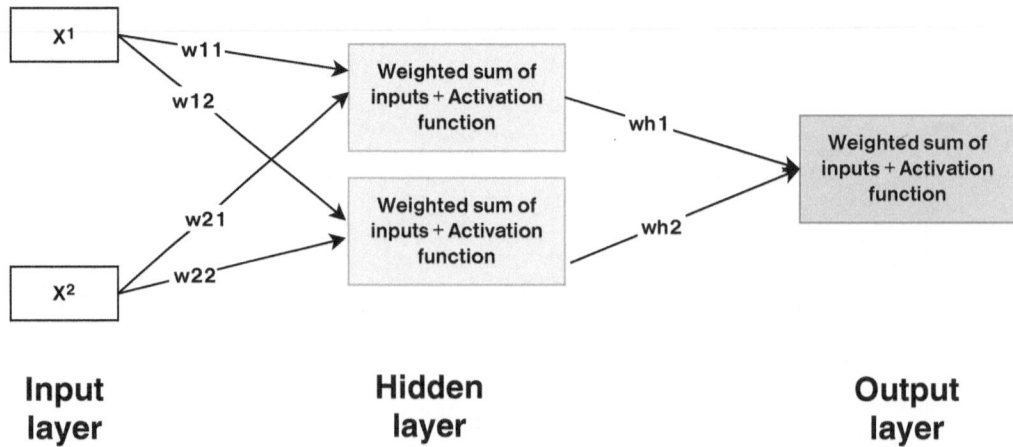

FIGURE 5.2 Multilayer algorithm.

The bias unit is not shown to simplify the diagram.

Adopting a feedforward model is an efficient way to solve this problem. Figure 5.2 illustrates a feedforward pass from the input to the output. In this diagram, a feedforward layered network includes a layer of input units on the left, an intermediate (hidden) layer in the middle, and a layer of output units on the right. In a feedforward network, information can only go one way, as shown in Figure 5.2, from left to right. Inputs on the left are computed using the initial weights to start with to get a weighted sum, which is then applied to the activation function. The result of the computation in the hidden layer, or their internal representation of the data, is propagated to the output layer. Such an internal representation is learned by the network, rather than fixed by hand.

5.2.3   Model optimization

In machine learning, a computer can provide multiple methods of finding the patterns, but only the method that has the lowest cost and performs best will be used. In model development, optimization plays a significant role in determining what the algorithm learns. Goodfellow et al. (2016) defined optimization as the task of either minimizing or maximizing some function $f(x)$ by altering x. The authors pointed out most optimization problems focus on minimizing $f(x)$, while maximization may be accomplished via a minimization algorithm by minimizing $-\mathbf{f(x)}$ (p. 80).

Goodfellow et al. (2016, p. 80) further clarified that the function to be minimized or maximized is called the objective function, or criterion. When it is minimized, it may also be called the cost function, loss function, or error function. Following the approach of Goodfellow et al. (2016), this book will use these terms interchangeably, while noticing that some machine learning publications assign special meaning to some of these terms.

Simply speaking, the cost function measures the difference between the correct answer (the ground truth) and the answer provided by the deep learning algorithm (Mueller & Massaron, 2019, Chapter 5). In both the perceptron (Figure 5.1) and the feedforward MLP (Figure 5.2), the loss of relevant model is calculated, for example, by using Mean Squared Error (MSE). MSE is a method to calculate loss function in machine learning. This method takes the square of the difference between a correct value and the value predicted by the algorithm. When the difference is great, the squared value is even greater, highlighting the algorithm error (Mueller & Massaron, 2019). For example, If the predicted outcome produced by the model $\hat{y}$ is 0.75, whereas the actual value of y is 1. The MSE value will be $(1-0.75)^2 = 0.0625$. By minimizing the difference between the correct value (label) and the predicted value, the cost function determines what the algorithm learns. During an optimization phase, the cost function provides feedback to a machine learning model on how well the model fits the data.

There are several different types of cost functions in machine learning. The choice depends on the specific task and the type of model. For example, mean squared error (MSE) is commonly used for regression problems, whereas cross entropy or log loss is usually used for classification problems.

The cost function is the total error of the performance of the network given a particular set of weights. To minimize this error, the model parameters (weights and biases) must be adjusted. These adjustments constitute a learning procedure. An algorithm for this procedure that is widely applied in networks of neuron-like units is backpropagation. According to Rumelhart et al. (1986), backpropagation repeatedly adjusts the weights of the connections in the network in order to minimize the cost error (p. 533).

Backpropagation is a gradient-based optimization method. Specifically, a technique called gradient descent is applied. It uses the derivative of a function (e.g., $y = f(x)$), which is denoted as $f'(x)$ or $\dfrac{dy}{dx}$. The derivative specifies how to scale a small change in the input to obtain the corresponding change in the output: $f(x) + \varepsilon = f(x) + \varepsilon f'(x)$ (see Goodfellow et al., 2016, p. 81). Here ε is a tiny number, close to zero. By repeatedly making a small move toward better configurations, the system is able to optimize the parameters of the network.

5.2.4 Deep learning

Deep learning models have achieved remarkable gains in many domains such as speech recognition, natural language processing, and transfer learning (Bengio et al., 2012; Lake et al., 2017, p. 1; LeCun et al., 2015; Schmidhuber, 2015). As LeCun et al. (2015) pointed out, deep learning discovers intricate structure in large data sets, which indicates how a machine should change its internal parameters that are used to compute the representation in each layer from the representation in the previous layer (p. 436).

Figure 5.3 illustrates a deep learning architecture. From left to right, each layer maps its input to output, which typically has a different number of dimensions. For example, the first input layer is one hot encoding. Each element is represented by a large, sparse vector. The general practice is that the first few layers reduce the dimensionality of the input, whereas the last few layers increase the dimensionality. The dimensionality of the encoded data in the middle, that is, data that expresses the input in a different representation space, is much less than the layers before and after. Specifically, there are three parts of deep learning architecture. The first part 'encoder' is related to input, which receives an input and generates an encoded data. Another part is called 'decoder', which takes the encoded data and converts it to the output representation space. The smallest representation of the data in the middle is the encoded data, or the context vector. The layers before this encoded

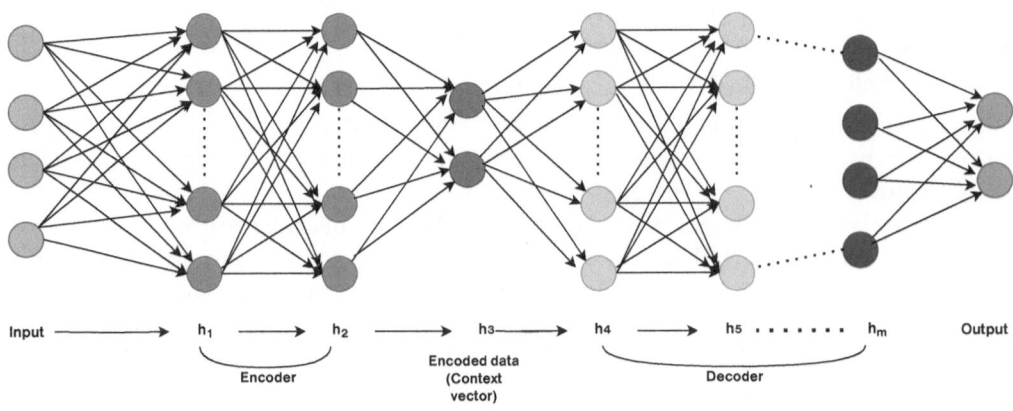

FIGURE 5.3 Deep learning architecture.

data are the encoder and the layers after are the decoder. All those in between the input and output layers are hidden layers.

The encoder-decoder architecture entails two fundamental types of tasks. The first one is based on the encoder, which is primarily a vectorization task from raw text to more abstract data representation. Through the encoded data, the system 'understands' the meaning, just like word embeddings. Thus, this task is focused on understanding. The second task is based on the decoder, which prioritizes producing outcomes. That is, the decoder is focused on data generation. Models that aim to generate new sequences must include a decoder. For example, Vaswani et al. (2017) proposed an encoder-decoder network architecture, the Transformer. This model is based solely on attention mechanisms, dispensing with recurrence and convolutions entirely. It is an efficient way to process sequential data such as language. Two famous applications of the Transformer model in the natural language field are ChatGPT and Bidirectional Encoder Representations from Transformers (BERT). While ChatGPT uses a multi-layer Transformer decoder for the language model (Radford et al., 2018), BERT is a multi-layer bidirectional Transformer encoder (Devlin et al., 2019).

5.2.5 Neural language models

A language model predicts what word comes next by assigning probability to a sequence of text (Wang & Sawyer, 2023, p. 52). To some degree, language models are communication models with noisy channels (see Section 5.1.2), with the calculation of probability as the core task. While a noisy channel model discussed in Section 5.1.2 includes a channel model and a language model, a neural language model can solve a cross-lingual task without the channel model. For example, in statistical machine translation, a noisy channel model includes a translation model to ensure the equivalency between the source and target text, as well as a language model to verify the fluency of the target text. In neural machine translation, the language model is based on deep learning artificial neural network (ANN), in which all information is embedded in the encoder-decoder network.

The ANN approach adopts connectionism, in which cognition is "not symbol manipulation but dynamic patterns of activity in a multilayered network of nodes or units with weighted positive and negative interconnections" (Harned, 1994). The key elements in this approach are the associative and statistical structure of the interactions in such networks. When the internal network constraints governing how the activations and connection strengths are adjusted based on new inputs, the patterns change as well. Such a system is by default able to 'learn' and to recognize patterns automatically.

Neural language models are an application of ANNs to deal with natural language tasks. Neural machine translation (MT) is a successful application of neural language models. In neural MT, a language model is fed with a group of observations (instances), x_i , in the real world. Through computing based on its parameters (weights, w_m and biases, b_m), the model produces a result $\hat{y}$, or the predicted outcome. In this context, the actual results are the natural language generated by humans, y_i, which is the ground truth for the language model to refer to. By measuring the accumulated distances between y_i and $\hat{y}$, that is, the cost function, one can apply the backpropagation learning procedure to find the most optimal model (defined by its parameters). The result the model produces can be as close to the ground truth (human produced labels).

In neural MT, the meaning of words is not defined by humans, but 'learned' by artificial neural networks themselves, in the form of word embeddings. Using word embeddings, the meanings of words are mapped onto a multidimensional space as real-valued vectors, where the distance and direction between vectors reflect the relationships among these words (see Mikolov et al., 2013a, 2013b). This mathematical interpretation of meaning aims to align with human understanding. However, each interpretation represents a different approach (mathematical vs. human intuitive) to the same problem (the understanding of meaning). Therefore, it is not surprising to find discrepancies in the results generated by machines and humans, respectively.

5.3 General considerations for multilingual language models

The implementation of neural language models and deep learning have revolutionized AI applications in natural language. Furthermore, when these models are developed to solve multilingual problems, there are a number of key factors that must be considered.

5.3.1 Cross-lingual representation learning

A multilingual neural language model enables cross-lingual understanding (XLU) and transfer learning across multiple languages. To begin, much of the work on multilinguality in language understanding has been at the word level (Conneau et al., 2018a, p. 2476). Mikolov et al. (2013c) first noticed that continuous word embedding spaces exhibit similar structures across languages, even when considering distant language pairs like English and Vietnamese (cited from Conneau et al., 2018b, p. 1). Such cross-lingual representation learning can be conducted in both a supervised and unsupervised manner. The method Mikolov et al. (2013c) adopted required a parallel lexicon (e.g., bilingual lexicon) to align two sets of source and target embeddings to the same space. Conneau et al. (2018b), however, introduced a model that did not employ any cross-lingual annotated data. Conneau et al. (2018b) used two large, unaligned monolingual corpora, one in the source and one in the target language.

The work on cross-lingual language understanding has been extended from word embeddings to sentence or paragraph representations. Conneau et al. (2018a) suggested universal cross-lingual encoders that can encode any sentence into a shared embedding space. To accomplish this goal, Conneau et al. (2018a) introduced a Cross-lingual Natural Language Inference (XNLI) corpus which includes 15 languages, based on monolingual Natural Language Inference (NLI) corpora. Their XNLI corpus consists of 7,500 human-annotated development and test examples in NLI three-way classification format in both low- and high-resource languages, resulting in a total of 112,500 annotated pairs.

As a cross-lingual task, machine translation is a useful auxiliary resource for other multilingual tasks. With machine translation, a monolingual communication activity can be directly converted to a multilingual one. For example, answers to questions in English can be translated into French, so that English speakers can communicate directly with their French counterparts. It is interesting to note that machine translation is not the only solution for cross-lingual tasks. Jiang et al. (2024), for example, used a unified model (a single encoder-decoder model) for both cross-lingual retrieval and multilingual question answering tasks.

Handling multiple languages in natural language understanding adds an extra layer of complexity to language models. For example, the cross-lingual language model (XLM) (Lample & Conneau, 2019) is used for XLU and transfer learning. This model contains multiple elements, including Causal Language Modeling, Masked Language Modeling (MLM), and Translation Language Modeling (TLM). Both the CLM and MLM training objectives are trained on monolingual data in an unsupervised way. TLM, however, is used to leverage parallel data to improve cross-lingual pretraining. TLM can be considered an extension of MLM. It follows the masked language modeling objective of Devlin et al. (2019), yet concatenating parallel sentences in different languages. According to Lample and Conneau (2019), a cross-lingual language model pretraining can be conducted with either CLM, MLM, or MLM used in combination with TLM.

In practice, some researchers differentiate multilingual and cross-lingual activities. For example, Ma et al. (2021) tested model performance of multilingual language generation tasks as well as cross-lingual language generation tasks. The multilingual language generation tasks include abstractive text summarization and question generation. In these tasks, the source and the target are in the same language. The model can handle these two tasks in multiple languages. In cross-lingual language generation tasks, however, the target language is different from the source language. For example, a cross-lingual text summarization task generates a summary of the input document in different languages. In this book, the term multilingual can serve as an overarching term encompassing both multilingual and cross-lingual tasks, while the nuances of these two types of tasks as Ma et al. (2021) indicated, have been noticed as well.

5.3.2 Language processing techniques

Language processing techniques used in multilingual settings must apply to characteristics of different language systems. For example, tokenization, a process to segment text into atomic units, plays a fundamental role in large-scale language model development. When the language in question is part of the Romance languages, such as English, French, and Spanish, tokens can be delimited using whitespaces. However, this technique does not work for languages that do not use whitespaces, for example, Chinese, Japanese, and Korean (see Si et al., 2023, p. 469). Moreover, this algorithm, which divides tokens according to whitespaces, will result in an extremely large vocabulary (Ahia et al., 2023, p. 9905). On the other hand, if tokens are defined as characters or bytes, it will make the associated sequences extremely long in terms of the number of tokens (see Mielke et al., 2021).

A commonly used solution in multilingual scenarios is to tokenize text into subword chunks, for example, Byte Pair Encoding (BPE). As Radford et al. (2019) pointed out, Byte Pair Encoding is a practical middle ground between character and word level language modeling. BPE effectively interpolates between word level inputs for frequent symbol sequences and character level inputs for infrequent symbol sequences. As Ahia et al. (2023, p. 9905) pointed out, for multilingual models containing data in a variety of scripts in different languages, even the base vocabulary of only characters (based on Unicode symbols) can be quite large with over 130K types. To address this problem, Radford et al. (2019) used a byte-level version of BPE that only requires a base vocabulary of size 256, in OpenAI's GPT model. The vocabulary size is much smaller than that in other versions.

When Lample and Conneau (2019) trained their cross-lingual language models, they processed all languages with the same shared sub-word vocabulary through Byte Pair Encoding (BPE). The BPE splits were learned on the concatenation of sentences sampled randomly from the monolingual corpora. Lample and Conneau (2019) reported that using shared sub-word vocabulary in the modeling process greatly improved the alignment of embedding spaces across languages that share either the same alphabet or anchor tokens such as digits.

5.3.3 Training data

In multilingual settings, language models are typically trained on parallel data through the supervised learning technique. For example, neural machine translation (NMT) systems are trained on parallel corpora, which include aligned source and target segments. In the context of deep learning architecture, a neural MT engine can take advantage of available computation and data to improve its performance. Unsurprisingly, there is a positive relationship between the amount of parallel data and neural MT performance.

However, linguistic resources vary depending on multiple factors, including mode of communication (e.g., spoken or written) and domain (e.g., business vs. biology). In high-resource languages, such as English, French, and Chinese, abundant resources are available, including parallel corpora, electronic bi- or multilingual dictionaries, and translators or bilingual (multilingual) linguists. However, as Magueresse et al. (2020) pointed out, most of today's research focuses on 20 of the 7,000 languages of the world. The vast majority of languages are understudied. These languages are often referred to as low-resource languages (LRLs). Thus, there is a significant imbalance concerning resources available to build language models that are meant to handle tasks in a variety of languages.

It is important to note that there are many current efforts to build parallel corpora to address the issue of imbalanced linguistic resources, e.g., Skadiņš et al. (2014). In the meantime, more studies have emerged using monolingual data to train cross-lingual models in an unsupervised manner. In the work of Artetxe et al. (2018), the authors used monolingual corpora to train their neural MT system. Their model was built upon the work surrounding unsupervised embedding mappings (Artetxe et al., 2017; Barone, 2016; Zhang et al., 2017).

5.3.4 Machine translation as a cross-lingual language task

Machine translation is inherently a cross lingual task. Before artificial neural networks were applied in machine translation, when more than one language pair was involved, for example, English to German and German to Russian translation, a statistical MT (SMT) engine heavily relied on language specific data. As discussed in Section 5.1.2, a SMT engine includes both a translation model (channel model) and a language model. Translation in each language pair must use bilingual data in their corresponding languages. Läubli et al. (2013) proposed an unweighted mode and weighted mode to train their SMT engines. In an unweighted mode, the in-domain, Europarl v7 (Koehn, 2005) and OpenSubtitles 2011 (Tiedemann, 2009) data were concatenated to train a combined translation and language model for each language pair. In a weighted language model mode, an interpolated language model was used in tandem with an unweighted translation model. The interpolation weights for translation and language models vary in each of the different language combinations. Overall, the training for SMT with multiple models is dependent on language combinations.

A neural MT system comprises a cross-lingual language model without a translation model. An encoder-decoder neural network is much simpler than a statistical MT with multiple models. Such a neural MT allows for a multilingual approach to language models. Specifically, multilingual systems are trained to process different languages in a single model. Such an approach has been applied to machine translation, as well as other types of natural language tasks, including text classification, syntactic analysis, and named-entity recognition (Wang et al., 2020). When compared to their monolingual counterparts, multilingual models possess two major advantages: (1) deploying a single multilingual model is much more resource efficient than deploying one model for each language under consideration; and (2) multilingual training makes it possible to transfer knowledge from high-resource languages to improve performance on low resource languages (Wang et al., 2020, p. 8526).

Johnson et al. (2017) proposed using a single neural MT model to translate between multiple languages. They introduced an artificial token at the beginning of the input sentence to specify the required target language. The rest of the model architecture, including an encoder, a decoder and an attention module, is shared across all languages.

The above studies highlighted transfer learning, which is a key feature for cross-lingual language models. Multilingual word embeddings provide an excellent mechanism for transfer learning. This mechanism allows a model trained in a resource-rich language to be transferred to a less-resourced one. Transfer learning has been applied to part-of-speech (POS) tagging, parsing, and document classification (see Artetxe et al., 2017, p. 451).

In the neural MT system developed by Artetxe et al. (2018), one encoder is shared by both languages involved. In this system, first a universal encoder aims to produce a language independent representation of the input text. Then each decoder transforms this shared representation into its corresponding language. This NMT system used pre-trained, fixed cross-lingual embeddings in the encoding process.

5.4   Multilingual large language models

When neural language models are trained on a sufficiently large and diverse dataset, they can perform well across a variety of domains and tasks. In addition to this scaling effect, multilingual large language models are exposed to data in multiple languages. These models can be used as a starting point, followed by two typical applications: (1) to be fine-tuned to do downstream tasks with a relatively small amount of data; and (2) to be prompted to do specific tasks with no data or a few shots of data.

5.4.1   RNN language models

Text data in natural language is sequential data, in which both the tokens in the sequence and their positions encode meaning. In this regard, recurrent neural networks (RNNs) are designed to process data sequentially, and further accomplish cross-lingual tasks such as machine translation. An RNN-based language model is organized as input, hidden, and output layers. RNN uses hidden states to capture the interdependencies of data sequences. In the hidden layer, the model computes the hidden state of the current input, which captures not only the state or meaning of this input, but also that of all the inputs before the current input. In other words, this hidden state can remember and use previous inputs for predictions in a short-term memory component.

RNN models align the position information of tokens to steps in computation time (Vaswani et al., 2017, p. 2). Computers process a sequence of tokens following time steps, which represent the position information of each token. The training is based on a technique called backpropagation through time (BPTT). As Mozer (2013) pointed out, the key feature of the architecture is a layer of self-connected hidden units that integrate their current value with the new input at each time step, to construct a static representation of the temporal input sequence. Using BPTT, the system can roll back the output to the previous time step and recalculate the error rate to adjust model weight accordingly.

RNNs have limitations in model performance. As Vaswani et al. (2017) pointed out, the inherently sequential nature of RNN "precludes parallelization within training examples, which becomes critical at longer sequence lengths, as memory constraints limit batching across examples" (p. 2). Vaswani et al. (2017) proposed the Transformer model, which is not only effective in addressing this issue, but more importantly, significantly scaling up language models in an attempt to leverage exponentially increasing computation power and data.

5.4.2 The Transformer and attention mechanism

Transformers have proved to perform effectively at modeling sequential data, such as natural language. Transformers are deep feed-forward artificial neural networks with a (self) attention mechanism (Phuong & Hutter, 2022, p. 1). The model was first proposed as a solution to accomplish machine translation tasks. As Vaswani et al. (2017) reported, the Transformer model achieved 28.4 BLEU on the Workshop of Machine Translation (WMT 2014) English–to–German translation task, improving over the existing best results, by over two BLEU scores.

The architecture of Transformers allows data sequences to be processed in parallel, using attention mechanisms. As all deep learning models, a Transformer model includes an encoder and a decoder. While the encoder maps an input sequence of symbol representations (text data) to a sequence of continuous representations (numeric data), the decoder generates an output sequence of symbols one element at a time from numeric representations of data.

The first set of continuous representations in the data flow from the input to the hidden layer are word embeddings without context. Word2vec, for example, as discussed in Chapter 4, is one way of converting text to numeric data that captures word meanings in a corpus. However, these embeddings are static. Suppose there are two sentences, "I eat an apple every day" and "My gray Apple laptop is out of power." Using out-of-context embeddings will produce the same vector for the word 'apple' in both sentences. However, the meanings of 'apple' in each context vary. Other words in each sentence can influence the meaning of 'apple'. For example, the verb 'eat' produces a few associations related to the word 'apple', such as its size, smell, and taste. The adjective 'gray' restricts the color of an Apple computer. To address these differences, the model must be able to update the embeddings, allowing other words in the context to inject meaning to the word 'apple'. This task can be accomplished by an attention mechanism.

Equation 5.5 is the formula of attention function (Vaswani et al., 2017, p. 4). This function contains three matrices, Q, K, and V, referring to sets of queries, keys and values, respectively. Queries and keys have a dimension of d_k. This function computes the dot products of the query with all keys, divides each by $\sqrt{d_k}$, and applies a softmax function to normalize the output values into a probability distribution. An attention function can be described as mapping a query and a set of key-value pairs to an output, where the query, keys, values, and output are all vectors. $\dfrac{1}{\sqrt{d_k}}$ is a scaling factor to counteract the effect that large values of d_k will push the softmax function into regions where it has extremely small gradients.

$$\text{Attention}\,(Q, K, V) = \text{softmax}\left(\frac{QK^T}{\sqrt{d_k}}\right)V \qquad\qquad \text{(Equation 5.5)}$$

The scaled dot-product attention function aims to measure how well a query matches each key. In a natural language instance, a query can be a word in investigation, such as 'apple'. Keys will be words before and after 'apple'. The number of words taken into consideration depends on the context size the model presets. The model deduces which words are relevant to the word the attention function will be able to identify. For example, 'eat' is relevant to 'apple' in "I eat an apple every day," whereas 'gray' and 'power' is relevant to 'Apple' in "My gray Apple laptop is out of power." The meaning of the relevant words will be passed to the embeddings of 'apple'. As a result, the model will generate two different, more refined embeddings for the word 'apple' in each sentence after applying the attention mechanism.

In practice, a multi-head attention mechanism consisting of several attention layers runs in parallel. Further, the above description is based on a self-attention mechanism, that is, the model processes the same set of data in training. For cross-lingual natural language tasks such as machine translation, cross attention is employed. Cross attention refers to a model that processes two distinct types of data, e.g., text in one language and text in another language, or an audio input of speech and an ongoing transcription. In this mechanism, key and query maps act on different data sets. In translation, the key comes from one language and the query comes from another. The attention map tells which word in one language corresponds to which word in another language.

The attention-based models enable parallelism in training, allowing a Transformer to train and process longer sequences in less time than an RNN does. The architecture of Transformers scales well with increased computational resources. These models can handle larger datasets and longer sequences more efficiently. Weights in these models are optimized for parallel computing, which graphic processing units (GPUs) offer for generative AI developments. Parallelism enables Transformers to scale massively and handle complex NLP tasks by building larger models. Transformers can process data sequences in parallel and use positional encoding to remember how each input relates to others. With the (self) attention mechanism, Transformers address the memory limitations and sequence interdependencies that RNNs have.

5.4.3 Large language models

There is a gradual evolution of language modeling, from supervised learning on specific tasks, to unsupervised learning to accomplish a variety of tasks. For example, machine translation was one of the first computer applications to be used for natural language tasks beginning in 1954 (see Hutchins, 2004, p. 1). Since that time, MT systems have gone through different iterations, from rule-based, to statistical, to neural MT. These systems are all dedicated to one special task, that is, machine translation. A specialized statistical and neural MT are trained on labeled datasets (parallel corpora) with clear training objectives. However, as Radford et al. (2019) pointed out, these systems, just like 'narrow experts', are brittle and sensitive to slight changes in data distribution and task specification. Radford et al. (2019) called for more general systems which can perform many tasks without the need to manually create and label a training dataset for each individual task. These models have been compared to 'competent generalists' by Radford et al. (2019).

What Radford et al. (2019) advocated for represents a new approach that influential research groups such as Google and OpenAI have pursued since the Transformer model architecture was released in 2017. This approach adopts generative pre-training (GPT) of a language model on a diverse corpus of unlabeled text, followed by discriminative fine-tuning on each specific task (see Radford et al., 2018, 2019; Devlin et al., 2018). Such an approach implies a two-stage training procedure: (1) using a language modeling objective on the unlabeled data to learn the initial parameters of a neural network model; and (2) adapting these parameters to a target task using the corresponding supervised objective (Radford et al., 2018, p. 2). At the first stage, while the primary task of training is language modeling, the performance of zero-shot domain transfer is also a significant indicator of the model capability.

The assumption is that in order to better predict and generate strings, which is the final training objective, a general language model with 'sufficient' capacity can also learn to infer and perform multiple necessary tasks to achieve this goal (Radford et al., 2019, p. 3). The scale of language models plays a significant role in boosting the model capacity and realizing the multitask learning goal (Radford et al., 2019). When a large language model is trained on a sufficiently large and diverse dataset, it is able to perform well across many domains and tasks. Kaplan et al. (2020) echoed this argumentation, finding empirical evidence to support the scaling law. Their empirical studies showed that language modeling performance improves smoothly as the model size, dataset size, and amount of computation used for training are scaled up in tandem.

The release of the Transformer architecture in 2017 enables such scaling up of language models with increased computational resources and large, diverse datasets (see Section 5.4.2). The two models discussed in Section 5.2.4, namely, the Generative Pre-Trained Transformer (GPT) developed by OpenAI (Brown et al., 2020; Ouyang et al., 2022; Radford et al., 2018, 2019) and Bidirectional Encoder Representations from Transformers (BERT) (Devlin et al., 2018), are large language models (LLMs) that are built on the Transformer. The former is based on the decoder of the Transformer, whereas the latter on the encoder, as the name of BERT indicates.

To a certain degree, being general, or task-agnostic, means the model does not have task specific goals. User (or developer) intentions can be injected to these models through fine-tuning or prompting. In a fine tuning approach, a general language model is further trained on task-specific data. For example, human labeled data is used to perform supervised learning for sentiment analysis tasks. Prompting does not rely on additional training. Users can directly interact with the model to retrieve relevant requested information from the system. Prompting is an example of direct human computer interaction.

The Stanford Institute for Human-Centered Artificial Intelligence (HAI) calls these generative, task-agnostic models 'foundation models' to "underscore their critically central yet incomplete character" (Bommasani et al. 2022, p. 1). Foundation models create pre-trained language representations, which can be further applied to downstream tasks, such as machine translation quality estimation and evaluation, which will be discussed in greater detail in Section 5.5.

In a fine-tuning approach, a system can be trained on the downstream tasks by simply fine-tuning all pretrained parameters. Fine tuning ensures the foundation model is task-aware during this process, to achieve effective transfer learning results. There is no need to make significant changes to the model architecture for different tasks. In other words, pre-trained representations reduce the need for many heavily engineered task-specific architectures. On the one hand, fine-tuning is focused on adding a thin layer of LLM parameter weights, to customize the model itself to work better within the context of a specific use case. On the other hand, prompt engineering does not involve modifying the actual LLMs. Rather, it focuses on adding information to the prompts, which can be conducted by regular users who do not have relevant engineering backgrounds. The assumption is that, the richer the context a prompt can provide to the system, the better the system will be able to understand users' requests. For example, if a user wants to ask the system to translate a sentence from English to French, the user can add a translation example.

5.4.4   Multilingual large language models

When a language model is trained on a large, diverse dataset from multiple languages, this model can learn some cross-lingual relations and transfer learning across languages. Typical examples include OpenAI's GPT models (Radford et al., 2018, 2019) and the multilingual BERT (mBERT) model (Devlin et al., 2019). Pires et al. (2019) reported that mBERT, a single language model pre-trained from monolingual corpora in 104 languages, can create multilingual representations, but these representations exhibit systematic deficiencies affecting certain language pairs. Through zero-shot cross-lingual model transfer, task-specific annotations in one language are used to fine-tune the model for evaluation in another language. The zero-shot cross-lingual transfer capabilities allow the multilingual language model to be adapted in a zero-shot manner to make predictions in a language that the model has not been trained on. However, such transfer works best between typologically similar languages (Pires et al., 2019). Furthermore, building on the encoder of the Transformer, BERT's functionality is limited in cross-lingual language understanding.

OpenAI's GPT models can handle some cross-lingual tasks. For example, Radford et al. (2019) reported GPT-2 has begun to learn how to translate from one language to another. However, Lai et al. (2023) pointed out that ChatGPT's zero-shot learning performance is generally worse than the state-of-the-art performance of the supervised learning models for a majority of cross-lingual tasks. In addition, ChatGPT's performance is generally better in English than in other languages. This is particularly true for higher-level tasks that require more complex reasoning abilities (e.g., named entity recognition, question answering, common sense reasoning, and summarization) (Lai et al., 2023, p. 13173).

To address the bias on languages, there is room for more research to develop multilingual models. Section 5.3.1 introduced a cross-lingual language model (XLM), which is a Transformer based architecture that is pre-trained using one of three language modeling objectives: (1) Causal Language Modeling—models the probability of a word given the previous words in a sentence, (2) Masked Language Modeling—the masked language modeling objective of BERT, and (3) Translation Language Modeling—a (new) translation language modeling objective for improving cross-lingual pre-training.

XLM-R is a Transformer-based masked language model, similar to BERT, trained on 100 languages, using more than two terabytes of filtered CommonCrawl data. Conneau et al. (2020) reported that XLM-R significantly outperforms mBERT on a variety of cross-lingual benchmarks, including Cross-lingual Natural Language Inference (XNLI), Cross-lingual Question Answering (MLQA), and NER (Named Entity Recognition). Conneau et al. (2020) pointed out that XLM-R performs particularly well on low-resource languages, such as Swahili and Urdu.

There has been an increasing amount of research which compares performance of different multilingual LLMs. For example, Ács et al. (2021) compared the effect of the choice of subword pooling on the downstream task performance in nine typologically diverse languages in mBERT (Devlin et al., 2019) and XLM-RoBERTa (Conneau et al., 2020). They found that XLM-RoBERTa is slightly better than mBERT in the majority of morphological and POS tagging tasks, while mBERT is better at name entity recognition (NER) in all languages.

5.5 Case study: applying LLMs to quality evaluation and estimation

LLMs are not only used to perform a task, but also to evaluate the performance of this task. As discussed in Section 5.4.3, there are two typical applications of LLMs: (1) to be fine-tuned to do conventional NLP tasks with a relatively small amount of data; and (2) to be prompted to do specific tasks with no data or a few shots of data. This section will use machine translation quality evaluation and estimation as an example to illustrate these two approaches.

5.5.1 *LLMs as evaluators of translation quality*

As Wang and Sawyer (2023) pointed out, there are two types of evaluation that depend on whether a reference translation is available: automatic metrics such as Bilingual Evaluation Understudy (BLEU), and quality estimation (p. 92). BLEU was one of the earliest automatic metrics. It requires a human translation as a reference to verify the quality of the final product. To conduct BLEU, parallel texts (i.e., a text and its translation) as well as an automatic translation of at least one of the texts, are needed. The alignment is determined in accordance with the similarity between the MT results of the source text and the target text sentences in the parallel corpus (Sennrich & Volk, 2010).

It is reasonable to use human translation as a 'gold' standard in an evaluation process, just like a quality decision is ultimately made by a human evaluator in the Turing Test.

However, simply relying on human efforts in an evaluation process will drag down the entire workflow. Other methods of using machines to verify performance are also needed. Quality Estimation (QE) is an effective tool to predict the quality of the MT output without relying on human references. For many applications, producing human references is both time-consuming and expensive (Scarton et al., 2016).

Zhao et al. (2024) categorized QE into handcrafted features-based, classic deep-learning-based, and LLM-based methods. The next section will use an example to illustrate the method that incorporates pre-trained LMs.

5.5.2   Fine tuning LLMs for machine translation quality evaluation tasks

Crosslingual Optimized Metric for Evaluation of Translation (COMET) is a neural framework for training multilingual machine translation (MT) evaluation models. This framework is designed to predict human judgments of MT quality (*COMET: The New Standard in MT Evaluation*, n.d.). Based on similarity of vector representations, COMET calculates the similarity between a machine translation output and a reference translation using token or sentence embeddings. Furthermore, COMET is an open-source framework for MT evaluation that can be used to train and develop new metrics (*COMET: High-Quality Machine Translation Evaluation — COMET 2.0.0 Documentation*, n.d.).

The primary building block of all the models in this framework is a pre-trained, cross-lingual model such as multilingual BERT (Devlin et al., 2019), XLM (Lample and Conneau, 2019) or XLM-RoBERTa (Conneau et al., 2020). These models contain several Transformer encoder layers to uncover the relationship between those tokens and the surrounding ones (Rei et al., 2020, p. 2686).

Given an input sequence, the encoder can produce embeddings for each token and each layer. The COMET framework focuses on three types of input, namely, the source, MT hypothesis (MT results), and reference (usually human translation as a reference). The goal is to map the three sets of embeddings into a shared feature space.

The approach to generate embeddings adopted by COMET follows Peters et al. (2018). The pool information from the most important encoder layers is projected into a single embedding for each token. The pretrained encoder and the pooling layer are the foundation for different models for MT quality evaluation (Rei et al., 2020, pp. 2686–8).

For example, in the estimator model, the source, hypothesis and reference are independently encoded using a pretrained cross-lingual encoder. The resulting word embeddings are then passed through a pooling layer to create a sentence embedding for each segment. Finally, the resulting sentence embeddings are combined and concatenated into one single vector that is passed to a feed-forward regressor.

In the translation ranking model, the encoder receives four segments: the source, the reference, a "better" hypothesis, and a "worse" one. These segments are independently encoded using a pretrained cross-lingual encoder and a pooling layer on top. Finally, the resulting embedding space is optimized to minimize the distance between the "better" hypothesis and the "anchors" (source and reference).

These two fine-tuned models are trained on data from three different corpora: the QT21 corpus, the DARR from the WMT Metrics shared task (2017 to 2019), and a proprietary MQM annotated corpus.

5.5.3 *Prompt engineering for quality assurance*

Since late 2022 when ChatGPT was released and accepted by the public, even novice users are able to work directly with foundation models through a prompt interface. In this approach, users 'prompt' a model to perform a specific natural language task. For example, a user might enter the prompt, "Translate this sentence into French" and give the source text that is supposed to be translated, for the model to perform a machine translation task. The recent hype of OpenAI GPT4 model is a good example. One success of this approach is that it effectively connects users' intentions with the model, allowing them to directly define and further unpack their real-life problems by experimenting solutions with the language model. This provides a higher quality of human–computer interaction, which means these NLP tools become more effective and relevant to the users. At the same time, exposing users directly to these models can also bring risks. Untrained users likely do not have sufficient knowledge and skills, or AI competence, to foresee risks, biases, or issues of fairness and transparency present in any real-world use of an LLM.

There are behavioral reasons behind the need for prompt engineering. A prompt results in an answer from machine intelligence, independent from human interference. By interacting with LLMs, humans are able to explore the potential of this system (see Kocmi & Federmann, 2023). When a task is accomplished through an 'narrow expert' system, for example, machine translation is produced by an MT system, this task only exhibits one aspect of its competence in a particular context. LLMs possess extensive knowledge bases and learning capabilities, biased or not, all of which can be further explored. Simply accomplishing some tasks will not reveal its full potential. LLMs are able to implicitly support a variety of tasks, even if the model has not been fine-tuned for that task. Just like a human is capable of doing tasks only when the need arises.

Kocmi and Federmann (2023) proposed using GEMBA (GPT Estimation Metric Based Assessment), a GPT-based metric, to assess translation quality, which works both with a reference translation (quality evaluation) and without (quality estimation). Below is an example of the prompt template for machine translation direct assessment, that is, an assessment without further annotation such as error types.

> Score the following translation from {source_lang} to {target_lang} **with respect to the human reference** on a continuous scale from 0 to 100, where score of zero means "no meaning preserved" and score of one hundred means "perfect meaning and grammar."
> {source_lang} source: "{source_seg}"
> {target_lang} human reference: {reference_seg}
> {target_lang} translation: "{target_seg}"
> Score:
>
> *(Output scores range from 0 – 100)*
> *(cited from Kocmi & Federmann, 2023)*

Kocmi and Federmann (2023) set the following parameters when assessing translation quality via prompting an LLM. For example, the prompt variant includes two scoring tasks (direct assessment and scalar quality metrics) and two classification tasks (one to five stars ranking and quality classes). Other prompt variants include source and target language names, e.g., 'Chinese' and 'English', as well as resources for evaluation, source segments, candidate translations (e.g., machine translation results), and optionally, human reference translations (two modes: with and without reference translation).

Kocmi and Federmann (2023) reported "state-of-the-art performance on the MQM 2022 test set across three language pairs." They also emphasized the importance of choosing the right LLM for implementing GEMBA, reporting only models beyond GPT 3.5 yielded promising results.

Note

1 Argmax is an operation that finds the argument that gives the maximum value from a target function.

6

MULTILINGUAL AND CROSS-LINGUAL INFORMATION RETRIEVAL

6.1 Information retrieval

In their book entitled *Introduction to Information Retrieval*, Manning et al. (2008, p. 1) defined information retrieval (IR) as "finding material (usually documents) of an unstructured nature (usually text) that satisfies an information need from within large collections (usually stored on computers)."

This conventional definition entails finding answers based on users' needs from information retrieval systems, rather than from people. Search engines such as Google can be considered an IR system, which has become a significant daily source of finding information. Information retrieval can also be a software program that deals with the organization, storage, retrieval, and evaluation of information from large collections of structured, semi-structured, and unstructured data. In both cases, information retrieval covers supporting users in browsing, filtering data collections, or further processing a set of retrieved information. To accomplish these goals, activities such as document clustering, indexing, and information analysis are needed.

In essence, what a user interacts with, e.g., Google or a dedicated IR computer program, is just an interface or frontend. What really supports the information retrieval functionality is the relevant data behind it. When large collections of information are stored on computers in a structured way, they make up a database. In this case, finding answers to users' questions from this system would consist of query and reporting activities, as well as database management to support needed functionality. Among different types of databases, as Manning et al. (2008) pointed out, "the canonical example of structured data is a relational database" (p. 1). Since the 1980s, relational databases have become dominant. In such databases, items are organized as a set of related tables with columns and rows. Such a way of organizing data provides an efficient and flexible way to access structured information. Nearly all relational databases use Structured Query Language (SQL), which is a programming language first developed at IBM in the 1970s, to query, manipulate, and define data, and to provide access control (Oracle, 2020).

DOI: 10.4324/9781003470557-8

Manning et al. (2008) also defined unstructured data as "data which does not have clear, semantically overt, easy-for-a-computer structure" (p. 1). To some degree, all language data, including both lexical resources and text data, has some kind of structure. Text data for human consumption, for example, contains some linguistic structure of human languages by default, such as headings, paragraphs, and footnotes. However, unless these semantic categories are annotated in a way that a computer system can directly recognize, such information is only implied in the text. This is a relatively easy task for humans to uncover the implied meaning. However, for computers, it might be a completely different story. A computer system must extract relevant embedded meaning to solve a certain problem within the text. In this context, this underlying meaning can also refer to certain features or characteristics of the text data.

There are cases when text data is organized in a semi-structured way, as a non-relational database, for example, using markup languages such as JSON (JavaScript Object Notation) and XML (eXtensible Markup Language). JSON and XML are examples of format frameworks for storing data in a machine-readable way; both languages can facilitate data exchange between applications, platforms, or systems in a standardized manner (*JSON Vs XML - Difference Between Data Representations - AWS*, n.d.). Both JSON and XML are self-descriptive. These languages contain both data and metadata, which describes the format, meaning, and other associated information concerning the data. XML is also a fundamental standard for more specific data storing and transporting formats used in translation and localization, such as TMX (Translation Memory Exchange) or TBX (TermBase eXchange). Semi-structured data is somewhere between structured and unstructured formats. It is unstructured as information has not been put under a particular relational database. On the other hand, it is structured as the text is annotated with tags or vital information that separates individual elements of the data (see Vidhyalakshmi & Priya, 2020).

Information retrieval for translation and localization in this chapter, includes both query/reporting activities in structured databases and feature extractions for unstructured multilingual text data. Metadata found in semi-structured data will be discussed from taxonomies and ontology perspectives. The annotation can help further narrow down the search area for relevant information. For example, the system can filter certain types of data, such as extracting only titles of the documents included in a semi-structured dataset.

6.1.1 *Interacting with an IR system*

Finding information using computer programs implies a set of underlying algorithmic considerations along with associated processing steps. No matter which methods an information retrieval system adopts, the starting place is always the problem space, from which a user can deduce their information need. According to Manning et al. (2008), an information need is the topic about which the user desires to know more (p. 5). To convert an information need to concrete actions, a user must be able to create queries, which is what the user conveys to the computer in an attempt to retrieve information needed. In this sense, queries are what a user provides to interact with an IR system.

Queries are situationally specific, depending on how much a user understands their problem space, as well as query structures pre-set by an IR system interface. Some IR systems are designed in an attempt for a user to follow a specific query format. In the United Nations Official Document System (United Nations, n.d.), for example, users must follow the pre-set filters, such as symbols, subject, and publication date, in order to have the best chance of retrieving documents that respond to the original user's needs. This query structure helps a user convert their information needs to executable requests for information. Queries serve as a potential link between information needed in a user's mind and the actual database behind the IR system. On the other hand, some IR systems such as Google allow a user to enter queries that are more intuitive to humans, using one simple input that may or may not capture their ideas. Such an IR system is designed to process more complex natural language queries, by 'paraphrasing' a user's need to perform the IR task. Sometimes, the 'paraphrase' as well as associated technical methods will produce results that align with human expectations. At other times, however, the problem space may be too ambiguous for computer programs to generate results that are consistent with how humans perceive things. In recent years, the advancements in deep learning techniques, large labeled datasets, and high-computing power have significantly improved the capabilities of IR systems to process complex natural language queries (Hambarde & Proença, 2023, p. 2). This topic will be discussed in greater detail in Section 6.2.2.

6.1.2 Indexing

One reason why an IR system is necessary is due to the significantly large volume of data involved. If it were just a handful of documents, a user can linearly scan through these documents, for example, using simple search or regular expressions, to extract information that they search for. However, if the needed information is buried in a large amount of data, this collection must be preprocessed. Indexing is one of the fundamental preprocessing techniques in information retrieval, with which a user can efficiently query the needed information. Indexing a collection of data in advance can avoid linearly scanning the texts for each query (Manning et al., 2008, p. 3).

Section 4.2.3 in Chapter 4 discussed a corpus-based word representation method, Term Frequency Inverse Document Frequency (TF-IDF). This example includes a corpus with two documents, each of which contains one sentence.

Document 1: Today is a cold, cold, wet day.
Document 2: Yesterday was a warm, warm, dry day.

Suppose a user aims to determine which document contains the words 'today' AND 'cold' AND NOT 'yesterday'. To find information needed for this query, a simple way is to scan through all the text, identifying each document whether it contains 'today' and 'cold' and excluding it from consideration if it contains the term 'yesterday'. This linear search is the simplest form of document retrieval. This process is commonly referred to as grepping through text (Manning et al., 2008, p. 3).

Alternatively, when the volume of data is significant, an IR system cannot reasonably conduct grepping. In this case, Boolean retrieval can be performed. In a Boolean retrieval model, all queries can be posted in the form of a Boolean expression of terms. Boolean expressions are combined with the operators AND, OR, and NOT, for example, 'today' AND 'cold' AND NOT 'yesterday' (see Manning et al., 2008, p. 4). This model views each document as just a set of words or terms. An IR system can record each document whether it contains each word out of all word types (unique words) in the corpus. The recording

TABLE 6.1 A term-document incidence matrix

Term	Document 1	Document 2
Today	1	0
is	1	0
a	1	1
cold	1	0
wet	1	0
day	1	1
Yesterday	0	1
was	0	1
warm	0	1
dry	0	1

result is a binary term-document incidence matrix, as in Table 6.1. To process the data, the two documents are first indexed as Document 1 and Document 2. Then each document is tokenized throughout (see Section 2.5.1.2 in Chapter 2). In this example, each token is a word. Each word type is a term, which is an indexed unit. The matrix in Table 6.1 contains two columns, namely, Document 1 and Document 2, as well as ten rows of terms. The value in each cell, or each matrix element (term, document), is 1 if the document column contains the word in the term row, and is 0 otherwise (See Manning et al., 2008, pp. 4–5).

It is worth noting that in database management, while indexing helps improve efficiency in queries, it may not necessarily achieve the same effect in other tasks. For example, when the user aims to use the application to connect and send commands to the database, such as inserting a new record, oftentimes indexing takes up more memory and slows down the insert operation. A user must select appropriate methods based on their business goals. In the next section, indexing is needed for a boolean search.

6.1.3 Boolean search

Based on the term-document incidence matrix, vector representations can be created for each term and/or each document. By examining the rows, each term can be represented as a vector, which shows the documents in which the term appears. For example, the vector for 'warm' is $[0, 1]$. From a column perspective, each document can be represented by a vector with each term as one of its dimensions, showing the terms that occur in it. For example, document 1 is represented as $[1, 1, 1, 1, 1, 1, 0, 0, 0, 0]$.

A conventional term-based retrieval, also known as Boolean retrieval, aims to match the terms in a query to the terms in a document (Manning et al., 2008). Based on the term-document incidence matrix in Table 6.1, a Boolean retrieval can be performed. For example, to answer the query of finding relevant documents that contain both the term 'today' AND the term 'cold', the vector of 'today' ($[1, 0]$) and the vector of 'cold' ($[1, 0]$) are added up. The adding logic follows bitwise AND operator (&), which compares each bit of the vector on the left operand $[1, 0]$ to the corresponding bit of the vector $[1, 0]$ on the right operand in an operation $[1, 0] + [1, 0]$. If both bits are 1, the corresponding result bit is set to 1. Otherwise, the corresponding result bit is set to 0 (*Bitwise AND Operator: & | Microsoft Learn*, 2021). Thus, adding up $[1, 0]$ and $[1, 0]$, the resulting vector is $[1, 0]$, meaning both 'today' and 'cold' appear in Document 1.

Term-based retrieval is widely used in practical applications, especially in small-scale information retrieval systems. This conventional approach is simple, fast, and easy to implement. However, it has limitations in handling synonyms, polysemy, and context (see Hambarde & Proença, 2023, pp. 3–4).

6.1.4   Feature extraction

Section 2.4.3 of Chapter 2 discussed feature extraction, as a data pre-processing technique. Feature is a representation of data, which "contains only the information that is relevant for the problem at hand" (Manolescu, 1998, p. 2). Section 2.4.2 provided an example of feature engineering for values of translator price quotes. In this example, the daily word count is raw data, which can be further classified in three categories (category 1: 3,000–3,500, category 2: 3,501–4,000, category 3: 4,001–4,500). This category information is a feature manually extracted, representing a specific attribute or variable to describe or characterize the observations.

Features can be extracted not only from original data, but also from other features. For example, part of speech (POS) and Term Frequency-Inverse Document Frequency (TF-IDF) can be extracted from a text corpus, using a fixed algorithm, or feature extractor. From these two features, a third feature, e.g., outstanding names, can be extracted manually.

The main goal of feature extraction is to map from a larger problem space into smaller feature space, which helps computer programs conduct information searches within large amounts of information and complex data (Manolescu, 1988, pp. 2–3). Through feature extraction, the original input variables are transformed into some new space "where, it is hoped, the pattern recognition problem will be easier to solve" (Bishop, 2006, p. 2). In software development, feature extraction is a function that computes an alternative, simpler representation of data, on the basis of the raw input data. A typical feature extraction function for text documents is automatic indexing. This function maps each document into a point in the k-dimensional keyword (or feature) space. Specifically, automatic indexing consists of a few pre-processing steps. For example, Manolescu (1988) clarified three steps to extract concepts from contents: (1) to remove common words like 'and', 'at', and 'the'; (2) to reduce the remaining words to their stem (e.g., 'computer' and 'computation' will be reduced to 'comput'); and (3) to assign each word-stem to a concept class. As a result of these steps, a keyword space is built, with each vector element corresponding to a concept class. In this feature space, only a few 'significant' features are considered when solving a problem, discarding the rest. Without feature extraction, searching a collection of documents requires a great amount of string matching operations. However, in the keyword space, documents are represented by vectors. Searching for documents in this space is much more efficient than string matching.

Thus, feature extraction enables scalable solutions for problems that deal with large amounts of information, providing a natural and low-overhead method to conduct similarity searches (Manolescu, 1998, p. 3). A keyword space presents simplified representations of the original data, and is considered a subset of original information. Such simplification also implies information loss while transforming data from one representation form to another. To conduct such a type of feature extraction, a software system does not need to 'understand' the contents when processing different types of complex information (see Manolescu,

1998, p. 4). Matching terms between queries and data is conducted on the surface structure of natural language. A computer program's 'understanding' involves deeper abstraction of the data to produce a pattern or a logic, which makes sense to a computer program, but not necessarily to humans. For example, a program can leverage a knowledge graph, which will be discussed in greater detail in Chapter 7, as well as embeddings, which are dense vectors that a system automatically learns from the database it was trained on.

The machine learning methods Term Frequency Inverse Document Frequency (TF-IDF) introduced in Section 4.2.3 is another model to retrieve information, or rather, extract features, from a corpus. The TF-IDF model uses one number to refer to the outstanding quality of a word in a corpus. In a similar vein, each document can be represented by TF-IDF numbers for all unique words in this document.

The association mining method, as discussed in Section 3.5.2 of Chapter 3, is a model to derive feature sets from pre-classified text documents. This method is applied to discover sets of associated words in the documents. Recommendation engines in streaming services as well as e-commerce, social media, and visual media platforms can be powered by this machine learning method.

6.2 Deep learning in information retrieval

While a general model such as generative pre-training (GPT) does not have task specific goals (see Section 5.4.3 of Chapter 5), information retrieval systems are dedicated to a particular natural language task. The fundamental problem of IR is to match information between the query and the data available. A simple and intuitive starting point mainly relies on the matching of terms between the query and the documents. However, term-based retrieval systems have limitations such as polysemy, synonymy, and context, as discussed in Section 6.1.3. The introduction of deep learning to the field of information retrieval has significantly modernized IR systems, enabling them to process complex queries using semantic retrieval and neural methods. To begin, vectors and vector databases are tools to leverage deep learning in this field.

6.2.1 *Vector search*

Vectors are mathematical representations of an object, such as a word, or a document. These representations contain certain knowledge, which informs a comprehensible, sharable model of how this object works. Depending on the algorithm, a vector implies a certain quality that a user might be interested in. A term-document incidence matrix as shown in Table 6.1, contains information about which word is included in which document. Section 4.4.3 of Chapter 4 discussed the word2vec model, which produces dense vectors to represent word meanings. In this model, a word representation in the form of a vector is created by training a classifier to predict whether a word is likely to appear nearby.

A database can be organized to store and manage vectors, in addition to raw data produced by humans, such as text, image, and sound. Such a database, also known as a vector database, is used to store high-dimensional data that cannot be characterized by traditional database management systems (Han et al., 2023). The mathematical representations of objects (e.g., words) rely on the meaning of these objects, such as relationships of one word/concept with other words/concepts, rather than on the form they adopt.

Information retrieval based on a vector database has the potential to be driven by meaning. In this type of database, data can be identified through similarity metrics, rather than exact matches, making it possible for a computer model to understand data contextually.

Once vectors are created and stored in a database, these vectors will be indexed to improve the search efficiency, just like indexing for word-based searches discussed in Section 6.1.2. However, as words and vectors have different characteristics, specific methods and considerations for each type of indexing might vary significantly. There are multiple techniques to index a vector database. For example, Google Cloud Spanner is a solution to find approximate nearest neighbors to index and query vector embeddings (Google Cloud, n.d.). The vector index used by Spanner is based on a tree-based structure to partition data into different sections. In a two-level tree configuration of Spanner, leaf nodes contain groups of closely related vectors along with their corresponding centroid. The root level consists of the centroids from all leaf nodes (Google Cloud, n.d.). In geometry, the term centroid refers to the center point of the object.

In addition to vectorizing text data that would be the basis for a search, queries will also be vectorized. The vector search system will match query vectors with those in the vector database, by means of similarity metrics. For example, cosine similarity measures the cosine of the angle between the query vector and vectors in the dataset, in order to assess how closely related these vectors are. Based on this metric, Boleda (2020) found that the vectors for words 'postdoc' and 'student' are closer in space than those of 'postdoc' and 'wealth' because their vector values are closer. The cosine of the angle between the two vectors 'post-doc' and 'student' is 0.99, which is greater than 0.37, the cosine between 'postdoc' and 'wealth'. The closer the vectors, the closer the cosines, the more similar the meaning (p. 3). This result is aligned with human's intuitive understanding, although the authors may not be aware of how accurate it is that a postdoc is more closely related to being a student than the concept of wealth in the eyes of most people.

Traditional search such as Boolean search relies on keyword matching and basic algorithms. Vector search is intelligent, as it uses AI and machine learning to draw comparisons, identify relationships, and understand context (see *What Is Vector Search?*, 2024). To some degree, keyword search technique fundamentally relies on human intelligence. However, the searching methods are limited when a computer program aims to align the way a computer works and human production such as words. The algorithm of Boolean search and operations are not intuitive for non-technical users. It requires a greater number of steps to convert a user's information need into actual queries, if that is possible at all. On the other hand, vector search leverages machine intelligence, relying not only human intuition, but also the machine's self-generated understanding of the text. For example, word2Vec generates corpus-based embeddings independently. In practice, often a hybrid search approach is adopted, which integrates both vector and keyword search techniques to provide versatile solutions to accommodate various scenarios. Such an approach can utilize both keyword search scores and vector-based similarity scores, and thus both human and machine intelligence.

6.2.2 *LLMs and information retrieval*

Large language models (LLMs) can be used to extract features, as well as evaluating the extracted results, through prompting or fine tuning. For example, a LLM can be fine-tuned to extract Named Entity Recognition (NER). This is a core task of information (feature) extraction, used in many applications, such as automatic news analysis, terminology extraction, and document classification. Malmasi et al. (2022) defined NER as identifying entities in text and recognizing their types (p. 3798). This definition implies two fundamental sub tasks of NER: one is to identify entities in the text data, the other is to group entities into conceptual categories according to their properties, such as names for a person, an organization, or a location.

For prompting, a user must select a modern large language model such as GPT4 with a functional prompt. The following is a prompt entered in ChatGPT 4o mini based on the prompt proposed by Constantin and Bernard (2023):

> The task is to create a dataset for entity recognition. Label as many entities, concepts, and ideas as possible in the input text. Use entity types in traditional NER Tasks such as more abstract concepts and ideas. Make sure the entity concept is not part of speech but something more meaningful. Avoid finding meaningless entities. Output format (separate entities with new lines, everything, including description, and entity concept is written in English):
> entity from the text: entity concept (description of entity group/concept)
> Input: <Mary worked in Ottawa in 2009.>

The output is as follows:

Mary: Person (An individual mentioned in the text, typically a proper noun referring to a human.)

Ottawa: Location (A city in Canada, serving as the capital and an important location for work and events.)

2009: Temporal Reference (A specific year, used to denote the time period in which an event occurred.)

(Output generated by ChatGPT 4o mini on August 27, 2024)

The above example illustrates how it is possible for a user to retrieve relevant NER features through prompting. However, such a method does not apply to large amounts of documents. In particular, there are confidentiality issues if the input data is sensitive in nature.

Furthermore, the NER problem space is much more complex than identifying and categorizing entities for input sentences such as "Mary worked in Ottawa in 2009." Some entity types can be linguistically complex. For example, entities in creative works may include complex noun phrases, gerunds, infinitives, or full clauses. These complexity factors impact the performance of a NER extractor. Meanwhile, a dataset with short and uncased text provides less informative context for entity extraction. Handling such low-context scenarios is also a challenge to develop an NER model. Moreover, entity distribution in the dataset can also vary significantly. For example, some documents have a large long-tail distribution (a dataset that includes a large number of a particular type of entity, such as location names). Such a distribution makes it hard to build representative training data (Malmasi, 2022, p. 3799).

6.3   Multilingual and cross-lingual information retrieval

When the problem of information retrieval is projected to a larger space, where multiple languages come into play, more factors must be taken into consideration. In such a space, an IR system must be able to accept queries for information in various languages and return objects (e.g., documents) of various languages. In practice, multilingual settings include various scenarios. For example, a user has to search for information in one language and read the returned results in another language. In a retrieval-augmented generation (RAG) pipeline, an LLM needs external information from multiple documents or multiple chunks of text to generate an answer. When these documents or chunks are written in different languages, it is a multilingual problem. This topic will be discussed in greater detail in Chapter 7.

While many people use multilingual or cross-lingual information retrieval interchangeably, some scholars differentiate these two terms. Yang et al. (2024), for example, defined Multilingual Information Retrieval (MLIR) as searches over a multilingual collection of monolingual documents to produce a single ranked list. The document retrieving and ranking activities are based only on query relevance, independent of document language. Conversely, in cross-language information retrieval (CLIR), queries and documents are in different languages. Yang et al. (2024) claimed that MLIR is harder to train than CLIR, because the MLIR model must assign comparable relevance scores to documents in different languages.

To tackle multilingual or cross-lingual IR problems, deep learning is an effective way to discover features or retrieve information in high-dimensional data with little or no human intervention. Cross-language transfer learning is a solution to address multilingual issues. The choice of vector storage, for example, is generally unaffected by whether the data is in English or another language. Cross-lingual language models provide extra resources to experiment for various options to solve problems in multilingual settings. For example, Eskander et al. (2020) adopted a fully unsupervised cross-lingual transfer approach for part-of-speech (POS) tagging. Their study, involving multiple source languages, either via projection or output combination, improved the tagging accuracy for most target languages (p. 4821).

6.3.1   Using statistical translation models for query expansion

One of the early methods to improve term-based retrieval systems focused on using query expansion (QE) techniques (Hambarde & Proença, 2023, p. 4). According to Vechtomova (2009), query expansion is "a process in Information Retrieval which consists of selecting and adding terms to the user's query with the goal of minimizing query-document mismatch and thereby improving retrieval performance." Some of the fundamental considerations for QE techniques include: (1) source of query expansion terms (e.g., hand-built knowledge resources such as dictionaries, thesauri, and ontologies), (2) techniques used for weighting query expansion terms, and (3) role and involvement of the user in the query expansion process (Vechtomova, 2009).

Riezler and Liu (2010) described an approach to query expansion that utilizes monolingual statistical machine translation (SMT) algorithms to improve retrieval effectiveness. Specifically, an SMT model was trained on large parallel data, with queries on the source side, and snippets of clicked search results on the target side. Snippets are short text fragments that represent the parts of the result pages that are most relevant to the queries (Riezler & Liu, 2010). This SMT system contains a query-to-snippet translation model and a query language model. The combination of these two models allow query expansion to incorporate contextual information into query extraction processes.

In the study of Riezler and Liu (2010), the SMT system is monolingual, that is, the user queries on the source side and snippets on the target side are in the same language. Early studies on using statistical translation models to improve information retrieval systems were also monolingual (Berger & Lafferty, 1999; Gao & Nie, 2012; Karimzadehgan & Zhai, 2010). These studies can be extended to multilingual settings.

6.3.2 Dense retrieval methods

Multilingual and cross-lingual information retrieval (CLIR) requires the ability to bridge the lexical gap between languages (Litschko et al., 2018). Traditional IR methods based on sparse text representations, such as word-based information retrieval, are not suitable for CLIR, as different languages do not share much of the vocabulary (Litschko et al., 2018). Representing text documents and queries in a continuous vector space, allowing for the utilization of neural network-based similarity measures, to rank documents and extract features are efficient in addressing the issues inherent in discrete retrieval methods (Hambarde & Proença, 2023).

As Section 4.4 of Chapter 4 discussed, embeddings are dense, real-valued, vector representations of linguistic units such as words. Embeddings capture the semantic meaning of natural language units. Theoretically, embeddings are language independent. In a multilingual setting, embeddings for words denoting similar concepts in different languages are very close in a shared cross-lingual word embedding space. For example, the positions of the embeddings for the English word 'method' must be very close to the French word 'méthode' in a vector space.

Vulić and Moens (2015) introduced a model to extract bilingual word embeddings for cross-lingual information retrieval. The model is trained on comparable corpora (see Section 2.5.3 of Chapter 5) in three language combinations (Spanish-English, Italian-English, and Dutch-English). Documents in these corpora are aligned by themes, that is, the aligned document pairs discuss similar themes. Throughout this study, neither direct translations for these aligned documents, nor other readily available translation resources such as pre-given bilingual lexicons. were involved. Vulić and Moens (2015) reported that their model significantly outperformed a series of strong baselines. This is a cross-lingual information retrieval (feature extraction) case study on learning bilingual lexicons from comparable corpora.

Gillick et al. (2018) pointed out that discrete, text-based information retrieval (IR) systems that index objects by words or phrases, have been augmented by models that use embeddings to measure similarity in continuous space. In an end-to-end continuous retrieval, standard approximate nearest neighbor (ANN) search replaces the discrete inverted index, and relies entirely on distances between learned embeddings. Gillick et al. (2018) reported their continuous retrieval model improved on a discrete baseline by 8% and 26% on two similar-question retrieval tasks. Karpukhin et al. (2020) also used neural networks to map documents and queries to a continuous space and applied a similarity measure to rank the documents.

6.3.3 Multilingual databases for MLIR and CLIR

When handling complex natural language queries, simply using LLMs may not suffice. Malmasi et al. (2022) argued that even the largest pre-trained transformers did not achieve top performance without external knowledge (see also *MultiCoNER 2*, n.d.). Specialized multilingual datasets are a good resource to address this issue. For example, Malmasi et al. (2022) and Fetahu et al. (2023) introduced MultiCoNER multilingual dataset versions one and two, which can be used to evaluate the robustness of the LLM-driven name entity recognition (NER) system, in multiple languages and under noisy scenarios. MultiCoNER version two claims to be able to handle complex NER in 12 languages, including low-resource languages such as Farsi and Hindi.

The MultiCoNER (version one) dataset represents three domains (wiki sentences, questions, and search queries) and includes 11 languages, including multilingual and code-mixed subsets. In the monolingual subsets, each of the 11 languages has their own subset with data from all domains. The multilingual subset contains randomly sampled data from all the languages mixed into a single subset. In addition, there is a code-mixing subset, which contains codemixed instances, where the entity is from one language and the rest of the text is written in another language. The multilingual and code-mixing subsets were designed to evaluate multilingual models and it is assumed that the languages present in an instance are unknown.

The MultiCoNER (version one) leverages the WNUT 2017 (Derczynski et al., 2017; cited from Malmasi et al., 2022) taxonomy entity types, and defines six NER categories, namely, person, location, corporation, groups, product, and creative-work (e.g., movie/ song/book titles). Later in MultiCoNER version two, Fetahu et al. (2023) created a taxonomy of 33 fine-grained NER classes across six coarse categories used in version one. Chapter 7 will discuss taxonomies and conceptual groups in greater detail.

6.3.4 Case study: cross-lingual terminology extraction for translation

Terminology extraction, also known as term extraction, is an information retrieval (feature extraction) task that is widely used in the language industry. For example, terminology is a significant instrument to aid translation, including both human and machine translation. Terminology is closely related to domain knowledge. As Cabré (1999, pp. 1–2) explained, terminology activities dated from 18th century research in chemistry or in botany and zoology, where the real protagonists were subject matter experts. For example, the Austrian E. Wster (1898–1977), considered the founder of modern terminology and the main representative of what is known as the Vienna School, came from the field of engineering, as did the Russian D. S. Lotte (1889–1950), founder of the Soviet School of Terminology.

Consequently, specialization, including both specialized knowledge and its corresponding special languages, is a definitive characteristic of terminology. As Faber and León-Araús (2016, p. 196) pointed out, terminology is "the study of how specialized knowledge concepts are structured, described, and designated in one or various languages within a specialized domain." Faber and León-Araús (2016) added, one of the practical tasks in terminology is the design and creation of terminological resources, with which users, including both human and machine, can effectively access concepts and associated information in order to understand, acquire, or produce specialized knowledge (p. 196).

The concept of terminology is enriched with both human and contextual interpretation, such as domains, languages, and purposes. For example, 'acute' can be a regular term in a daily dialogue, but a specialized term in the medical domain, when a doctor asks the patient to describe their pain level. It also involves segmentation problems, or the meaning unit. For example, 'birds of a feather' is one phrase, rather than 'birds', 'of', 'a feather'. The identification and categorization of specialized terms would benefit from human external human knowledge, such as taxonomies and ontology. Terminology related tasks usually involve both deep learning and symbolic knowledge.

Deep learning applications started to help terminologists who work in this space. For example, through prompting, LLMs can return relevant terms. However, these extracted terms usually need human verification. Sometimes, such human intervention can also be automated, through techniques such as rule mining.

For example, authors Dai and Song (2019) investigated two types of terms in product reviews, aspect terms (those that describe a product's properties or attributes) and opinion terms (those that correspond to the reviewer's sentiments towards the product or an aspect of the product). To improve the performance of neural-network-based aspect and opinion term extractions on product reviews, the authors proposed an algorithm to automatically mine extraction rules from existing training examples. These mined rules are applied to label data. Both the data automatically labeled by the rules, together with a small amount of data accurately annotated by humans, were used to train a neural model.

Monolingual terminology extraction algorithms are based on how the word 'terminology' is defined. For example, the Term Frequency Inverse Document Frequency (TF-IDF) technique focuses on which words are more outstanding in a specific document, when compared with other documents in the corpus (see Section 4.2.3 of Chapter 4). The design of these algorithms is based on human knowledge about how they think a term is defined. Other algorithms are related to the process of how pieces of conceptual network are mapped into linguistic terms.

In translation, multilingual or cross-lingual terminology extraction is helpful for both human and machine translation. Depending on how abstract the algorithm and conceptual mappings are, the degree of alignment between the extracted terminology lists from a collection of text data in multilingual languages vary. Broadly speaking, there are two scenarios for term alignment in multilingual settings. The first of which is separate term lists can be extracted from comparable corpora in multiple languages, which are chosen in accordance with topics, themes, or other criteria. For example, regarding the topic of movie reviews for a particular title, a person can collect English texts and French texts accordingly. These texts are not translated but naturally generated in human communication. The terms extracted from English and French texts are probably related, even though they may not necessarily be the direct translation of each other. Another scenario is that extracted terms are aligned by translation. Usually these terms are extracted from parallel corpora; for example, a collection of sentences in both English and their French translations.

In Computer-Assisted Translation (CAT) software, aligned terms with direct translation is often a linguistic resource that a CAT tool can manage. In many cases, the translation of a term is not the direct translation of this term, but extracted from the target texts in a parallel corpus, such as translation memory, aligned source, and target segments (usually sentences, or paragraphs and documents). Although the relationship between aligned segments is also based on translation, the translation is on larger units, such as sentences, paragraphs, and even documents. The capture of larger context in parallel corpora is assumed to help the translation of words rely more on meaning, rather than word-for-word literal translation.

Non-neural bilingual or multilingual terminology extraction systems often integrate both statistical and rule-based algorithms to extract terms. The technique Macken et al. (2013) used started with discovering confident terminology pairs and then extracted rules for correspondence between terms in different languages. For example, the rule for French-Dutch aligned terms is noun + adjective corresponding to adjective + noun.

In the study of Baisa et al. (2015), a bilingual terminology is retrieved from parallel corpora combining a monolingual terminology extraction and a co-occurrence of statistics. Specifically the parallel corpora, stored as monolingual corpora, are aligned on segment level. To extract cross-lingual terminology, the monolingual terminology is extracted in both languages. Next, the algorithm computes co-occurrence statistics for all aligned structures and for all candidate pairs occurring within the aligned structures. The resulting list of all term pairs can be sorted by various scores. In Kilgarriff et al. (2014), identifying the grammatical shape of a term in a language is an important technique to extract terms for multiple languages.

7

AUGMENTING LLM PERFORMANCE WITH HUMAN KNOWLEDGE

7.1 LLM performance and human knowledge

As discussed in Chapter 1, Shannon's framework surrounding the mathematical theory of communication applies to human–to–human exchanges, as well as information flow from an engineering perspective, such as data transmission within deep learning. The focus in this holistic communication process is on the problem of how to communicate perfectly over imperfect (noisy) communication channels. In multilingual settings, humans use natural language symbols to think, communicate with others, and organize internal knowledge. If a listener cannot understand the language the speaker speaks, it may be classified as a noise. The noisy channel theory as discussed in Section 5.1.2 in Chapter 5 can be applied to the translation problem where the noise is the foreign language.

Deep learning weaves one of the simplest, yet most efficient and intricate networks to transmit data across layers, including from human to machine, within machine, and finally from machine to human. The data transmitted can be either symbolic (e.g., natural language symbols) or subsymbolic (e.g., vectors or other mathematical forms). In a multi-layered deep learning system, such a transmission process involves both human–to–human communication results at the input and the output layers, and the communication within the system at the intermediate, hidden layers.

According to Shannon's theoretical framework, data is the raw component to be passed along in both human and machine communication. From an engineering perspective, data can be either binary or non-binary. From a sociocultural perspective, data represent facts about the world, as well as peoples' conceptualizations of or reflections on these facts. Information consists of the facts (data) that are systematically presented in the context of a problem space. According to Section 2.2 of Chapter 2, context provides guidance to organize, structure, and process raw data, compiling the data in a meaningful manner that is relevant to the person or entity according to their purposes or business goals. The holistic view of data as well as communication that carries it to flow across interfaces, establishes a common ground between the human and machine approaches, enabling them to be communicable, comparable, or analogous. In terms of knowledge, on the one hand, it is

DOI: 10.4324/9781003470557-9

internalized to an individual cognition. On the other hand, when it is used to communicate with external entities, such as another individual or within a computer system, it informs a comprehensible, shareable model of data representations. For humans, knowledge models can evolve over a lifetime. For machines, when knowledge can be represented in such a way that they can read and compute, machines can act on their own to generate answers to new questions.

In this sense, Large Language Models (LLMs) are data transformation systems at various levels of abstraction or degrees of data compression, which are analogous to human brains. According to MacKay (2003), brains "are the ultimate compression and communication systems" (p. v). The information theory applies to both LLMs and human brains, when communicating data across layers. Using human intelligence to augment the performance of LLMs will also help improve the explainability of AI. As discussed in Section 6.3.3, even the largest pre-trained Transformers did not achieve top performance without external human knowledge (see Malmasi et al., 2022; *MultiCoNER 2*, n.d.).

There are a few primary considerations to achieve this goal. First, it is important to allocate tasks in response to strengths and natural abilities of both humans and machines, to improve the performance and explainability of LLMs, while simultaneously keeping everything running as it should. Second, what aspect of human knowledge is the starting point to ensure accuracy of LLM applications. For example, is the LLM generation result accurate when compared with human creation? Or, are LLMs heading in a direction that is not what humans expected? Third, is it possible for individual, internalized human knowledge to be leveraged as a shareable model that LLMs can read and compute? If so, what are the specific methods to accomplish this? Sections 7.2 to 7.4 will address these three questions in detail.

7.2   Complementing deep learning with human knowledge

Deep learning is efficient in forming its own 'understanding' from data, by recognizing patterns, without or with minimal human intervention. Despite its undeniable success, this bottom-up approach leads to a number of shortcomings, including data inefficiency, poor generalization, and a lack of interpretability (Garnelo & Shanahan, 2019, p. 17). It should be noted that the shortcomings of deep learning align with the strengths of symbolic AI, which closely resembles a top-down approach; this is particularly true when applying high-level abstractions to real-life instances. To begin, symbolic representations promote data efficiency as they lend themselves to re-use in much more than a single task. Second, symbolic representations tend to be high-level and abstract, which facilitates generalization. Third, symbolic representations are language-like and align with the logic of human reasoning. Thus they are more comprehensible and interpretable to humans (see Garnelo & Shanahan, 2019, pp. 17–18).

Deep learning has tremendous potential to leverage external human knowledge. The key is understanding how to properly communicate high-level, abstract human knowledge to computer programs. This involves mapping personalized, subjective knowledge onto a shareable model of representation that other systems can leverage, which falls under the category of knowledge representation in computer science and information systems. Knowledge representation "deals with the encoding of knowledge in a form that can be used for computer based problem solving" (Das, 2003, p. 33). Sowa (2000) emphasized the role of logic and ontology in this concept, pointing out that knowledge representation "is the application of logic and ontology to the task of constructing computable models for some domain" (p. xii). Such a model focuses on analyzing knowledge about the real world and mapping it to a computable form (Sowa, 2000, p. xi).

Intuitively, humans have their own way of organizing knowledge, for example, using concepts as a unit of knowledge management and analysis. Such concepts are typically based on a relatively limited amount of observations (data), unlike deep learning, which relies on large-scale data to train the model. When it comes to mapping human concepts onto computer systems, there are multiple theories at play. For example, the Conceptual Dependency (CD) Framework (Schank, 1972; Schank & Tesler, 1969) is one of the early models of Natural Language Understanding. In this framework, the term 'concept' is used to align with meaning. A concept "may be considered to be an unambiguous word-sense" (Schank & Tesler, 1969, p. 4). At the conceptual level, meaning is independent of the words used. For example, two sentences can be composed of different sequences of words. However, these two sentences may be identical in meaning. In that case, these sentences would have a single representation of meaning, or 'interlingua' as indicated in Vauquois Triangle (Vauquois, 1968, p. 335; see Section 3.2 in Chapter 3). Specifically, the Conceptual Dependency framework is a stratified linguistic system that attempts to provide a computational theory of simulative performance. The highest level of the stratification system is a conceptual base, which can also be considered an interlingua. Such a conceptual base consists of a network of concepts that applies to all languages.

Conceptual Dependency Framework can be applied to construct symbolic, concept-based natural language parsers, which are computer programs that automatically parse the grammatical structure of sentences.[1] Schank and Tesler (1969) claimed that their parser is conceptual, rather than syntactic, as its output is not concerned with the syntax of the input language (p. 569). However, conceptual and syntactic elements are more in a parasitic relationship than in one excluding each other. In the CD framework, Schank and Tesler (1969) also employed knowledge of grammar, though semantics-based, as part of a more complete linguistic system. Schank and Tesler (1969) proposed the grammar of the CD framework consists of two parts: (1) a universal grammar exemplified by the conceptual rules; and (2) a language-specific part that is made up of realization rules. Through these realization rules, pieces of the conceptual network are mapped into linguistic items. The realization rules may be used for both parsing and generating (Schank & Tesler, 1969, p. 569). In an automatic sentence parser, a system aims to analyze a sentence in a way analogous to the human method. The system

> handles input one word at a time as it is encountered, checks potential linkings with its own knowledge of the world and past experience, and places its output into a language-free formulation that can be operated on, realized in a paraphrase, or translated.
> *(Schank & Testler, 1969, p. 572)*

In this process, there is a knowledge base for computers to process and understand, which is based on the previous accumulation of concepts and their relationships.

Conceptual Dependency, as well as other methodologies, such as Conceptual Graphs and Formal Concept Analysis, assumes natural language is conceptual. When using such an approach, semantics carried by texts are transformed into semantics of conceptual models at a high level of abstraction (Bogatyrey & Samoduroy, 2016, pp. 13–14). Conceptual graphs use graph-based structures to represent concepts and their relationships to one another (Bogatyrey & Samoduroy, 2016; Sowa, 2000; Wille, 1997). A Formal Concept Analysis uses matrix models as a "formal context" from which to analyze data, in terms of how objects can be hierarchically grouped together, according to their common attributes (Bogatyrey & Samoduroy, 2016, pp. 13–14).

7.3 The starting point to ensure accuracy and explainability

Humans are experts in using concepts to analyze and solve problems. Terminologists, for example, are linguists who specialize in terminology as well as term-level knowledge management. They use concepts and concept maps to create definitions for terms in specialized domains. However, concepts are challenging for computers to grapple with. A concept is abstract, complex, and deconstructable. Schank (1972) claimed that people always decompose complex concepts into primitives. Conceptual primitives cannot be further broken down. These primitives were often combined into semantic structures to represent contents.

However, if a model can pass a benchmark or definitive knowledge structure to a deep learning system, the strengths of both human cognition and machine intelligence can be leveraged. The primary concern is whether accuracy and explainability can be ensured by injecting defining knowledge to a system that can autonomously form its own understanding.

7.3.1 Terminology knowledge base

One definitive element of knowledge is terminology. Section 6.3.4 of Chapter 6 discussed terminology extraction as a case study of information retrieval. From a knowledge perspective, terminology plays a significant role in domain knowledge representation. As Meyer et al. (1992) proposed, "the vision of a hybrid between a term bank and a knowledge base, or terminological knowledge base (TKB), has recently been paralleled in computational lexicology by the concept of a lexical knowledge base (LKB)" (p. 159). Meyer at al. (1992) built a prototype TKB entitled COGNITERM that was constructed at the Artificial Intelligence Lab at the University of Ottawa. This was a pioneering effort to combine knowledge engineering with term management.

In practice, the majority of people approach knowledge through terminology. For example, they use terms to associate certain concepts with particular positions in their knowledge structure. When searching for specific pieces of knowledge in their brains, sometimes people refer to these terms as keywords. Both terms or keywords, regardless of how people address them, are used to represent concepts. A definition for a concept applies to terms in various languages. The meaning of one concept relies on the relationships between this concept and its adjacent concepts. For example, to describe a wine, an individual can use its different aspects/attributes: its color (e.g. white wine), its flavor (e.g. dry), its grape variety (e.g. Pinot Grigio), its origin (e.g. Germany), and its growing region (e.g. Kaiserstuhl), as well as its quality (e.g. Kabinett). With these (and other) keywords, a wine like the "Oberbergener Baßgeige Grauburgunder" from 2017 could now be labeled so that users can navigate this knowledge, for example, quickly finding it in an online catalog (see Herwartz, 2019).

7.3.2 Taxonomies

Terms and keywords are useful to organize knowledge and quickly find what one is looking for. Furthermore, structuring these terms as hierarchically ordered elements improves efficiency in capturing the complexity of human knowledge. Section 4.2.1 of Chapter 4 discussed WordNet, which is a synonym-based structured large lexical database of English symbols. Using meaning relationships such as synonyms is an efficient way for computers to capture the complexity of terminological knowledge.

Another way to capture the semantic relationships between words is through hypernym (a word that acts as the name of the category) and hyponym (a word with specific meaning that falls under a category). In the context of terminology, taxonomy is a method of organizing concepts and vocabulary according to their sub or superordinate relationships (see Herwartz, 2019). For example, the concept of 'animal' has a few subordinates such as 'dog', 'cat', and 'rabbit'. Note that in this framework, terms such as 'dog', 'cat', and 'rabbit' represent one way to label concepts. If the taxonomy is presented to a French community, 'animals' or 'animale' (French feminine) probably will be used, rather than 'animal'. In other words, labeling the concepts is a simplified way to communicate ideas. Thus, concepts can be identified by numbers, as what is more significant is not how the concept is identified, but the relationship between concepts. For example, the concept of 'animal' is labeled as concept #1, which has subordinates such as concept #2 ('cat') and concept #3 ('dog'). Taxonomies define the hierarchical relationships between concepts #1 to #3: A cat is one type of animal, so is a dog.

Oftentimes, there are multiple ways to organize concepts in a subordinate or superordinate way. This uncertainty leads to different taxonomies for the same groups of concepts. For example, a wine can be organized according to country of origin, or according to color. In the line of country, there could be multiple subordinates, such as Germany, France, and Australia. Under color, a wine could be white, red, or pink. These two starting points lead to different hierarchical relationships about the concept of wine. Thus, before designing a taxonomy, it is important to decide where to start conceptually (see Herwartz, 2019). To ensure machine generated results are under control, it is crucial for humans to identify the starting point, e.g., whether taxonomy begins in the branch of color or country of origin in the context of wine. Otherwise, the remaining tasks that a deep learning system accomplished can lead to unexpected results. Changing decisions at the root tends to cost more than minor changes in the leaves (details).

From a high-level perspective, taxonomies can be applied to real-life instances, in the form of metadata. An annotation schema based on taxonomies allows users to classify the content according to a hierarchical sequence of sub and superordinate terms. For example, the taxonomy identifies 'dog is a type of animal' and 'Shih Tzu is a type of dog'. The metadata include 'dog' and 'animal', with the former as the subordinate of the latter. If this schema is used to annotate an English sentence "Shih Tzus are very gentle animals" and a French sentence "Les Shih Tzus sont des animaux très doux," 'Shih Tzus' and 'Les Shih Tzus' are annotated as 'dog', and 'animals' and 'des animaux' as 'animal'. In this way, the taxonomy helps users capture the high-level relationships, that is, Shih Tzus are a type of animal. Such categorization is language-independent, just like the annotation applies to both English and French sentences. As mentioned in the wine example, different taxonomies (e.g., country of origin vs. color) lead to different categorization results, depending on the purposes of data annotation and analysis.

7.3.3 Term definitions

Definitions are another significant element at the root of navigation. The relationship between concepts as well as their associated terms is established through definitions. In this regard, terminologists have accumulated rich experiences. Their work begins with definitions, which is based on concepts, as well as relationships between concepts (e.g. concept maps). The primary goal of a terminologist is to define an object. In order to create an accurate and useful definition, a terminologist begins with a concept and analyzes its adjacent concepts. Oftentimes, concept maps are leveraged by terminologists in their effort to define an object. The definition based on such analysis is useful and qualified to be repeatedly referred to in various scenarios. For example, in the domain of 'Document Type', terms are defined as:

> "administrator guide | Administrationsanleitung: document type that refers to information on the management of a technical system"
>
> "assembly instructions | Montageanleitung: document type that refers to information on how parts are put together to complete a specific product so that it fulfills its intended use"
>
> "bill of materials | Stückliste: document type that refers to formal tabulation of the physical assemblies, subassemblies, and components needed to fabricate a product"
>
> *(Source: iiRDS - The International Standard for Intelligent Information Request and Delivery—tekom iiRDS: iiRDS—intelligent information Request and Delivery Standard, extracted from Tekom termXplorer (termtechnologies.com))*

The above definitions are associated with concepts. Although each one may be represented by different terms, concepts as well as their visual representations such as concept maps, transcend the boundaries of form and language. Perhaps maps look different in some way for each language. However, they can be combined into one system in which the relationships between concepts apply to all languages, so that they can be customized to language-specific subsystems if needed. As the above definitions show, the linguistic structure of these definitions are consistent, indicating the attribute that they come from the same system, starting with "document type that refers to...".

Terminology is an effective tool to represent specialized knowledge. For example, *Pandemology*[2] is an online platform for a multilingual database for terminology that focuses on knowledge related to COVID-19. The database is open, inviting both translators and medical professionals to add new concept entries.

7.3.4 Case study: adding term definitions to LLM prompts

Definitions of terms are useful elements to guide the performance of LLMs. For example, the following prompt incorporated definitions given by the intelligent information Request and Delivery Standard (iiRDS). These definitions are included in a *ChatGPT* prompt:

Build a taxonomy based on these terms and definitions:

1 administrator guide: *document type that refers to* information on the management of a technical system;

2 assembly instructions: *document type that refers to* information on how parts are put together to complete a specific product so that it fulfills its intended use;
3 has a document type: *document's property* that references its document type.

(Source: Tekom termXplorer (termtechnologies.com).
Note: The italicization is added by the authors.
The three italicized phrases will be discussed at the end of this section)

The response ChatGPT returns includes a taxonomy and an explanation:

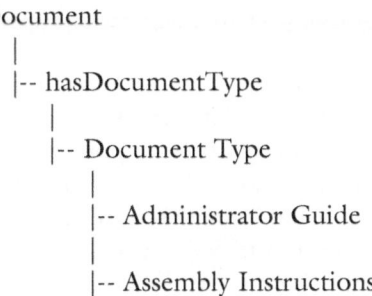

```
Document
  |
  |-- hasDocumentType
      |
      |-- Document Type
          |
          |-- Administrator Guide
          |
          |-- Assembly Instructions
```

In this taxonomy:

Document is the root category.
hasDocumentType is a property that connects documents to their specific types.
Document Type includes various specific types like **Administrator Guide** and **Assembly Instructions**, which are more detailed classifications of documents.

As shown in this example, the Large Language Model is able to create a reasonable taxonomy. These definitions, both in their linguistic structures and content blocks, offer clear instructions for the LLM agent to process and summarize the hierarchical relationships between these concepts. The concepts of 'administrator guide' and 'assembly instructions' are at the same level in this hierarchy, which is indicated by the shared structure and linguistic descriptions in these two definitions, that is, "document type that refers to…". The iiRDS system includes a 'has a document type' concept, describing its attributes as 'document's property' in its definition. Such a system not only facilitates intelligent search and organization of terms as well as their associated concepts, but also takes hierarchical relationships into consideration, which encodes taxonomy information in its terminology system.

By adding the definitions in a system that encodes meaning about both concepts and concept relationship in a prompt, an LLM is able to leverage terminological expertise and its generated results are easier to trace.

7.4 Knowledge representation methods and their implementations

Terms and their definitions are effective methods to describe and represent terminological knowledge. As a convenient starting point of understanding, taxonomies (see Section 7.3.2) focus on defining concepts using sub or superordinates. However, real-life relationships between objects contain more than what taxonomies can summarize. To explicitly specify knowledge beyond terminology, a data model must capture more complex relationships in order to accurately represent them within a reusable and shareable knowledge framework.

Structured knowledge representations about the world are used in a variety of subjects and computer applications such as artificial intelligence, semantic webs, software/system engineering, and library sciences. Although the same name may be used to identify a method, such as ontology, there could be nuances when different subjects are involved. For example, in the context of big data analysis, ontologies are used as formal systems that assign data objects to classes and that relate classes to other classes (Berman, 2013, pp. 35–6). Such a classification becomes a hierarchy of data objects, helping data analysts determine how things relate to other things. Berman (2013) illustrated six principles to which this hierarchy must conform (p. 37). These principles are summarized based on Big Data analysis. In another application area such as software engineering, these principles can serve as a starting point to be further reexamined according to specific research goals and business purposes.

Regardless of subject, knowledge representation methods as well as their implementations are significantly reliant on context. For example, 'Chardonnay' represents a specific 'instance' within a class of "wine recommendations," but in the domain of a "restaurant" (with a wine cellar), in which the individual "wine bottles" represent the specific instances, it can refer to a subclass of a certain type of wine (see Herwartz, 2019).

To avoid confusion, working definitions of knowledge representation methods covered in this section primarily target a specific area of application, namely, semantic webs. Readers can apply these frameworks in other areas by integrating appropriate contextual information. A semantic web refers to "an extension of the current web in which information is given well-defined meaning, better enabling computers and people to work in cooperation" (Berners-Lee et al., 2001).

7.4.1 Semantic webs

In the context of semantic webs, webs are considered Big Data resources. Different from traditional webs, the meaning of the information in semantic webs is made explicit through methods such as taxonomies and ontologies. These methods aim to decode meaning by turning raw data into classified, structured, and standardized knowledge representations. When humans are exposed to a stream of sensory information, they sort it into a set of objects, and then assign the individual objects to general classes. For example, a piece of writing is classified as 'administrator guide', and this 'administrator guide' is subclassified under a larger grouping, such as 'document' (see Section 7.3.4). A culturally determined classification of objects for the world helps individuals avoid becoming overwhelmed by floods of sensory input, remembering these objects, drawing inferences, as well as searching for information to address specific questions as they arise in real-life communication (see Berman, 2013, p. 36).

This classification process can be simulated by machines, using structural frameworks to capture meaning in knowledge. In the same vein as human brains, a computer system can become a 'sorting machine' to classify unstructured, raw data. While there are multiple ways to classify input data, some methods of grouping data objects, such as by similarity (e.g., WordNet), can be misleading. According to Berman (2013), simply counting similarities should not be used as the basis for constructing a classification in the context of

Big Data (p. 37). On the other hand, some methodologies, such as ontology, proves to be useful when sharing common understanding of the structure of information/knowledge among people or software agents (De Luna, 2020, p. 61). A software product with such a functionality is referred to as an 'agent', capable of performing tasks in an intelligent way. For example, Google Translate is a machine translator. Ontologies are significant components of semantic webs. As a reusable and shared knowledge/data model, ontologies enable computers and people to work in cooperation.

7.4.2 Ontologies

Simply speaking, a classification is a form of ontology, in which each class is limited to one parent class (Berman, 2013, pp. 37–9). In this classification system, the classes are built on relationships among class members. Ontologies also define terms to label classes, just like taxonomies. However, compared with taxonomy, ontologies provide a more complex hierarchy, going beyond the scope of defining terms and concepts within a domain. An ontology can represent much wider and more complex relationships between concepts. For example, in a sentence "The dog bit a person," 'dog' is not a sub or superordinate of 'person', or vice versa. However, there is a relationship between these two entities. That relationship is established through the word 'bite'. This is a do (action) relationship, rather than a be (is-a) relationship in taxonomies, which are used to define terms. As De Luna (2020) pointed out, ontologies can describe relationships and intricate interconnectedness, and thus are suitable for modeling high-quality, coherent, and linked data (pp. 56–61).

Unlike a terminologist who focuses on defining concepts and terms, an ontologist must accomplish these tasks: (1) to define classes (i.e., find the properties that define a class and extend to the subclasses of the class), (2) to assign instances to classes, (3) to position classes within the hierarchy, and (4) to test and validate all of the above (Berman, 2013, p. 37). The constructed classification becomes a hierarchy of data objects conforming to a set of properties or rules. According to these explicit rules, the system can determine which class members can be included in the category or subcategory, and which ones are unrelated. There are other principles that an ontology must comply with. For example, in a hierarchical classification, each subclass may have no more than one parent class and the root (top) class has no parent class (see Berman, 2013, p. 37).

In the context of semantic webs, ontologies are part of the World Wide Web Consortium (W3C) standards stack. Ontologies provide users with the necessary structure to link one piece of information to other pieces of information on the Web of Linked Data (De Luna, 2020, p. 57). Thus, ontologies enable database interoperability, cross-database searches, and smooth knowledge management (De Luna, 2020, p. 57). By establishing essential relationships between built-in concepts, ontologies help in the automated reasoning of data. The way ontologies reason with concepts parallels the way in which humans comprehend interlinked concepts. In addition to reasoning, ontologies allow users to efficiently navigate from one concept to another within the ontological structure (see De Luna & Albuero, 2020, p. 59).

In multilingual settings, ontologies are language independent, focusing on relationships between concepts, rather than specific words that are used to represent them. In this sense, relationships play a more significant role than the data objects or classes involved.

7.4.3 Major components of semantic webs

In addition to ontologies representing relationships between classes and subclasses, a set of standards and best practices is needed, in order for different Big Data systems to communicate with one another. This set of standards in semantic webs include the Resource Description Framework (RDF) model, RDF schema, and SPARQL Protocol and RDF Query Language (SPARQL).

Resource Description Framework (RDF) is a solution provided by the W3C consortium. It is a practical method whereby data can be intelligibly organized into classes and shared over the Internet (Berman, 2013, pp. 44–5). Using RDF, Big Data resources can design a scaffold for their information that can be understood by humans, parsed by computers, and shared by other Big Data resources. The RDF is used for encoding knowledge on Web pages which makes it understandable to users (De Luna, 2020, p. 61). As a standard model for data interchange on the Web, RDF syntax supports an Entity-Attribute-Value (EAV) pattern, in which the subject is the entity, the predicate is the attribute, and the object is the value. The combination of the three parts is referred to as a 'triple'. Each triple has a Unique Resource Identifier (URI). Multiple triples are linked together to form a RDF model to represent knowledge for a specific domain. For example, the statements "Fred Flinstone's wife is Wilma Flintstone" and "Fred Flinstone is 25 years old" can be translated into RDF knowledge representation in *The Flintstones* animation:

The RDF schema (RDFS) is a standard model for data interchange on the Web. It contains the vocabulary that is used for describing different properties and classes of a variety of resources that are dependent on the Resource Description Framework. For example, according to the RDFS, the definition of the 'hasSpouse' attribute entails that the subject and object in this relationship are both humans. Thus, if Wilma is Fred's wife, it can be inferred that Fred and Wilma are humans. The RDFS also defines that humans are mammals, which means that Fred and Wilma are mammals (see GraphDB, 2024).

When data is stored in RDF format, a user can search for relevant information using an RDF query language. While there are multiple computer languages for database query, SPARQL has emerged as the standard RDF query language (Bikakis et al., 2016). In 2008, SPARQL became a W3C recommendation (Prud'hommeaux & Seaborne, 2008).

7.4.4 RDF knowledge graphs

When knowledge is externalized, it can be stored and managed using structured databases such as knowledge bases. A conventional database model is a flat (or table) model, which consists of a single, two-dimensional array of data elements. For example, to describe a person, there are a few columns listing their attributes, such as first name, last name, and gender. Each row describes different attributes for a single person. Furthermore, knowledge can be represented by a graph database model. A knowledge graph is simply a knowledge base organized as a graph. A graph model consists of nodes and edges, where the nodes represent concepts or classes, and the edges represent relationships between them. Such a model can be represented using the Entity-Attribute-Value pattern in the RDF model. RDF graphs can represent more complex relationships, such as super/subordinate, or non-hierarchical (e.g., action).

TABLE 7.1 An example of a triple

Subject (Entity)	Predicate (Attribute)	Object (Value)
:Fred Flintstone	:hasSpouse	:Wilma Flintstone
:Fred Flinstone	:hasAge	25

Source: Adapted from GraphDB (2024).

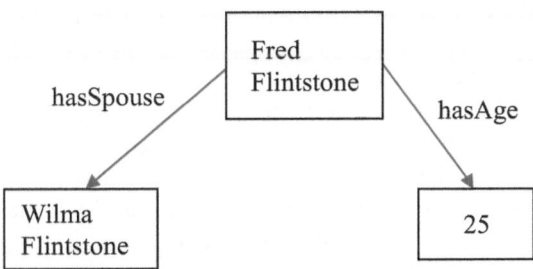

FIGURE 7.1   RDF knowledge graph for the entity 'Fred Flintstone'.

Using RDF as a graph data model that describes the meaning of information, the example as shown in Table 7.1 can be visualized as a graph (see Figure 7.1). Furthermore, the relationships are encoded with extra meaning embedded in RDFS. For example, the 'has-Spouse' relationship indicates that Fred and Wilma are both humans. Knowledge graphs can also be integrated with or without ontology. Without ontology, a knowledge graph is simply a structure that captures interlinked data. With ontology, an extra layer of contextual richness is added, which leads to contextual knowledge creation as well as relevant comprehensive analysis. Thus, knowledge graphs provide more dense relationships and capture more contextually derived meaning, than conventional relational databases.

In essence, a knowledge graph is primarily a data solution. A graph database enables sharing and reuse of knowledge, not only among people, but also with computer systems. As Schmidt and Leoncio (2023) pointed out, knowledge graphs aim to define the semantic relations between entities, which is central to providing humans and machines with context and means for automated reasoning.

7.4.5 Using knowledge graphs in Retrieval Augmented Generation (RAG)

There are multiple ways for individuals and organizations to leverage human knowledge in deep learning. For example, humans can be assigned to tasks to review and verify results generated by machines. A human translator can post-edit machine translation results, or a terminologist can verify the alignment and accuracy of bilingual terms extracted by a computer program. However, directly injecting human knowledge to an AI solution can help significantly scale up human intelligence. In this regard, Retrieval-Augmented Generation (RAG) with knowledge graphs helps enhance the performance of LLMs, by retrieving the most relevant information from external databases and incorporating it into the LLM-generated output. As Qiu et al. (2024) pointed out, explicitly augmenting LLMs with retrieved external knowledge from reliable data sources can enable LLMs to generate content that exhibits less deviation from the truth, and benefit downstream knowledge-intensive tasks.

In a conventional prompting process, a user inputs a question to prompt a large language model (e.g., OpenAI's GPT) to return a response. In a RAG process, a retrieval step is added to this process before response generation. During the retrieval process, a set of AI methods, such as embedding models and similarity vector search, are used to identify contextually pertinent information. An LLM based on the retrieved context can generate more meaningful responses. The following is a RAG case study based on Neo4j, which is a graph database management system developed by Neo4j Inc. The Neo4j graph data structure includes three fundamental elements: (1) nodes, (2) edges connecting nodes, and (3) attributes of nodes and edges.

To begin, large language models are trained on publicly available data. While each organization may store and manage their own knowledge bases, an LLM cannot be trained on this proprietary data. If a LLM is asked with questions such as "who do I need to contact if I want to update my profile," the LLM will probably not be able to provide a meaningful answer. However, a company may have a knowledge base, or a documentation system, which includes a group of documents, some of them related to the procedure of updating a user's profile. In this case, a Neo4j knowledge graph can be created to represent different documents (nodes) and relations between these documents. Using Retrieval Augmented Generation, the knowledge stored in a knowledge graph can be transferred to the LLM. Such a knowledge injection enables a LLM to provide more accurate answers to a question such as "who do I need to contact if I want to update my profile."

Specifically, a series of transformations is implemented, including (1) retrieving text representation of nodes in the knowledge graph, (2) using an embedding model to retrieve embeddings of these text documents, (3) storing embeddings as node properties in the graph, and (4) creating a vector index to allow efficient similarity vector search in the graph database. Next, another series of transformations can be established to provide context to the questions sent to LLMs. First, embeddings for the user's question (e.g., "who do I need to contact if I want to update my profile") is retrieved using the same embedding model as that which is used to embed nodes. The resulting vector represents the question in this embedding space. Then the embedding vector of the question is used to query the vector index, which will return nodes that are most similar to the question vector. To find other documents that may be related to the question, the returned nodes can be used to further query the knowledge graph to explore the properties and relationships for these nodes. As a result, a group of documents that are related to the question the user asked will be retrieved. Then the question asked by the user can be augmented with the information retrieved by the knowledge graph. The resulting augmented question is based on the context provided by the internal documents. When this augmented question is sent to an LLM, the LLM will be able to generate a more accurate and meaningful answer.

Notes

1 see https://nlp.stanford.edu/software/lex-parser.html.
2 https://pandemology.org.

PART THREE

Culture and multicultural AI

8

MULTILINGUAL AI IN PRACTICE

Transformer-based large language models have reached a new level of usage in society–they are increasingly present tools such as chatbots in your car or in the software system that operates the customer service contact center for your bank. Behind the scenes they play key roles today in a wide and widening variety of legal, business, industry, and governmental workflows and online systems. This "mass integration" of language algorithms in our daily lives presents both visible benefits as well as very concrete risks and harms–how can NLP researchers and practitioners practice responsibly in this ethical space? What is fairness in the context of LLMs, and how can we consider the social impact of language model use? And in particular, how are these challenges answered for language models that are increasingly multicultural?

8.1 A first focus on multilingual data

As was outlined in detail in Chapter 5 and developed in chapters throughout this book, the paradigm established by BERT is still an important one today: today's LLMs are most often pre-trained on a select set of training data and later fine-tuned for downstream tasks (Rogers et al., 2020). Writers who consider the ethical and fairness issues in this standard workflow have focused on both the data as well as the model elements of that flow. And as we covered in Chapter 2, today's large language models and other machine learning tools make use of linguistic data—multilingual corpora of text or speech that have been assembled, organized, and cleaned—for initial training data.

It is a recent trend that we have more information about the training data sources of open source models, as the makers of commercial and proprietary LLMs, more often than not today, do not disclose their training data in detail. For example, we know that the training data corpus for a product such as OpenAI's GPT 3.5 draws primarily from sources such as Wikipedia and the Common Crawl.

We have already examined the languages which are the focus of most major, free LLMs to date—with English predominating. More recent developments such as the 2024 arrival of the Google *Gemini* model do foreshadow more focus on large, multilingual

DOI: 10.4324/9781003470557-11

models. 2024's open-source models such as *Mistral* and Llama-2 are also known for their multilingual nature.

Yet even with English-predominant modeling, it is critical to remember that the enormous sizes of available training corpora do not ensure that they are bias-free. As Bender et al. (2021) pointed out, there is often the assumption that because the amount of scraped training data is so noticeably large, that these data must certainly be representative of all voices and views. But we know that not to be the case.

Indeed, one case in point: it is now better understood that the Common Crawl, a large collection of "data collected over 8 years of web crawling" that is used in many language models, is heavily influenced by the factors that narrow down internet participation. We know that these data over-represent young Internet users from developed and generally more wealthy countries. And specific tools such as Reddit, a specific source in the scraping process of models such as GPT-2, are known to skew more than 60% male and more than 60% between the ages of 18 and 20.

Another common source for both English-centric and multilingual models is Wikipedia, where early studies confirm fewer than 15% female among users and editors (Barera, 2020). And Wikipedia scholars do note this gender bias as

one if its two greatest flaws, as seen in statistics such as: of the nearly 2 million biographies present even in English Wikipedia alone, only 18.6% are currently about women; and only 8–15% of Wikipedians (editors) in the U.S. are females as of 2020.

(Barera, 2020)

Initially to note: one form of "systemic bias" in Wikipedia is geographical bias, where coverage of history and politics (in the English Wikipedia) skews heavily toward North America, Western Europe, Australia, and New Zealand, with "mediocre" or "poor" coverage for Latin America, the Middle East, North Africa, and South Asia, and notably "poor" coverage of Sub-Saharan Africa.

The effects of training data marked by gender, race, and geographical biases can generally be seen in both English-centric as well as more multilingual models today. For years, researchers have shown that language automation tools, most recently LLMs, are marked by biases such as those that de-center and disadvantage those of African origin, Hispanic, and other ethnic groups. And studies such as Abid et al. (2021) found marked anti-Muslim bias in prompts to early versions of the GPT model set. To be concrete about these findings, when the prompt included the word "Muslim," outputs in that study were more likely to include violent language ("killing" or "shooting") than when the word was not present. Similar biases were also explicated by Naous et al. (2023).

8.2 Multilingual and massively multilingual models emerge

Following the early success of BERT, an array of language-specific versions of that model methodology began to appear. The field quickly saw cleverly titled examples such as FlauBERT (Le et al., 2019) and CamemBERT (Martin et al., 2019) for the French market and in Dutch we saw BERTje (de Vries et al., 2019), Versions also began to appear for lower-resourced languages such as Basque with BERTeus (Agerri et al., 2020), or versions for larger language groupings such as IndicBERT (Doddapaneni et al., 2022). However, training such language-specific models relied heavily on the available data and computational resources, and was not sustainable as an approach to the world's 7,000+ languages.

A case in point is CamemBERT. Essentially a large, pre-trained monolingual model in a language other than English, CamemBERT developed using the BERT methodology and at that time recently released multilingual corpora with French holdings. This trend of developing monolingual models for a wide range of languages was popular following the emergence of BERT, drawing on training data such as Wikipedia or the Common Crawl (Martin et al., 2019, p. 2). Martin and colleagues utilized whole word masking and a model architecture similar to the $BERT_{BASE}$ configuration, resulting in 110M parameters, a very small model by today's standards. On standard NLP tasks such as part-of-speech tagging (POS) and named entity recognition (NER), the model outperformed several competing models, including the multilingual model mBERT (Martin et al., 2019).

Another interesting example is HyperCLOVA X (Yoo et al., 2024), a model "tailored to the Korean linguistic and cultural framework and are capable of understanding and generating English," a model that was "initially pre-trained using an evenly distributed mixture of Korean, English, and programming source code data" (p. 2). This model, focusing on Korean and English as well as coding, was developed to increase performance in Korean in particular, and was tested on "extensive experiments on a collection of major benchmarks on reasoning, knowledge, commonsense, factuality, coding, math, chatting, and instruction-following, as well as harmlessness, in both Korean and English." Hyper-CLOVA X was and is available via the NAVER Cloud Platform and the resulting chat service is available at the Naver website. This example model is not technically monolingual, while at the same time not fully multilingual in nature.

During the development of Korean models under the Naver umbrella, scholars did point out early critical questions. Kim et al. (2021) describe the early development of a "billions-scale" GPT-style model centered on Korean, noting that in comparison to English-dominant models, comparatively "we know little about how to train similar models in another language with different linguistic properties" (p. 1). Those authors note that even processes such as data crawl and collection, as well as data cleaning will be affected by the linguistic properties of Korean. And certainly Korean provides an excellent example here, as an agglutinative language. Among the other innovations this work highlights was a focus on improved methods for tokenization in Korean, a vital step that is critical for the downstream performance during model construction and application.

Gurgurov et al. (2024) provide a basic history and overview of multilingual models. Multilingual BERT, or mBERT, is a multilingual model which also deserves detailed attention. Devlin (2019) overviews the development of mBERT, which was trained with Wikipedia data to serve 104 languages, via a single model, and the Devlin team noted at the time that "they do not plan to release more single-language models." And mBERT proved surprisingly capable of performing NLP tasks across languages other than English.

By the same token, researchers almost immediately began to ask if, even in a single model, "all languages are created equal" (Wu & Drezde, 2020). Researchers pointed out that for the 104 top Wikipedia languages utilized in the training of the model, training data set size varied significantly by language, with languages such as English, German, Spanish, French, and Russian representing with an order of magnitude more data. And when Wu and Drezde (2020) examined the NLP capabilities of the model for languages in the bottom 30% languages by training dataset size, the model performed much worse.

Another example multilingual model, XLM, appeared quickly on the scene as well (Lample & Conneau, 2019). XLM expanded the thinking around training data types for multilingual language model training, combining unsupervised learning centered on monolingual data in multiple languages with supervised learning that levered parallel data, of the sort often found in locations such as bilingual parliamentary transcripts (Canada) or political entities such as the EU where significant translation of official documents and proceedings is baked into the organization (citation for bilingual data type). This approach resulted in a model better able to tackle cross-lingual challenges such as machine translation, in addition to more traditional NLP tasks.

The theme of language representation continues to draw attention. Sitaram et al. (2023) tackled the issue of "*massively* multilingual models" and their emergence on the scene more recently. As training data set sizes multiply and model architectures grow in complexity, a similarly first question those researchers ask is: "Are our technologies progressively getting more linguistically inclusive and diverse?" With models such as GPT frequently cited for a training dataset that is 93.7% English, models such as BLOOM with training data only 30.4% English,and a more balanced set of 46 languages in the training set, are emerging (p. 46). Other cited examples include XLM-R and mBERT (Sitaram et al., 2023). 2024 has also seen intentionally multilingual model products such as Cohere/Aya appear on the scene.

To state the question concretely: how much linguistic "coverage" do today's multilingual and massively multilingual models afford? In truth, the answer is: in the broader scope of the world's languages, this coverage remains fairly limited. Joshi et al. (2020) provides a recognized framework for thinking about linguistic diversity in NLP. Their work helps NLP researchers and practitioners to classify and think about the world's languages, from those such as English, Spanish, and French, which have a dominant digital and online presence, through language of the globe that have smaller labeled and unlabeled datasets to those that have exceptionally limited online/digital resources at all.

In sum, the taxonomy provided by Joshi and colleagues categorizes and labels approximately 2,500 of the world's estimated 6,000–7,000 total languages, drawing from the University of Pennsylvania's Linguistic Data Catalog, and cross-referencing with Wikipedia for detailed information on individual languages.

It is perhaps no surprise that this look at the "state and fate" of world languages has been widely cited for classifying languages as "haves" and "have nots" from a digital sense. In that classification, languages such as English, Spanish, French, German, and Japanese are "The Winners," with a dominant online presence and marked by massive industrial and government investments in the development of resources and technologies for these languages. A group of 18 languages, "The Underdogs," follows closely behind: Russian, Hungarian, Vietnamese, Dutch, and Korean are examples—where one finds a large amount of unlabeled data, and a lesser amount of labeled data. A group of 28 languages forms the next tier, languages such as Indonesian, Ukrainian, Cebuano, Afrikaans, and Hebrew are cited—these languages are marked by a strong web presence and thriving online communities, but with lesser amounts of labeled data available for model development. Nineteen languages form "The Hopefuls"—as represented by Zulu, Lao, Maltese, and Irish—and more than 220 are labeled "The Scraping Bys," with Cherokee, Fijian, Greenlandic, and Navajo as exemplars. And finally a major grouping of "The Left-Behinds" as languages, more than 2,000 in number, ex. Dahalo or Walpiri, have exceptionally limited digital resources and "a monumental, probably impossible lift" to advance them in the digital space.

And with new and newer versions of LLMs appearing daily as of this writing (2024), one increasing focus is on the increasingly multilingual nature of the models themselves. Although many proprietary models are released or updated without full documentation on the training data utilized or the model training process, there are some notable exceptions to that rule.

The Aya model family from Cohere serves as a recent example here, described by Ustun et al. (2024). The Aya team set out to create an "open-source multilingual instruction-finetuned LLM with diverse linguistic representation," addressing issues such as linguistic diversity with a target of 101 languages, more than 50% of which were generally considered lower-resource languages. They also strived to make instruction fine-tuning (IFT), truly multilingual as well, with volunteer linguists and contributors working globally for more than a year on assembling prompt-response datasets in languages other than English, for the training of the instructional model. This model team also invested heavily in expanding existing work on truly multilingual evaluation and a more multilingual approach to model safety, including important work, for example, on the detection of toxicity, social bias, and gender bias across the languages and cultures represented in the model work.

Sitaram and colleagues note, at the start, that there are a myriad of challenges in constructing more multilingual models, from gaps in quantity of data across language in widely used data sources such as the Common Crawl, where better representation is found in the top 25 languages, when nearly 60 languages represent only 0.001% of data assets in that collection. There are additional data gaps by language across available domains as well (Gao et al., 2020), and challenges in the quality of data in languages actually represented (Kreutzer et al., 2022). Quality challenges are seen in incorrect language identification (especially across similar languages with poorer data quality), machine generated data, and limited tooling to identify toxic and adult content across languages and cultures. And as in any large-scale data collection initiative, governmental agencies and academic institutions doing this work frequently face complex issues of identifying data custodians and rights holders of the datasets in question.

Doddapaneni et al. (2021) also offer a primer around the construction of pretrained, multilingual language models.

More recently, Xu et al. (2024) offer a comprehensive overview of the evolution of the multilingual LLM research and practice space. Tracing the evolution from English-centric large language models, through language-specific (non-English) models, to finally reach the current growth cycle in multilingual and "massively multilingual models." Xu and colleagues present descriptive information on more than 40 multilingual large language models or "MLLMs," including key details for each model such as: release date; parameter size; context length; pretraining file size; architecture; and pretraining function in addition to the model's primary modality(-ties). They also discuss such additional factors as training the reward model (RM) of an MLLM, as well as fine-tuning (or instruction-tuning) of multilingual models for downstream tasks.

On the theme of multilingual training corpora utilized by each of the MLLMs reviewed, Xu and colleagues do publish the "language proportion" details for given multilingual models. For example, although mBERT is advertised as being trained in Wikipedia data in 104 languages, the actual breakout percentages of training data by language are not published. The multilingual model XLM-R, with training data drawn from open source and CC-Net repository, states upfront that the percentage proportions of training data for the model are: English (12.56%); Russian (11.61%); Others (63.89%); Indonesian (6.19%); and Vietnamese (5.73%) (p. 7). The BLOOM model, a multilingual project sourcing in France during 2002, also shows a less English-centric training data set drawn from Web-crawl and BigScience Catalog data: English (30.03%); Simplified Chinese (16.16%); French (12.9%); Spanish (10.85%); Portuguese (4.91%); Arabic (4.6%); and others (20.55%).

And there are unique issues of benchmarks and evaluating multilingual LLMs: similar to the rise of monolingual and multilingual models, the research space has also seen the emergence of both primarily monolingual benchmarks, as well as more multilingual banks of test metrics. In point, early benchmarks such as GLUE and SuperGLUE are collections of scored performance tasks for language models, with prompts made and responses expected in English. When the first collection of GLUE "language understanding" tasks of sentence and sentence pair classification as well as tests of language inference routinely saw models generating scores exceeding human performance (Nangia & Bowman, 2019), more difficult or "stickier" tasks such as varying types of question answering were assembled into the SuperGLUE benchmark set (Wang et al., 2019).

Early monolingual benchmarking carried out primarily in English was followed by language-specific benchmarks in specific language and culture settings, such as KLUE (Korean Language Understanding Evaluation) (Park et al., 2021), CLUE (Chinese Language Understanding Evaluation) (Xu et al., 2020), ALUE (Arabic Language Understanding Evaluation) (Seelawi et al., 2021), and Russian SuperGLUE (Shavrina et al., 2020).

Similar then to the evolutionary path of the models themselves, often monolingual followed by multilingual development, multilingual benchmarking test sets began their emergence as well.

Metrics and benchmark sets are now available in multilingual information retrieval, question answering, and machine translation to name a few. One widely used standard benchmark is XNLI (Conneau et al., 2018a), which boasts training data for Natural Language Inferencing tasks in English and test data for 15 languages including English.

In addition to XNLI, other beginning multilinguial test benches included XGLUE (Liang et al., 2020) (a cross-lingual evaluation benchmark including elements such as named entity recognition, parts of speech identification, news classification, and other tasks), and XTREME (Hu et al., 2020), also itself a collection of cross-lingual test benches) and additional new test sets appear regularly. And more specialized multilingual and multicultural benchmarks in areas such as toxicity and bias have also come onto the market.

And of course major challenges such as gender bias/representation, widely researched in English with English-predominant models, take on additional layers of complexity in a multilingual and multicultural setting. Xu et al. (2024) also neatly summarizes the issue of bias in multilingual LLMs, suggesting that bias can arise from unmoderated training data, model design, or biased word embeddings (p. 13). They point out that bias can refer to a model's uneven behavior toward "specific gender, race, ethnicity, or other social groups" and that bias can be seen not only in model output but also in evaluation ("evaluation bias"), when this disproportionate activity exists in evaluation metrics as well.

One famous example of bias in widely used models is the representation of professions relative to gender. This example came to fore when readers noted clear trends in a major public tool, Google Translate, and its handling of professions such as "doctor" and "nurse," with utterances co-referencing "doctor" more often associated with masculine pronouns, and feminine pronouns being more prevalent for "nurse."

In the multilingual model ecosphere, additional factors do come into play as well. Touileb et al. (2022), as an example, examined how gender representation presented in both monolingual Norwegian and multilingual models, finding that monolingual models more accurately represented the demographic distribution of occupations in Norwegian society. And staying within the Scandinavian context, Touileb and Nozza (2022) were surprised to find harmful and gender-based stereotypes in monolingual models across several Scandinavian languages, despite the region's reputation for gender equality. And to move this particular research area forward, new evaluation metrics for the example case of gender-bias are emerging, for the evaluation of performance by both monolingual (primarily English) and multilingual models. One example of a multilingual bias benchmark is MozArt, which uses fill-in-the-gap cloze tests across languages to suss out model bias, a measure used by Piqueras and Søgaard (2022) as a case in point. Those writers used the MozArt metric to test for group bias in three major multilingual models—mBERT, XLM-R, and mT5—and found that not only are biases present in these model tests, that the models also differ in their results by language, that is that the models are not equally fair across languages.

And into late 2024, the focus on massively multilingual models continues, with new arrivals on the scene such as EMMA-500, a project offering a "comprehensive multilingual dataset...curated across multiple domains" and the resulting models trained from this dataset (Ji et al., 2024). Language models specific to the European Union's language set are also appearing, as these supported major projects respond in context to challenges of training data, model construction, model evaluation, and model use within multilingual and highly multilingual settings (Martins et al., 2024). Even major international conferences such as the 2024 meeting of the Translation Automation Society feature this topic, with the gathering titled "TAUS Massively Multilingual AI Conference Albuquerque."

8.3   Complex issues and a curse

We will end this chapter with two more complex, almost philosophical questions. First, how do multilingual LLMs "do what they do," how do they represent their constituent languages in vector space, and are there cross-lingual phenomena? This debate is complex from an engineering and a linguistic perspective and considering the issues around internal language representations across the families of multilingual LLMs also depends on whether parallel corpora are utilized or not, as well as approaches used for alignment of languages in model space (Xu et al., 2024, p. 10).

One set of authors (Wendler et al., 2024) delves into these issues with a more catchy, understandable title: "Do Llamas work in English?" They asked: what is the "latent language" of multilingual transformer models? The example model used in this particular analysis was Llama-2 a family of large open source models, which allowed the author to "look inside the model" to determine whether the model itself, trained predominantly on English language data, "pivoted" through English when prompted to solve a task in a language other than English. This ability to crack open a model, referred to broadly as mechanistic interpretability, is a rapidly developing field in computational linguistics, and allowed the authors to examine the internal workings of the model and led to a "tempting conclusion" that in the case of Llama-2, the model does show signs of using English as an implicit pivot. They do add the additional nuance that how not only "language spaces" but also "concept spaces" are created within a model may be at play in their results.

One additional area of research, and an important concept, is that of cross-lingual transfer learning. This issue came to the foreground in 2022, when early generative AI tools, essentially massive, pre-trained English language models began to show abilities in languages other than English (Blevins & Zettlemeyer, 2022). Referred to by both vendors and researchers with the unfortunate moniker of "language contamination," Blevins and Zettlemeyer conclude that due to massive scale of data collection for pre-training, models such as the GPT family boast "corpora [that] actually contain significant amounts of non-English text: even when less than 1% of data is not English ..., this leads to hundreds of millions of foreign language tokens in large-scale datasets." For example, GPT3.5 is thought to be "contaminated" with approximately 7% non-English tokens in the training data. Blevins and Zettlemeyer go on to demonstrate that "even small percentages of non-English data facilitate cross-lingual transfer for models trained on them, with target language performance strongly correlated to the amount of in-language data seen during pre-training" (p. 1). The suggest in the end that no modern, massive-scale model "is truly monolingual when pre-trained at scale."

What is cross-lingual transfer? In short, it is the idea that knowledge of, say, one language—considered here as set of linguistic features, from the syntactic to the lexical and sociolinguistic—might be "learned" by the model and applied in other language settings, where less training data may be present. There is a significant history of this concept in machine translation, particularly in the case of translation involving a low- or lower-resource language. One example is provided by researchers Tars et al. (2022), who explored fine-tuning a pre-trained neural machine translation model, trained on languages such as Finnish and Estonian, with smaller amounts of tuning data for low-resource language of the Finno-Ugric language family, Livonian. Instead of training a model from scratch focusing on Livonian, they "leverage the knowledge transfer" in the model from related languages with richer availability of training data, achieving significantly better NMT output in language pairs including Livonian, a southern Finnic language spoken on the shores of the Gulf of Riga, once considered extinct, today claiming one (p. 1) native speakers and fewer than 250 proficient speakers today.

There is considerable research as well interpreting and attempting to explain how cross-lingual transfer may work in large language models. In their strikingly titled "Same Neurons, Different Languages: Probing Morphosyntax in Multilingual Pre-trained Models," Stańczak and colleagues (2022) probe open LLMs to determine if specific neurons or groups of neurons in the trained model encode particular morphosyntactic features—features such as animacy, aspect, case, definiteness, gender, mood, number, person, and tense—across languages, finding a striking level of "cross-lingual overlap," although the interpretation of these findings is complex and may depend on language proximity (an example of closer language proximity would be Spanish and Portuguese, for example) and training data set size. Yet it is important to note that scholars continue to debate, at both the linguistic level as well as at the level of reasoning-based tasks, whether these "emergent abilities of LLMs" actually exist (Lu et al., 2023).

However, even the choice of multilingual model has complexity and consequences. To that point, Choudhury and Deshpande (2021) ask: "How linguistically fair are multilingual pre-trained language models?" These researchers tackle the perhaps more philosophical "multilingual model selection problem," asking the examining complex questions of fairness present in selecting MLLM A vs. MLLM B for a given task. They describe this often-seen dilemma this way:

> *Imagine that a researcher has come up with two MultiLMs, A and B. She decides to test her models on a standard benchmark, say XNLI (Conneau et al. 2018), which has training data for Natural Language Inferencing task in English and test data for 15 languages including English. She observes that A performs better than B on 10 languages, B performs better than A on 3 languages, and on the remaining two, the models perform equally well. Should she declare that model A is better than B because it outperforms the latter on most of the languages in XNLI? Or should she declare the one with higher average accuracy as the winner?*

They note that which multilingual model a researcher selects for a given experiment or an engineer chooses for an applied task in the real world draws on discussions of fairness in machine learning, ethics, social choice theory, as well as economics and decision theory. Given that there are "extremely skewed" distribution of resources across languages in multilingual NLP, how do we achieve the Rawlsian idea of "distributive justice," isolating and using, for research or utilitarian purposes, models which maximize the minimum performance across all the languages present in the models and work?

Last and importantly, Chang et al. (2023) raise the issue of the "curse of multilinguality." This complex and long-standing question asks: what are the trade-offs in utilizing generalist vs. specialist models, broadly multilingual models vs. a model trained or fine-tuned in a specific language or language family, for NLP or specifically translation tasks? Those writers pre-trained over 10,000 monolingual and multilingual language models for over 250 languages, finding that while high-resource languages "consistently perform worse in multilingual pre-training scenarios," adding that multilingual data improves low-resource language modeling performance, although this is somewhat dependent on the linguistic similarity of the added languages. As the dataset sizes increase toward the largest of models, the addition of multilingual data "begins to hurt the performance for both low-resource and high-resource languages" due to limitations of model capacity, which is known as the "curse of multilinguality" (p. 1).

9

MULTICULTURAL AI

9.1 Definitions and models of culture

Between 2017 and 2023, the research literature on "culturally aware and adapted NLP" has become one of the hottest research topics in computation and language, more than tripling the number of research articles yearly (Liu et al., 2024). What is culture, and why should an AI researcher or practitioner of NLP care? How can definitions and frameworks of culture help us as NLP researchers, practitioners, and students? And how is culture being considered as emerging computed tools such as LLMs come onto the scene?

Naturally, NLP and AI practitioners and researchers would want emerging models to function adequately across a broad range of geographical and cultural contexts. Why is this critical? If models are biased to the values of one particular region or demographic, or consistently make language usage choices or mis-represent the day-to-day workings of like in a given country or cultural context, research shows that users will react negatively. Chaves and Gerosa (2019), in the early days of chatbot evolution, noted that users clearly desired chat tools that were socially "mannered" in speech and interaction, avoided stereotyping culturally, adapted to interlocutors interests and humor—all deeply culturally challenging for automated tools. The research of Haoyue and Cho (2024) goes even further, pointing out that systems such as chatbots that are not culturally aware can alienate users, leading to mistrust and eventual abandonment of the system.

Why is it so hard to create a tool such as a chatbot that is culturally aware? One of the most challenging aspects of the word culture is its definition itself. In fact, so many definitions of this word exist, in so many subject areas and domains, that culture is widely cited as one of the most difficult words or concepts to define. It has been defined in such terms as "things shared by a group of people," "collective programming of the mind," from "a complex whole" to a "deposit of knowledge" or a "pattern of shared basic assumptions." Some writers have used culture as a synonym for "social reality" or "the real world." And yet others see culture as a "dynamic, ongoing group process" or even a verb which denotes an active process of meaning making and discovering. More recent conceptualizations of culture stress this fluid, process-based approach, with Brian Fay (1996, pp. 62–3) calling

DOI: 10.4324/9781003470557-12

culture "an evolving, connected activity, not a thing," not wanting to give the impression that culture is "static, closed and given" (1996, pp. 62–3). Zhu (2014) provides an excellent overview of these definitions that is very readable.

Adilazuarda et al. (2024) rightly point out in their overview of "culture in LLMs" that this definitional chaos has left us with a literature that is broad in scope and purpose. Some researchers focus their work on "deep issues" of values, emotions, opinions, and beliefs. Whereas others may focus on more "surface" issues such as behaviors, norms, language usage, or cultural artifacts. Liu et al. (2024) provide one taxonomy in an attempt to encapsulate what is an age-old problem in cultural studies of both differentiating but also integrating "deeper," values-based approaches to the concept of culture with the operational and every-day "facts and features of life" in a given cultural setting.

Why should students and practitioners of NLP care? Gumperz and Levinson (1991) sum it up nicely: "Communication relies on [these] shared meanings and strategies of interpretation. However, this common ground is distributed in a complex way through social networks" (p. 12). We cannot consider communication (from utterances to whole texts) outside of the context of culture and its "webs of significance." In short, multilingual AI *is* multicultural AI!

Going beyond the challenge of deciding on a definition of culture, scholars and researchers have provided more complex frameworks for describing and "operationalizing" culture and the values at its heart. Perhaps the most widely used, modern, values-based model of culture came from Professor Geert Hofstede et al. (2010), who collected his initial data via large-scale surveys in the workplaces of a global company (later revealed to be IBM) during the late 1960s and 1970s. The Hofstede model and international data collection with this model continue to today, and his model is still seen broadly in the humanities, social sciences, business, and other research areas in assessing the role of culture (Minkov & Hofstede, 2011). And although this descriptivist approach and research practice has come in for criticism and more recently for major reformulation (Minkov & Kaasa, 2021), it remains the most commonly seen "grand model" for the description of culture across the research disciplines and in scholarly circles.

In the Hofstede approach, national culture serves as the primary organizational tool, and within country definitions, nations overall are assigned scores (on a normalized 0–100 scale) for factors such as the well-known individualism vs. collectivism dimension, where country-level scores are provided along a spectrum from the most individual-oriented to the most group/family oriented based on continued, widespread survey sampling (cite current Hofstede company/annual report).

How has this framework been used in NLP-style research? One example of the Hofstede framework applied to a natural language corpus is Yu et al. (2016). Those researchers utilized the Google n-GramViewer to track the use of first person personal pronouns over the past 60 years, with the first person singular pronoun ("I") standing in for more individualistic expressions, and the first person plural ("we") representing more collectivist expressions. In this approach, they found that across a variety of languages associated with cultures that the Hofstede database had labeled as more individualistic (ex., English, German) and even languages associated with collectivist countries (Chinese, Russian), there were clear trends toward more I-based language. In their findings, Yu and colleagues summarized that a majority of cultures that they examined skewed heavily with a trend toward individualism.

In the decades since the Hofstede framework appeared, other scholars have used large-scale survey research to discover patterns of cultural values and value clusters in national culture settings. Examples here include the GLOBE Project on business leadership across cultures and the World Values Survey (WVS).[1] WVS is a long-standing, international research survey initiative which collects "social, political, economic, religious and cultural values of people in the world." Data in this ongoing project are sampled from more than 120 countries in a cadence of survey "waves," providing time-series data for almost 40 years, which have been analyzed by more than 150 national research teams and are being represented in more than 30,000 research publications, rivaling Hofstede for the range of its use in research. Like Hofstede, the WVS makes use of a wide variety of survey research, and it is especially known for its data visualizations, including groupings of countries according to country-level outcomes on given values or value-driven question prompts.

And there are definitely other theories and frameworks which consider cultural values and the interaction of cultures, and which focus less on description of cultural dimensions and on the dynamism of culture and cultural identity. Cultural globalization theory (Pieterse, 2003), as just one example, centers on the cross-national transmission or spread of "media forms, symbols, lifestyles, and attitudes." Indeed, one concept that has emerged in this school of thought posits that individuals globally are assimilating into a global cultural context, which is replacing globally spread behaviors and preferences for those from their traditional, local cultures, due to the technological interconnectedness worldwide today. The result, those authors argue, is the growth of cultures "without a clear anchorage in any one territory."

One of the "big, open questions" of cultural research at present is whether the interconnected nature of the world today is causing cultures to become more alike, noted in the term "cultural convergence" (Kaasa & Minkov, 2020). Some scholarssuggest that intercultural encounters lead to a form of acculturation to other cultures or even a global culture, leading to newly learned social skills, changed expectations, attitudes, and values, and updated cultural identities and self-identities, whereas others suggest the process is more complex (Ryder, Alden, and Paulhus, 2000). This speaks, however, to one of the "promises" of language technologies in general, and the value of global digital interconnectedness. One domain where these changes in attitude and behavior globally are widely seen and studied is in the area of e-commerce, where local consumer culture and a more globalized framework for consumer activities are being studied by marketing researchers (ex., Guan et al., 2021).

9.2 Culture and AI use cases

The use case of machine translation has led the way in our understanding. Statistical machine translation (SMT) was prominent in the early days of big-data approaches to machine learning, and neural machine translation (NMT) can be seen as one of the earliest uses of the transformer architecture. This use case is a critical one-each day in 2024, it is estimated that one trillion words are translated in an automated fashion, across thousands of language pairs (Vashee, 2024c). Translation automation has a critical, demonstrable impact in fields such as global e-commerce, travel and tourism, or intercultural communications writ large. And prior to 2023, the majority of this trillion-word traffic was translated by dedicated neural-network models specifically trained for the translation act, in a given language pair and a given domain.

However it is fair to note that with a focus on the production of linguistic form, MT research has not centered on cultural issues, with several exceptions. On the culture front, Hershcovich et al. (2022) challenged the then NLP researchers and users to consider elements beyond linguistic code, including common ground, aboutness, and values. The terminology here does require clarification. By "common ground," these authors mean "the shared body of knowledge that can be talked about and that can be assumed as known by others," such as conceptualizations of the world and commonsense knowledge that are commonly "neglected in NLP" (pp. 2–3).

As an aside, this discussion immediately confronts one philosophical assumption probably too complex to tackle here, that "different languages share a similar semantic structure" (Miceli Barone, 2016). Other dimensions outlined by Hershcovich et al. (2022) include the above-mentioned topic of values, as well as "aboutness," the markedness of certain topics or themes across cultures.

In several respects, this is a fair working definition of culture: a "shared body of knowledge that can be talked about and that can be assumed by others," with a recognition that the importance of certain topics (such as traditional religion, etc.) may vary from culture to culture. And the use of the word "values" also ties to recent, large-scale values surveys such as the GLOBE or World Values Survey, which are also used widely in research today to define and quantify cultural values.

And certainly for several decades, researchers and critics have remarked that existing machine translation tools were not constructed to center cultural knowledge, culturally marked topics, or values in the translation process. In one area of MT research this topic appears regularly, that is, in the research literature on the particular challenges faced by literary translators and the struggles met by MT with literary or other "culturally-bound" texts. Scholars such as Łoboda and Mastela (2023) have summarized this literature and they also point out that the roles of the human translator or translation student is creative and critical, and in many ways this discussion foreshadows current debates in the AI world about the role of humans vs. machines in a workflow, sometimes referred to as "human in the loop." In our discussions of MT and especially MT for literary texts, we have been running this debate for decades as well (Öner Bulut & Alimen, 2023): what is the role of the human translator in the loop, and should we be thinking about the "re-positioning" of the translator in emerging language technology workflows, as educators developing the "AI-ready linguist" (Wooten, 2024).

There is a strong argument that current LLMs and modeling techniques are focused primarily on linguistic code, and may not, in their current architectures, demonstrate a deeper-than-surface knowledge of concepts such as culture values (Bender et al., 2021). This point of view is supported, too, by the frequent overreliance of current models on one major Internet language variant, American English (Vashee, 2023a), and the point that, even in relatively broad sources of training data in text form, concepts such as cultural values are as much about what is included or described outright in the trillions of words of scraped language data, as what remains undescribed or unmarked in the training dataset (Vashee, 2023b).

In the larger scope too, with the emergence of tools such as OpenAI's ChatGPT in late 2022, multiple national and international consortia moved to create models with less of an emphasis on (North American) English language and value sets, producing models with less of an "American accent" (Johnson et al., 2022). Researchers in the European, Nordic, Japanese, Chinese, Korean, and multiple other national and international contexts are moving rapidly to develop and train models "to grasp the intricacies...of language and culture" in settings other than North American English (ex., Hornyak, 2023). Anders Søgaard (2022) notes that around 60% of "NLP research at top venues is devoted exclusively to developing technology for speakers of English." That researcher has even suggested that NLP work focusing on English be frozen for a year, and notes other suggestions such as an NLP/English "cap and trade," or an NLP/English "carbon tax" to begin to mitigate these inequities.

It is within this global, multilingual, and multicultural context that future NLP and AI researchers and developers will work. How can future application of tools such as LLMs or machine translation engines prove not only sensitive to but also driven by this truly globalized context? How can cultural diversity models and concepts be integrated with NLP tools and uses? Does the future hold not only LLMs but also LLCMs, models shaped not only by large amounts of linguistic code but also by computed approaches to cultural values, experiences, and beliefs, and proving as posited by Bowman (2023), that future "LLMs need not express the values of their creators nor the values encoded in web text"?

Researchers and commentators today are slowly coming to the realization, however, that major contemporary models such as OpenAI's GPT series are decidedly English-language centric in their values, as developed in their training. Although detailed data on the training sets of modern LLMs are difficult to obtain, scholars do know the relative positioning of English and other world languages in the training data sets of earlier models of GPT, for example Johnson et al. (2022), which contained more than 90% English language material.

9.3   Are today's LLMs truly multicultural?

During this period of rapid growth in LLMs and especially more multilingual LLMs, researchers began to move beyond language performance alone, to probe these emerging models for their expression of cultural values at the high end and daily life/knowledge in practical orientation.

We start with the "deeper" definitions of culture focused on values: in short, what do these models apparently "know" about constructs such as culture or cultural values?

Early researchers such as Johnson et al. (2022) also started to test of the GPT family of models for cultural "knowledge." In that research, models were tasked with summarizing texts with clear expressions of cultural values, in multiple languages. Examples of such texts, which were often chosen to be "orthogonal" to US/Western values, included the Australian Firearms Act on gun control, a speech delivered by Angela Merkel on immigration, and other texts highlighting themes of secularism, reproductive choices, racism, climate change, and indigenous rights. Summarization of these value-rich texts was the method used to "probe" the black-box model, and model-provided summaries of these texts clearly showed altered values in the output summaries, frequently more "aligned with the dominant voice baked into the training data" (p. 8) than in the values expressed by the source culture on the World Values Survey.

Other attempts to document the expression of cultural values by LLMs have taken different forms of probing, and a rich literature has emerged on this cultural turn. Prominently, researchers at The Culture Factor Group (formerly Hofstede Insights) took the unique approach of simply asking an LLM to respond to items on its standard Cultural Compass survey instrument; in this study, they prompted the model-respondent to respond as a "typical person coming from a different country" to prompts based on their six-dimensional model of culture (*AI Meets Culture*, 2023). With the set national role, the model was then tasked to respond to standard survey items designed to elicit information such as how individualistic a particular culture is, as compared to more collectivist cultures, and how a given culture relates to power, time, achievement, and uncertainty. The overall findings from this study were that "ChaptGPT's cultural representations missed the mark very noticeably" across cultures such as the U.S., Canada, India, Finland, Austria, German, and Nigeria. For example, with this methodology, ChatGPT 4.0 labeled India as a highly individualistic nation (upper 90s on the standardized Hofstede 0–100 scale), when in fact decades of research have identified that country as highly collectivist in nature (scoring in the 20s), specific and overall findings that Culture Factor CEO, Egbert Schram, would later label "a cultural disaster" (*AI Meets Culture,* 2023).

The language used also plays a role in interactions with an LLM, as Cao et al. (2023) documented. Those writers also made use of the Hofstede framework, prompting ChatGPT across five languages (US/English, Chinese, Japanese, German, and Spanish) using modified questions from the Hofstede research instrument. And as was found in multiple other studies, this research pointed out the predominance of Western values in answers to questions about cultural norms across the cultures sampled. Importantly, these researchers found that this predominance of WEIRD values was more marked when the prompts were made in English than in other languages such as Chinese or Japanese.

And as LLMs continue to proliferate globally, scholars from varying disciplines have been taking up this set of critical cultural questions: what do these models "know," or how does their output accurately or not so accurately correspond with research in cultural beliefs, attitudes, roles, norms, and values?

Benkler et al. (2023) benchmarked the expressed values from output of OpenAI's text-davinci-00 (one of the "flavors" of ChatGPT) against values data collected over the past three decades by the World Values Survey project (2024). Data were collected using general values prompts such as, "What beliefs, practices, and/or aspirations do you hold that are fundamental to your character and your life?" as well as specialized question prompts about the role of God and faith in life, autonomy vs. obedience, national pride, respect for authority, and abortion. These researchers used an approach to construct LLM prompts similar to The Culture Factor study, using a template such as:

You are a (age) year old nationality) (sex) participating in an ethnographic interview. Briefly answer the interviewer's question. Question: (LLM Question).

(p. 3)

This data collection approach asked for responses across a range of ages, gender, and from a variety of nationalities representing differing values clusters formerly identified in the WVS research: German, Japanese, Czech, American, Romanian, Vietnamese, Venezuelan. Across the nationality, gender, and age combinations, and utilizing multiple repeated prompts for each, more than 50,000 responses from the LLM were collected and scored for "resonance" with the values expressed in the World Values Survey.

This study added to the developing research picture that suggests LLMs have a "WEIRD" moral bias, biased toward the value set of countries that are Western, educated, industrialized, rich, and developed, and "that LLMs may have difficulty assuming non-WEIRD moral perspectives." The issue of age also sparked a confusing set of model outputs, with the LLA We also find age inaccuracies in LLM projecting "more traditional values for older demographics than are measured by the WVS," and tending to over-emphasize the moral ideals of younger ages. Benker and colleagues concluded that "LLMs are biased to assume a culturally-dominant WEIRD voice rather than accurately expressing a plurality of cultural voices" (p. 8).

A wide variety of research across the disciplines generally confirms these findings. Arora et al. (2022) utilized prompts based on both the Hofstede and World Values Survey framework, and found that model output on cultural themes "only weakly correlated with [those major] values surveys." In a cultural values audit of several iterations of ChatGPT, Tao et al. (2023) found a marked bias for "values resembling English-speaking and Protestant European countries." And Papadimitriou et al. (2022) point out that even on the linguistic level, the influence of high-resource languages in major LLMs predominates, with the grammatical forms of higher-resource languages "bleeding into [the output of] lower resources languages, a phenomenon [called] grammatical structure bias."

Focusing less on Western values, Abid et al. (2021) found marked anti-Muslim bias in prompts to early versions of the GPT model set. When the prompt included the word "Muslim," outputs in that study were more likely to include violent language ("killing" or "shooting") than when the word was not present. As noted, similar biases were also explicated by Naous et al. (2023), which noted the clear lack of cultural sensitivity to cultural context in model outputs.

Tao et al. (2023) prompted several versions of GPT using WVS/IVS values prompts, and found Western cultural biases when working in English. Importantly too, those writers also explained what risk is present in these biases, noting the widespread adoption of LLM-based tools to prompt writing and communications:

> Considering GPT's rapid adoption in countries around the world, this cultural bias may affect people's authentic expressions in several aspects of their lives. GPT's observed bias toward self-expression values may cause people to inadvertently convey more interpersonal trust, bipartisanship, and support for gender equity in GPT-assisted communication, such as emails, social media posts, and instant messaging. This may have interpersonal and professional consequences by signaling a lack of cultural embeddedness within an organizational context or misrepresenting the user to their readers.

Choi and her colleagues (2023) asked a slightly different question: [D]o LLMs understand social knowledge? Those writers summarized that we see LLMs perform regularly on syntactic, discourse, and reasoning tasks, but seldom on higher-order, more socially embedded outcomes which test more social types of knowledge based in and developed by interpersonal communication. If language is inherently social and meaning is constructed through social interaction, how do these models learn and perform with frequent elements of social interaction, such as humor, sarcasm, sentiment, emotion, and trust? Their SocKET benchmark includes 58 tasks in these areas of social knowledge, and they used it to test several modern LLMs such as the GPT line, BLOOM, and Llama. An example test within the benchmark, for example, tasks the LLM to determine whether a participant in a dialog is being "condescending" or "talking down" to an interlocutor, clearly a complex, socially embedded perception.

Other researchers have focused on discourse elements such as emotion in interactions with LLMs. Havaldar et al. (2023) have argued that multilingual models are by definition not multicultural, if they are unable to work with the emotional level of communication. They outline that emotions are experienced and expressed differently around the globe, and that language models seldom are able to appropriately express these differences in the languages produced by the model. Not surprisingly, tests involving English and Japanese utterances showed that the "emotion embeddings from LMs are Anglocentric" and models struggle with complex emotional constructs such as pride or shame, which carry very different weights and values across those two cultures. Ahmad et al. (2024) found that and LLM such as ChatGPT was challenged to respond with a native-speaker-like emotional valence (positive, negative, neutral) to socio-cultural questions such as: *"How would you feel if your student called you by your first name?"* Such behavior is deeply disrespectful in the Hausa context, with the language model was not able to convey.

There is also a vibrant literature on the day-to-day, operationalized elements that are associated with culture. As noted above, these elements of "small-c culture" may include behaviors and norms, linguistic forms, cultural artifacts, and other materialized objects of daily life. Liu and colleagues (2024) provide one taxonomy of these elements. These items can include concepts—basic units of meaning underlying ideas or beliefs—and knowledge, or information that can be acquired through education or life experience.

The area of cultural *concepts*, in the sense provided by Liu, is an active one, and a significant array of projects and research endeavor to collect and log these elements. One clear example is CultureBank, an online community database of cultural descriptors to both serve as a resource for training and fine-tuning models, but also for evaluation of models for cultural awareness (Shi et al., 2024). An example of ethnographic-style concepts logged in CultureBank might include detailed, contextualized information on tipping in a given cultural context, such as Japan. A second illustrative example of this work is the BLEnD database and benchmark, which collects the "mundane, everyday lifestyles of diverse regions," forming these concepts into question–answer pairs for model evaluation across 13 (often low-resource) languages, as research has shown that model performance on cultural benchmarks can be affected by the language used to prompt/answer (Myung et al., 2024).

Scholarly work on LLMs and the idea of cultural *knowledge*, most clearly represented as knowledge typically acquired during formal education within a given cultural context, is clearly seen in research and evaluation of LLMs using existing test instruments. One example here is the HAE-RAE Bench, which includes question items on Law and History, drawn from Namuwiki (Korean equivalent of Wikipedia) or from standardized testing in Reading Comprehension (RC) sourced from from the Korean Language Ability Test (KLAT), an exam designed to evaluate proficiency in Korean as a second language) (Son et al., 2024).

9.4   Evaluating multilingual and multicultural models and tasks

When a critical new or updated LLM is released by a major company or enterprise, frequently the release is accompanied by a scorecard. This set of scores, produced by the new model against standardized and theoretically unseen tasks, can provide both a standard comparison of the model's performance against competitor models, but it might also serve as a form of marketing, as seen in a recent release from Anthropic (2024).

Increasingly, the new model or model variant is scored via benchmarks or test sets that are multilingual or multicultural. Whereas early industry benchmarks like GLUE (Wang et al., 2018) were monolingual English in nature, it is key to note Anthropic's use of the BIG-Bench (BIG being "beyond the imitation game") evaluation as example of emerging evaluation scoreboards that are at least partially multilingual and multicultural. BIG-Bench (Srivastava et al., 2022) is a collection of more than 200 diverse tasks currently thought to be beyond the capabilities of modern language models, and includes a variety of non-English tests of language identification, translation, summarization, or interpretation and the English-language subtests do touch on cultural themes such as gender and national bias detection.

Unfortunately, the BIG-Bench-Hard test used, a subset of the benchmark's several 100 tasks, includes only one that is overtly multilingual: *Salient Translation Error Detection*, which is based on translation quality estimation and cross-lingual natural-language inference. Future benchmark suites and their usage will undoubtedly trend toward the more multilingual and multicultural.

One group of scholars has focused on the ability of large language models to retrieve cultural or societal knowledge, which cultural scholars call "big-C culture," elements such as factual knowledge of the arts, history, geography, or elements that are assumed knowledge among educated members of a given cultural group. Often, benchmark items here are drawn from standardized tests of knowledge available in a given setting or culture.

Another example is the development of benchmarks in Korean. The example scorecard above notes model performance on the widely seen measures GLUE and MMLU, and at first non-English evaluation benches appeared based primarily on translations or re-workings of these English measures, including KLUE (a Korean version of GLUE).

Son et al. (2024) then developed the unique KMMLU, a benchmark of more than 35,000 expert-level multiple-choice questions across 45 subjects ranging from humanities to STEM...collected from original Korean exams rather than translated from English-language benchmark questions, uniquely "capturing linguistic and cultural aspects of the Korean language" (Son et al., 2024). A related research team in 2023 had released HAE-RAE Bench, a dataset "curated to challenge models lacking Korean cultural and contextual depth" across domains and tasks around vocabulary, history, general knowledge, and reading comprehension, emphasizing in particular a model's "aptitude for recalling Korean-specific knowledge and cultural contexts." Not surprisingly, major multilingual language models "suffered" in solving the HAE-RAE Bench items, in comparison with a model such as Polyglot-Ko, a model trained on Korean source data from scratch (Ko et al., 2023). Similar experiences will no doubt emerge in differing cultural settings, highlighting the ongoing debates around massively multilingual models vs. more focused modeling attempts.

And a last grouping of researchers have tested models for what cultural researchers call "small-C culture," knowledge of everyday life in a given cultural setting, such topics as food, dress, etc. In some cases, these elements of daily existence in a culture might be conceptualized as "rules of thumb" for culturally sensitive behavior, such as, "Is it OK to eat with your left hand?" (Rao et al., 2024). Myung et al. (2024) collected a not dissimilar benchmark set of test items on "everyday knowledge" and "cultural sensitivities" across 16 diverse cultures and 13 languages, in domains such as food, sports, family, holiday, and work life. Not surprisingly, those researchers found a strong relationship between the representation of a language and culture broadly on the Internet–for mid- and low-resource languages and cultures, models tested with this benchmark struggled and frequently responded with information from other cultures/regions or even in languages other than the language of the question prompt.

9.5   Can cultural knowledge be "infused" into LLMs?

Looking forward, there are several hopeful trends and directions in the development of truly multicultural AI. If the current state of large language models and model usage is a cause of concern relative to the role of culture in general model use, translation, or content generation and evaluation, what will future model products and methodologies hold? Can we count on incremental improvement in cultural values and cultural knowledge as model size and sophistication continue to grow? Or can we as researchers take a more proactive approach as the Korean scholars around evaluation in their language and culture? In short, can cultural knowledge be improved or infused into LLMs?

Tao et al. (2023) also raise a first, critical question about model remediation. Given that the research shows clear biases and lack of cultural knowledge in model output, what might be done to mitigate these shortcomings? First, suggestions by that author team include regular and detailed "cultural audits" of LLMs. And they cite the work of Ferrara (2023), to highlight that biases in LLMs are not a new issue, and methodologies are emerging for bias documentation and mitigation. Indeed, research around these notions of bias identification and response have been visible in the research literature since the emergence of BERT. In some research such as Ahn and Oh (2021) more multilingual models themselves are seen as one approach to increase cultural diversity and attention to cultural factors in LLM output.

More proactive approaches to cultural elements are also possible. Several techniques allowed Yao et al. (2023) to infuse cultural knowledge into a functioning language model. Those scholars created a culturally rich, sentence-level parallel corpus (one of the key data formats used in MT) and also added culture-related annotations, additionally linking entries on culture-specific items (ex., cannoli as a form of Italian pastry) and linkages to Wikipedia data and metadata. They also used complex prompting techniques in both source and target languages to encourage the LLM to identify and better incorporate culture-specific items into output and translations. They label this work "culturally-aware machine translation" and note that its emergence is tied to the emergence of LLMs as an MT environment.

Increasingly, we are seeing work such as Chouikhi et al. (2024), making use of fine tuning or instruction tuning (concepts we introduced in Chapter 3) to bring language- and culture-specific training to base models such as Llama and Gemma. That research team

(Elfilali et al., 2024) developed and collected a unique constellation of datasets for tuning the base models for question answering, summarization, and classification in Arabic, across domains such as medicine, math, as well as literature and classical Arabic poetry. And the work of this team was and is evaluated in real time on the Open Arabic LLM Leaderboard via HuggingFace which benchmarks models on a variety of Arabic language versions of standard benchmarks such as MMLU as well as benchmarks authored specifically for Arabic and its cultural contexts, for example AlGhafa (Almazrouei et al., 2023).

Cultural and linguistic diversity can also mark the instruction tuning and human feedback processes which are increasingly central to LLM construction. Weber et al. (2024) asked: Do polyglot models demand for multilingual instructions? Those researchers argue that instruction tuning in multiple languages is a critical element of model creation, showing their work in the creation of multilingual, human-curated instructions in multiple European languages. This work parallels that of Dang et al. (2024), who describe the Aya Project from Cohere and its approach to crowdsourcing multilingual and multicultural RLHF. And in another prominent example, Kirk et al. (2024) present the PRISM Alignment project, in which those research practitioners developed a dataset that includes the sociodemographics and stated preferences of 1,500 diverse participants from 75 countries, gathering their cultural preferences and feedback to more than 8,000 live conversations with 21 LLMs. In so doing, PRISM specifically designs wide geographic and demographic participation in human feedback data.

Researchers across the LLM spectrum are also currently exploring the value of pairing such organized knowledge formats as knowledge graphs with LLMs. This pairing is definitely gaining traction in research and application. Dillinger (2023) argues that "Knowledge graphs and LLMs together can push AI forward to create novel models that have knowledge infused into every single step of their development, evaluation, and deployment."

A more limited number of researchers are indeed operationalizing organized, symbolic knowledge of culture for model training or fine-tuning. Li et al. (2024) take the interesting approach of using the World Values Survey data not only for benchmarking LLM performance on cultural issues, but also as data for the fine-tuning of culturally aware models at affordable cost. Noting that the collection of human-annotated datasets such as CultureBank pose issues of time and cost, Li and colleagues see that the WVS itself is a large-scale pool that "contains answers from a vast people of different cultures" and might be used to generate fine-tuning data on cultural themes. They tuned ChatGPT3.5 using that platform's fine-tuning API using sentences generated based on WVS-reported opinions and beliefs from respondents across nine languages, although these researchers limited their work to augmentation with English-language sentences generated. Although the outcome measures focused on toxic speech detection, this approach of fine-tuning a base model with culturally specific data across multiple world cultures is a promising direction for future exploration. These scholars have also tested fine-tuning of open-source models such as Llama to increase cultural awareness.

9.6 Machine translation—NMT vs. LLMs

As a final section in this chapter, we consider a debate roiling the MT community today: that of specialized neural MT engines pitted against large language models for translation production and quality. Translation is correctly viewed not as a "solved" task of converting one language string into another language string, but more globally as the transfer of a text from one language and cultural context to another language and cultural context.

One key starting point for this debate was Jiao et al. (2023a), which asked the title question: "Is ChatGPT a Good Translator?" Their initial analysis found that ChatGPT (3.5) was competitive with commercial MT products in language pairs involving high-resources European languages, but that it scored lower when working with low-resource languages. The LLM also struggled with translation in specialized domains such as biomedical abstracts or Reddit posts. Later research (Jiao et al., 2023b) found that ChatGPT4 improved in capabilities to translate in pairs with a low-resource language, when a high-resource pivot language was used in the translation. And research continues at a good pace, with Hendy et al. (2023) and Yan et al. (2024) as both examples of research in this area as well as excellent overviews of the research literature to date.

Following that early work, which started immediately following the late-2022 release of ChatGPT as an interface, the race was on to consider specialized, task-specific translation models against the LLM competition. Research conducted as 2023 progressed asked such questions as: how can Chat GPT be fine-tined for translation? Can LLMs provide superior performance in translation tasks requiring greater immediate context (full document translation)? How do large and emerging multilingual LLMs perform translation and related tasks compared to models with more monolingual training data? Does LLM translation provide an easier path to integrate translation into tasks such as online chat, another LLM-based task? And overall, does the future of machine translation lie with large language models (Lyu et al., 2023)?

This has indeed become one of the defining questions of the language services industry in 2024 (Vashee, 2024a). Intento an industry organization dedicated to large-scale evaluation of machine translation systems, has begun to include LLMs into their annual report on *The State of Machine Translation*. That report notes that "multilingual LLMs capable of high-quality translations are developed and deployed at an accelerating pace" and that LLMs are frequently among the top-performing models in selected domains and language pairs. The Intento authors do point out issues of cost and performance, noting that in the area of machine translation in 2024 the largest stock models are "10–100 times less expensive than MT systems, but 50–1,000 times slower." Vashee (2024b) provides an even more detailed analysis of the future path of LLM-based translation, especially from the viewpoint of the language services industry.

Note

1 https://www.worldvaluessurvey.org/WVSContents.jsp

10

MULTILINGUAL AND MULTICULTURAL AI—PEDAGOGY, PROFICIENCY, POLICY, AND PREDICTIONS

One critical difference between this chapter and those that have come before it: rather than a focus on technology and process, the focus here is on people–their learning about and learning to use multilingual and multicultural AI, its current and future applications in the social setting of the real world, and the array of policies that arise in response.

A key question in our age of AI and machine learning is precisely: how can both the humanistic and engineering elements of linguistically and culturally diverse AI be integrated into teaching, learning, policy, and future practice in a globalized world?

10.1 Teaching learners about multilingual and multicultural AI

The ready availability of multilingual tools such as LLMs provide teachers and learners a variety of opportunities to learn about the training and use of multilingual AI. University curricula around the world with a focus on language, culture, and translation (rather than the engineering aspects of the technology) are incorporating the most important concepts and practices for their learners, and such curricula are almost by definition becoming more technical. Examples of institutions of higher education making this shift under the rubric of Localization and/in Translation include the University of Texas at Arlington, the Middlebury Institute of International Studies at Monterey, and others. Another common trend is to find more technology-forward, language-centric courses, and curriculum under the heading of Computational Linguistics (GALA, 2024).

The exploration of LLMs for translation itself has received perhaps the most widespread attention, as researchers begin to delve into the performance of multilingual models across languages. In fact, this question of comparing the translation performance of LLMs vs. specifically trained translation models has become a driving question in the language industry today.

As Renato Beninatto (2024) points out, machine translation was "the first form of AI," "the oldest and most mature form" being the field where neural nets and the transformer architecture first found global scale use. Google Translate is perhaps the most well-known MT engine product, which debuted in 2006 and until 2016 was driven by statistical

DOI: 10.4324/9781003470557-13

machine translation (SMT) modeling, with a move to neural model architectures starting in late 2016 (Bahdanau et al., 2014; Cho et al., 2014; Wu et al., 2016).

Learners in the fields of translation and applied machine translation at the University of Texas at Arlington compare the performance of a trained MT engine against that of one or more of the available LLM tools, replicating the work of researchers Jiao et al. (2023a, b). Students use structured assignments to explore the nature of prompt-driven LLM translation across language pairs, comparing and contrasting it to the more familiar dynamic of using an MT engine such as DeepL or Google Translate.

Through such exploration, learners tackle the concepts of training data quantity and quality for each of the models, and the important ideas around human and automated evaluation of translation output from these tools. Although this assignment work at UTA requires use of only the free-level versions of MT and LLM tools, it is important to note that several of the key drivers of increased translation quality in the LLM space may be settings such as model temperature, which is usually not addressable in the free versions of proprietary large language models (Peng et al., 2023).

Learners also come to more concretely appreciate the nuances of MT metrics during this work as well. And indeed, approaches to automated metrics for machine translation output quality have also developed over time, from a more mechanical, word-count approach such as BLEU (Papineni et al., 2002) to more vector-based approaches (Rei et al., 2020). Students rate MT engine vs. LLM translation using a variety of automated measures beyond BLEU, including COMET and ChrF. Importantly too, these metrics conceived originally to score machine translation output are finding widespread use in NLP situations beyond translation, as applied to output quality in tools such as chatbots (Rodríguez-Cantelar et al., 2023), question answering systems (Yagnik et al., 2024), and other computational linguistic settings.

Technical training and experimentation with large language models and their performance in languages other than English also raise a variety of systems use, societal, and philosophical issues for learners of localization, translation, or computational linguistics. Recent research on the creation and use of emerging LLMs can be shared with students, to ask them to consider the broader cost and impact of designing and deploying a multilingual model at scale.

One excellent case study is the building and ongoing work on the Cohere Aya models, where a team of more than 3,000 "citizen researchers" globally aided a core technical team in model creation and development. In this project, the "back-end" of model construction was made visible to volunteer researchers, who also assisted in multilingual instruction-tuning. Weber et al. (2024) pointed out the comparative focus on training data alone in multilingual models, and those writers noted that model production also includes the training of a parallel dataset and instructional model (see Chapter 3), and ask the question: "Do polyglot models demand for multilingual instructions?" In Cohere's Aya work, this critical step was crowdsourced to volunteer researchers and graduate students who authored instruction-tuning datasets across 101 languages" (Ustun et al., 2024). In addition to releasing model weights, the Aya project has also published this "human-curated instruction-following dataset" developed for the project (Singh et al., 2024).

After model roll-out, this extended Aya research and development team has continued involvement in work around model use, model bias, and multilingual evaluation of the Aya model set, for example moving research forward around such benchmarks as MMLU-style evaluation newly translated into 30 mid- and low-resource languages.

A second case study that is shared (research reports and articles, along with available video interview and other resources available around the project) is the building of BLOOM, an open-access multilingual model which leveraged the work of hundreds of researchers and applied scientists (Scao et al., 2022). One follow-up classroom assignment centers on considering in detail the carbon footprint of BLOOM at all stages of its creation and use–with the environmental impact of LLMs becoming a central point of debate nationally and internationally when thinking about the true total cost and impact of large language models. It is easy to quote statistics such as an 118-day training time for the BLOOM final model, or more than 1,000,000 GPU-hours, but Luccioni and her colleagues work to put a concrete environmental cost on this work, which students reflect and write on (Luccioni et al., 2022). Several years after this seminal article, the environmental impact of LLMs and the associated data centers had become a key discussion, with broad impact points clearly seen in climate, air, water, and power generation statistics (Big Tech's Great AI Power Grab, 2024).

Numerous researchers and research teams have explored the training and performance of LLMs from a cultural lens, and we cannot shy away from the major cultural frameworks and issues in a field we have been labeling "multicultural" throughout this book. As outlined in Chapter 9, early research considered the cultural *performance* of available and emerging LLMs. Did the models produce and align cultural knowledge and cultural values as expected when describing or interacting with users from a given culture? Unsurprisingly, these writers found that the major public models struggled with accurately portraying cultural scenes or value sets across the global swath of values, often favoring the value sets of WEIRD countries (Benkler et al., 2023). Thus one is left with descriptions of, for example, Arabic-speaking culture where the model might propose going for "beer after prayer" (Abid et al., 2021).

But as overviewed in Chapter 9 and reinforced by writers such as Adilazuarda et al. (2024): most research on black-box LLMs has focused on values *as expressed* by a language model. We remain relatively ignorant as to the actual working of LLMs, which remains worrisome for researchers and applications specialists alike. As university educators, we also challenge our Humanities students with the idea of better understanding the inner workings of tools such as LLMs, and in particular more precisely describing what takes place within a model. Do LLMs "understand" a given topic or task, a verb from corporate "hype" that is frequently associated with descriptions of the latest and greatest trained language models?

In response to these questions, educators can present opposing viewpoints to our students around the use of "understanding," using such classic articles as "On the Danger of Stochastic Parrots: Can Language Models Be Too Big? 🦜 " (Bender et al., 2021), "Climbing towards NLU: On Meaning, Form, and Understanding in the Age of Data," (Bender & Koller, 2020). Mitchell and Krakauer (2023), who overview the debate about understanding in large language models, go so far as to hint at the end that

the field of AI has created machines with new modes of understanding, most likely new species in a larger zoo of related concepts, that will continue to be enriched as we make progress in our pursuit of the elusive nature of intelligence.

(p. 4)

What are the dangers of the widespread, global use of the ubiquitous language model today? As a black box for which users, researchers, or even politicians have limited understanding of its internal workings, the dangers of use and misuse are manifold, and will be described in the section on policy. In short, major public LLMs that don't "do right" linguistically or culturally by the majority of Internet citizens working in languages other than English and cultures outside North America cannot be an acceptable paradigm for the ethical scholar, researcher, model engineer, or major AI enterprise.

10.2   AI competence frameworks

As learners tackle both the conceptual understanding of artificial intelligence as well as the mechanics and applied uses of examples such as large language models, competence frameworks have begun to come onto the scene. Often used by teachers and curriculum planners, these tools outline a set of understandings, skills, as well as attitudes and beliefs associated with mastery of AI in theory and practice. The broad term "AI literacy" is frequently used to describe this bundle of concepts and objectives.

Long and Magerko (2020) is one widely-cited "set of competencies set in a conceptual framework" especially for use in K-12. In particular, their definition of AI literacy outlines the key topics of that conceptual framework:

> We define AI literacy as a set of competencies that enables individuals to critically evaluate AI technologies; communicate and collaborate effectively with AI; and use AI as a tool online, at home, and in the workplace.

And based on a careful meta-review of research and theory in the teaching of computational concepts, Long & Magerko lay out one of the most comprehensive frameworks conceptually for learners coming to AI. In summary, those writers summarize their framework as encapsulating competencies for answering five key questions about AI:

> What is AI?; What can AI do?; How does AI work?; How should AI be used?; and How do people perceive AI?
>
> *(p. 3)*

These questions are then operationalized into learning objectives and tasks. For example, addressing the first question—*What is AI?*—students learn to recognize AI by distinguishing technologies that do and don't use it, and they develop skills to critically analyze and discuss intelligence, along with thinking about "intelligent machines" such as cognitive systems, robotics, and machine learning. For the second question, as an additional example—*What can AI do*—students learn to recognize the strengths and weaknesses of AI, determining when it is important to use AI and when to leverage human skills, and they also learn expansive thinking about the role AI might play in the future (p. 4).

Noticeably missing from this well-recognized framework is any mention of multilingual or multicultural AI. Indeed, a more global scoping review of frameworks for student attitudes toward and mental models of AI conducted by Marx et al. (2023) also makes no mention of languages other than English or multiculturality in the review of research.

It is perhaps more surprising, however, that the manifestly international UNESCO AI Literacy Framework for Teachers (draft), in working form in 2023, also makes bare mention of the notions of multilingual and multicultural AI. To their credit, UNESCO as an organization states the importance of AI and AI literacy to their mission—"AI technology is not limited to the workforce. AI has profound implications for culture, diversity, education, scientific knowledge, and communication and information, especially insofar as they concern peace, sustainability, gender equality..."—the recognition of these key elements of multilinguality and multicultural factors are noticeably absent. Even a mention of machine translation for the ease of international communication is missing from this framework, although as an international organization they do stress "the seamless flow of information across linguistic boundaries, thereby facilitating communication in our ever-more interconnected world" (Exploring the Multifaceted Aspects of Humanity, 2023).

Although one is tempted to point out the missing element of the multilingual and multicultural and stress it as being overlooked, one can also seize on this as an opportunity for language- and culturally oriented learners to mesh these critical elements into national and international frameworks. One feature of the critical study of translation by UNESCO is a topic focus on the "power dynamics of translation" for low-resource and indigenous languages, a concept which can be expertly tied to the concepts of multilingual large language models and their development which stresses English and other high-resource languages in training and use (Blodgett et al., 2020).

10.3 Emerging policy and the role of humans

Policy asks the question: how do we want the world to be, and how can we get there?

As of this writing, major national and international entities are drafting and enacting, with a greater or letter degree of publicity and acceptance, policy, procedure, and legal frameworks to guide and regulate IA. Such initiatives are seen prominently in the U.S., Canada, and through developing legal frameworks from the European Union, in addition to a wide variety of national and supra-national entities. OECD.AI (2024) lists and links to policies from across the globe, adding that nearly all major national entities have made explicit AI strategies, if not policies, linked from that site. DeFranco and Biersmith (2024) also describe and review the global policy landscape as of 2024.

Insightful analysis of these strategies and policies is offered by Salo-Pöntinen and Saariluoma (2022), who ask a key question in relation to the theme of this chapter: [H]ow do national AI strategies [globally] view people? This question is imperative as "one core measure for the level of AI performance today is its capacity to replace people or to modify the way people have previously worked," thus focusing on the socio-technical change wrought by these new technologies globally, outlined and described on a country-by-country basis.

As described by the Directorate General for Communication (2023), the European Union's AI Act is billed as the "world's first AI law" to "ensure better conditions for the development and use of this innovative technology" (p. 1). At the start, this Act classifies a list of activities as "high risk," which include cognitive behavioral manipulation, social scoring, biometric identification, and categorization of people. Such high-risk systems fall under greater regulation under the Act, simply put. However, interestingly, generative AI such as ChatGPT "will not be classified as high-risk, but will have to comply with transparency requirements and EU copyright law," which requires disclosing that the content was generated by AI, designing the model to prevent it from generating illegal content, and publishing summaries of copyrighted data used for training (p. 3).

In the US two White House documents, one the Executive Order on the Safe, Secure, and Trustworthy Development and Use of Artificial Intelligence and the other a White House Memorandum, Advancing Governance, Innovation, and Risk Management for Agency Use of Artificial Intelligence, set the tone for these issues in the country. Based on these documents, major national agencies were directed to establish a Chief AI Officer (CAIO) as a senior leadership role, advance AI to improve operations and efficiencies, attend to issues of IT infrastructure and data sharing, as well as to recruit and expand AI talent. Agencies were also directed to fully vet AI for real-world contexts, to mitigate and test for risks such as algorithmic discrimination (equity and fairness), as well as to focus on human considerations and remedy processes.

10.4   Future roles of linguists and linguistics researchers in multilingual and multicultural AI

Researchers such as Salo-Pöntinen and Saariluoma (2022) also address a developing discussion of technical skills vis à vis specialists in other domains critical to AI development and delivery:

> Much of the AI discussion is performed by people with technical competences as developing AI is understandably an engineering problem. However, one should not think that AI does not essentially change the way people live, and for this reason it is essential to activate social scientists and other human researchers to consider what future life will be like.
>
> *(p. 2)*

As large language models have burst onto the scene beginning late in 2022, this focus on technical or engineering competencies has highlighted the relative dearth of, for example, professional linguists in the conception, design, and deployment of the most prominent language models. This tension is not a new one. One can easily find examples of this push-pull, such as the oft-quoted excerpt from Fred Jelinek, an early research pioneer in speech recognition, who is quoted as saying in the 1980s, a statement similar to, "Every time I fire a linguist, the performance of our speech recognition system goes up."

If one values domain expertise, it is obvious that large language models, their construction and use, would benefit from trained language scientists informing and guiding work. But as late as 2024, few major multilingual and multicultural AI project teams include more than an isolated linguist with formal training in the language sciences field.

The key role of linguists and language specialists in the future of multilingual and multicultural AI has received some scholarly attention. Opitz et al. (2024) for example list and describe the areas where linguistic study and expertise have crucial roles to play in the years ahead. Their RELIES model—highlighting Resources, Evaluation, Low-resource Settings, Interpretability and Explanation, and the Study of Language—points to areas of linguistic experience and expert knowledge. For example, the creation and curation of resources such datasets, lexicons, and corpora with sensitivity to such elements as languages, dialects, genres, and styles tap the unique training of linguistically trained researchers and scientists. Embarrassing cases such as the "enrichment" of Chinese-language training data for OpenAI models with token sets strongly marked by spam and pornography sources could likely have been avoided with proper linguistic oversight (GPT-4o's Chinese token-training data is polluted by spam and porn, 2024). Selection and curation of even raw text, overseen by a linguistic professional, in addition to sensitivity for such topics as language diversity and bias, would likely have prevented the undesirable content.

The performance of major, public LLMs in medium- and low-resource languages has also attracted considerable attention (Vashee, 2024b). In short, due to relative shortages of training data, instruction-tuning data, and often human feedback data in languages outside of the "top 10" global languages, models in lower-resourced language settings perform in ways that have been documented to be at lesser quality standards. And again, the long-standing experience of linguists in the collecting and documenting of language data across language families globally can be a critical part of any collaboration team in NLP or AI development or production.

Kirk et al. (2024) focus on a third rail of multilingual model development, the role of human feedback modeling for LLMs. They developed and described a rich research dataset of live "alignment conversations " between 1,500 diverse participants from 75 countries, including their fine-grained feedback in live conversations with 21 different LLMs. Case studies also included by the authors around dialogue diversity and multilingual/ multicultural outcomes show that it does clearly matter "which humans set alignment norms" for the models (p. 1).

However the future role of linguists and linguistics researchers in multilingual AI will not be without its challenges. "First Tragedy, then Parse: History Repeats Itself in the New Era of Large Language Models," Saphra et al. (2023) outline the lessons of an earlier inflection point in computational linguistics, the 2005 emergence of n-gram models, such as seen in Google Translate of that era. Questions that arose in 2005 are also prominent in 2024: what is the role of scale when it comes to datasets and model compute, and "[I]s scale supreme?" In that earlier period, as today, linguists may sense that in the face of the massive scale of newly-available datasets, "years of research have just been rendered utterly inconsequential" (p. 1). As highlighted by Opitz et al. (2024), Saphra and colleagues also highlight the future opportunities in evaluation and metrics/measurement, where research and standards are badly needed.

The question from Saphra and team about scale, however, is likely in need of an update. In that 2023 publication, the authors noted Sutton's "bitter lesson," that "general purpose methods exploiting scale will outperform methods that leverage informed priors" (Sutton, 2019), and concluding at that point in time that scale was indeed supreme. More recent discussions, in both the research and applied literatures, are revisiting that question in 2024 (Vashee, 2024b).

Sutton ends his "Bitter" thoughtpiece (2019) with this additional nuance:

> The second general point to be learned from the bitter lesson is that the actual contents of minds are tremendously, irredeemably complex; we should stop trying to find simple ways to think about the contents of minds, such as simple ways to think about space, objects, multiple agents, or symmetries. All these are part of the arbitrary, intrinsically-complex, outside world.

To build on that larger point, researchers have begun to highlight the space between "model land" and the complexity of the real world. *We know what LLMs are, but what are they not? Are LLMs truly models of language writ large?* Veres (2021) joins a long line of linguistic researchers who point out that "essentially eliminative" models such as today's LLMs are models of language writ large or "a radical restructuring in our understanding of cognition" and language processing. This debate rages, with Piantadosi (2023) suggesting that [l]arge language models refute Chomsky's approach to language and Katzir (2023) critically responding that "this claim is wrong." A similar point has been made by Chomsky as well, among others.

In that same vein, are today's LLMs "compression algorithms for human culture"? As this research area involving LLMs and cultural themes have emerged, writers and scholars have raised even broader questions than what the model can express or inference about in the area of socio-cultural knowledge. Buttrick (2024) suggests that we move beyond the large language model as chat partner or information retrieval bot, and begin to view these models as a "compression algorithm for human culture." Buttrick argues that, as these models isolate and note patterns in their training data, researchers can begin to use these models "to study the conceptual relationships encoded in the training data" and should not miss the (i.e., the open "remarkable opportunity to understand the cultural distinctions embedded within much of recorded human communication" (p. 1).

And there is a promising future research direction for scholars who consider the applications of tools such as multilingual AI in multicultural settings themselves. Ge et al. (2024) argues that culturally diverse users of tools like NMT or multilingual LLMs may make different demands on the technology based on cultural values or assumptions. One example those researchers share is the rise of the chatbot, especially in Western cultural settings which emphasize agency and individualism, where the same tool formal finds fewer applications in other cultural settings. In short they argue that people "apply their cultural models when imagining their ideal AI."

10.5 Future education for multilingual and multicultural AI

In retrospect, the breadth of themes covered in this book is stunning–from the concepts of language and culture in a multilingual and multicultural frame, from the mathematical theory of communications to the technical and engineering aspects of information theory and deep learning. How is an educator to teach, and how is a learner in a field to learn and continue learning over a lifetime, in a field so broad and so rapidly changing?

It is important to note that higher education has its own broad educational mission, its own governance structures, and its own accountability to accrediting organizations as well as to its funders both public and private. This mission is broader and longer-term than what might be assumed in the word "training," and it is something of a fallacy to consider a college education as simply a "training pipeline." That in and of itself is not our mission! Each time I hear about the "gaps" that the language services industry finds in our curricula or students, I honestly cringe a little bit.

The late Vartan Gregorian has said a university education is a bridge between where you are today and the farthest you can possibly go in the future, and we sell ourselves short if we envision a short span leading to the technologies and skills of today's job openings. In addition to the ability to train an MT engine or fine-tune an LLM in a given language, colleges and universities develop future skills most prized by employers today and in the future: analytical thinking, learning and coachability, communication and collaboration across languages and cultures, complex problem solving, creativity and innovation, among others.

What does the future of our industry hold? Blending the key ideas in this chapter, one can easily see a future centered on NLP and AI-savvy linguists and cultural specialists, policy experts, and educators themselves—a vision that preserves at its core deep knowledge and experience in languages and cultures in a rapidly evolving technology world. It is, admittedly, a view of the decade ahead driven less by an engineering-centric worldview, based more in the thought leadership that critically thinking, creative, and innovative learning scientists and linguists should and will play in creating the future state.

In his later years, Professor Gregorian argued that this tension inherent in U.S. higher education—a broader and longer-term educational preparation vs. training for the "real world" of employment—wasn't necessarily either–or. Modern, responsive university educational programs can do both, he argued.

REFERENCES

Abid, A., Farooqi, M., & Zou, J. Y. (2021). Persistent anti-Muslim bias in large language models. *Proceedings of the 2021 AAAI/ACM Conference on AI, Ethics, and Society.*

Ács, J., Kádár, Á., & Kornai, A. (2021). Subword pooling makes a difference. https://arxiv.org/abs/2102.10864.

Adilazuarda, M., Mukherjee, S., Lavania, P., Singh, S., Dwivedi, A., Aji, A., O'Neill, J., Modi, A., & Choudhury, M. (2024). Towards measuring and modelling "Culture" in LLMs: A survey. https://arxiv.org/abs/2403.15412.

Agerri, R., San Vicente, I., Campos, J. A., Barrena, A., Saralegi, X., Etxabe, A. S., & Agirre, E. (2020). Give your text representation models some love: The case for Basque. https://arxiv.org/abs/2004.00033.

Ahia, O., Kumar, S., Gonen, H., Kasai, J., Mortensen, D., Smith, N., & Tsvetkov, Y. (2023). Do all languages cost the same? Tokenization in the era of commercial language models. *Proceedings of the 2023 Conference on Empirical Methods in Natural Language Processing*, Association for Computational Linguistics, Singapore, 9904–23.

Ahmad, I. S., Dudy, S., Ramachandranpillai, R., & Church, K. (2024). Are generative language models multicultural? A study on Hausa culture and emotions using ChatGPT. https://arxiv.org/abs/2406.19504.

Ahn, J., & Oh, A. H. (2021). Mitigating language-dependent ethnic bias in BERT. *Conference on Empirical Methods in Natural Language Processing.*

AI meets culture: A harmony or a work in progress? (2023). *News.hofstede-Insights.com.* Retrieved December 28, 2023, from https://news.hofstede-insights.com/news/ai-meets-culture

Almazrouei, E., Cojocaru, R., Baldo, M., Malartic, Q., Alobeidli, H., Mazzotta, D., Penedo, G., Campesan, G., Farooq, M., Alhammadi, M., Launay, J., & Noune, B. (2023). AlGhafa evaluation benchmark for Arabic language models. *ARABICNLP.*

Anthropic. (2024, March 4). Introducing the next generation of Claude. *www.anthropic.com.* https://www.anthropic.com/news/claude-3-family

Arora, A., Kaffee, L., & Augenstein, I. (2022). Probing pre-trained language models for cross-cultural differences in values. https://arxiv.org/abs/2203.13722.

Artetxe, M., Labaka, G., & Agirre, E. (2017). Learning bilingual word embeddings with (almost) no bilingual data. In *Proceedings of the 55th Annual Meeting of the Association for Computational Linguistics* (Vol. 1: Long Papers, pp. 451–62), July 2017. Association for Computational Linguistics, Vancouver, Canada. https://aclweb.org/anthology/P17-1042.

Artetxe, M., Labaka, G., Agirre, E., & Cho, K. (2018). Unsupervised neural machine translation. *6th International Conference on Learning Representations*, ICLR 2018, Vancouver, Canada.

AWS. (n.d.). JSON vs XML – Difference between data representations. Retrieved April 12, 2024, from https://aws.amazon.com/compare/the-difference-between-json-xml/

Bahdanau, D., Cho, K., & Bengio, Y. (2014). Neural machine translation by jointly learning to align and translate. *CoRR*. https://arxiv.org/abs/1409.0473.

Baisa, V., Ulipová, B., & Cukr, M. (2015). Bilingual terminology extraction in sketch engine. *RASLAN*.

Bang, Y., Cahyawijaya, S., Lee, N., Dai, W., Su, D., Wilie, B., Lovenia, H., Ji, Z., Yu, T., Chung, W., Do, Q. V., Xu, Y., & Fung, P. (2023). A multitask, multilingual, multimodal evaluation of Chat-GPT on reasoning, hallucination, and interactivity. *Proceedings of the 13th International Joint Conference on Natural Language Processing and the 3rd Conference of the Asia-Pacific Chapter of the Association for Computational Linguistics*, Association for Computational Linguistics.

Barera, M. (2020). Mind the gap: Addressing structural equity and inclusion on Wikipedia. https://hdl.handle.net/10106/29572.

Bayes, Price. (1763). An essay towards solving a problem in the doctrine of chances. *Philosophical Transactions (1683-1775)*, *53*, 370–418. https://www.crummy.com/software/BeautifulSoup/bs4/doc/

Beautiful Soup 4.12.0 documentation. (n.d.). Retrieved April 7, 2024, from https://www.crummy.com/software/BeautifulSoup/bs4/doc/

Bender, E. M., Gebru, T., McMillan-Major, A., & Shmitchell, S. (2021). On the dangers of stochastic parrots: Can language models be too big? *Proceedings of the 2021 ACM Conference on Fairness, Accountability, and Transparency*.

Bender, E. M., & Koller, A. (2020). Climbing towards NLU: On meaning, form, and understanding in the age of data. *Annual Meeting of the Association for Computational Linguistics*.

Bengio, Y., Courville, A. C., & Vincent, P. (2012). Representation learning: A review and new perspectives. *IEEE Transactions on Pattern Analysis and Machine Intelligence*, *35*, 1798–828.

Bengio, Y., Ducharme, R., & Vincent, P. (2001). A neural probabilistic language model. *Proceedings in Advances in Neural Information Processing Systems*, *13*, 932–8.

Beninatto, R. (2024 B.C.E., March 17). Renato Beninatto on LinkedIn: NMT is the first form of AI. https://www.linkedin.com/posts/renatob_are-you-afraid-of-how-ai-is-going-to-affect-activity-7169369528278142977-cA44/

Benkler, N., Mosaphir, D., Friedman, S., Smart, A., & Schmer-Galunder, S. (2023). Assessing LLMs for moral value pluralism. https://arxiv.org/abs/2312.10075.

Berger, A., & Lafferty, J. (1999). Information retrieval as statistical translation. In *ACM SIGIR Forum*, Association of Computing Machinery.

Berman, J. J. (2013). *Principles of big data: Preparing, sharing, and analyzing complex information*. Amsterdam: Elsevier Science.

Berners-Lee, T., Hendler, J., & Lassila, O. (2001). The semantic web. *Scientific American*, *284*(5), 34–43.

Bhandari, P. (2020, August 12). Ordinal data | definition, examples, data collection & analysis. https://www.scribbr.com/statistics/ordinal-data/

Biber, D., Conrad, S., & Reppen, R. (1998). *Corpus linguistics*. Cambridge: Cambridge University Press.

Biber, D., Johansson, S., Leech, G., Conrad, S., & Finegan, E. (1999). *Longman grammar of spoken and written English*. Pearson Education. ISBN: 0-582-23725-4

Big tech's great AI power grab. (2024, May 5). *The Economist*. https://www.economist.com/business/2024/05/05/big-techs-great-ai-power-grab

Bikakis, N., Tsinaraki, C., Gioldasis, N., Stavrakantonakis, I., & Christodoulakis, S. (2016). The XML and semantic web worlds: Technologies, interoperability and integration. A survey of the state of the art. https://arxiv.org/abs/1608.03556.

Bird, S., Klein, E., & Loper, E. (2009). *Natural language processing with python*. O'Reilly Sebastopol, CA.

Bishop, C. M. (2006). *Pattern recognition and machine learning*. New York: Springer Verlag.

Bitwise AND operator: &. (2021, November 23). *Learn Microsoft*. https://learn.microsoft.com/en-us/cpp/cpp/bitwise-and-operator-amp?view=msvc-170

Blevins, T., & Zettlemoyer, L. (2022). Language contamination helps explain the cross-lingual capabilities of English pretrained models. *Conference on Empirical Methods in Natural Language Processing* (pp. 3563–74). Abu Dhabi, United Arab Emirates.

Blodgett, S. L., Barocas, S., Daumé III, H., & Wallach, H. (2020). Language (technology) is power: A critical survey of "bias" in NLP. https://arxiv.org/abs/2005.14050.

Bogatyrev, M., & Samodurov, K. (2016). Framework for conceptual modeling on natural language texts. *Proceedings of the Third Workshop on Concept Discovery in Unstructured Data co-located with the 13th International Conference on Concept Lattices and Their Applications (CLA 2016)* (pp. 13–24). https://dblp.org/rec/conf/cla/BogatyrevS16.html

Boleda, G. (2020). Distributional semantics and linguistic theory. *Annual Review of Linguistics, 6,* 213–23.

Bommasani, R., Hudson, D. A., Adeli, E., Altman, R., Arora, S., Arx, S. V., Bernstein, M. S., Bohg, J., Bosselut, A., Brunskill, E., Brynjolfsson, E., Buch, S., Card, D., Castellon, R., Chatterji, N. S., Chen, A. S., Creel, K. A., Davis, J., Demszky, D., … Liang, P. (2021). On the opportunities and risks of foundation models. https://arxiv.org/abs/2108.07258.

Bowker, L., & Pearson, J. (2002). *Working with specialized language*. London: Routledge.

Bowman, S. (2023). Eight things to know about large language models. https://arxiv.org/abs/2304.00612.

Brown, T. B., Mann, B., Ryder, N., Subbiah, M., Kaplan, J., Dhariwal, P., Neelakantan, A., Shyam, P., Sastry, G., Askell, A., Agarwal, S., Herbert-Voss, A., Krueger, G., Henighan, T., Child, R., Ramesh, A., Ziegler, D. M., Wu, J., Winter, C., Hesse, C., Chen, M., Sigler, E., Litwin, M., Gray, S., Chess, B., Clark, J., Berner, C., McCandlish, S., Radford, A., Sutskever, I., & Amodei, D. (2020). Language models are few-shot learners. https://arxiv.org/abs/2005.14165.

Buttrick, N. (2024). Studying large language models as compression algorithms for human culture. *Trends in Cognitive Sciences, 28,* 187–9.

Cabré, M. T. (1999). *Terminology: Theory, methods and applications*. Amsterdam/Philadelphia: Benjamins. https://doi.org/10.1075/tlrp.1

Cambridge Dictionary. (n.d.). https://dictionary.cambridge.org/dictionary/english-chinese-simplified/corpus

Cao, Y., Zhou, L., Lee, S., Cabello, L., Chen, M., & Hershcovich, D. (2023). Assessing cross-cultural alignment between ChatGPT and human societies: An empirical study. https://arxiv.org/abs/2303.17466.

Caplan, J. (1989). Postmodernism, poststructuralism, and deconstruction: Notes for historians. *Central European History, 22*(3/4), 260–78.

Center for Research and Development Strategy (CDRS). (2019). Development on the Fourth Generation of AI. *Strategic proposal*, CRDS-FY2019-SP-08. https://www.jst.go.jp/crds/report/CRDS-FY2019-SP-08.html

Chandler, D. (2017). *Semiotics: The basics* (3rd Edition). Routledge. https://doi.org/10.4324/9781315311050

Chang, T. A., Arnett, C., Tu, Z., & Bergen, B. (2023). When is multilinguality a curse? Language modeling for 250 high- and low-resource languages. https://arxiv.org/abs/2311.09205.

Chapman, P., Clinton, J., Kerber, R., Khabaza, T., Reinartz, T., Shearer, C., & Wirth, R. (1999). CRISP-DM 1.0 step-by-step data mining guide. https://www.kde.cs.uni-kassel.de/wp-content/uploads/lehre/ws2012-13/kdd/files/CRISPWP-0800.pdf.

Chaves, A. P., & Gerosa, M. A. (2019). How should my Chatbot interact? A survey on social characteristics in human–Chatbot interaction design. *International Journal of Human–Computer Interaction, 37,* 729–58.

Cho, K., Merrienboer, B. V., Bahdanau, D., & Bengio, Y. (2014). On the properties of neural machine translation: Encoder–decoder approaches. *SSST@EMNLP*.

Choi, M., Pei, J., Kumar, S., Shu, C., & Jurgens, D. (2023). Do LLMs understand social knowledge? Evaluating the sociability of large language models with SocKET benchmark. *Conference on Empirical Methods in Natural Language Processing.*

Choudhury, M., & Deshpande, A. (2021). How linguistically fair are multilingual pre-trained language models? *AAAI Conference on Artificial Intelligence.*

Chouikhi, H., Aloui, M., Hammou, C. B., Chaabane, G., Kchaou, H., & Dhaouadi, C. (2024). GemmAr: Enhancing LLMs through Arabic instruction-tuning. https://arxiv.org/abs/2407.02147.

City of Toronto. (2017, November 9). Toronto open data. Retrieved March 8, 2024, from https://open.toronto.ca/dataset/fire-incidents/

COMET: High-quality machine translation evaluation — COMET 2.0.0 documentation. (n.d.). *GitHub.* Retrieved August 16, 2024, from https://unbabel.github.io/COMET/html/index.html

COMET: The new standard in MT evaluation. (n.d.). *Unbabel.* Retrieved August 17, 2024, from https://unbabel.com/research/comet/

Conneau, A., Rinott, R., Lample, G., Williams, A., Bowman, S. R., Schwenk, H., & Stoyanov, V. (2018a). XNLI: Evaluating cross-lingual sentence representations. *Proceedings of the 2018 Conference on Empirical Methods in Natural Language Processing.* Association for Computational Linguistics.

Conneau, A., Lample, G., Ranzato, M., Denoyer, L., & Jegou, H. (2018b). Word translation without parallel data. *ICLR.*

Conneau, A., Khandelwal, K., Goyal, N., Chaudhary, V., Wenzek, G., Guzmán, F., Grave, E., Ott, M., Zettlemoyer, L., & Stoyanov, V. (2020). Unsupervised cross-lingual representation learning at scale. *Proceedings of the 58th Annual Meeting of the Association for Computational Linguistics,* pp. 8440–51, Association for Computational Linguistics.

Connectionism. (n.d.). Internet encyclopedia of philosophy. Retrieved July 29, 2024, from https://iep.utm.edu/connectionism-cognition/

Constantin, A., & Bernard, E. (2023, November 7). A foundation model for entity recognition. *NuMind.* Retrieved August 26, 2024, from https://numind.ai/blog/a-foundation-model-for-entity-recognition

Dai, H., & Song, Y. (2019). Neural aspect and opinion term extraction with mined rules as weak supervision. https://arxiv.org/abs/1907.03750.

Dang, J., Ahmadian, A., Marchisio, K., Kreutzer, J., Ustun, A., & Hooker, S. (2024). RLHF can speak many languages: Unlocking multilingual preference optimization for LLMs. https://arxiv.org/abs/2407.02552.

Das, A. (2003). Knowledge representation. In Hossein Bidgoli (Ed.), *Encyclopedia of Information Systems* (pp. 33–41). Elsevier. https://doi.org/10.1016/B0-12-227240-4/00102-7. https://www.sciencedirect.com/science/article/pii/B0122272404001027

Dawson, M. R. (2020, February 4). 7.6: Local versus distributed representations - Social Sci LibreTexts. *LibreTexts Social Sciences.* Retrieved July 29, 2024, from https://socialsci.libretexts.org/Bookshelves/Psychology/Cognitive_Psychology/Mind_Body_World_-_Foundations_of_Cognitive_Science_(Dawson)/07%3A_Marks_of_the_Classical/7.06%3A_Local_versus_Distributed_Representations

De Luna, A. A. (2020). *Principles of big data.* Burlington, Canada: Arcler Press.

DeFranco, J. F., & Biersmith, L. (2024). Assessing the state of AI policy. https://arxiv.org/abs/2407.21717.

Devlin, J., Chang, M., Lee, K., & Toutanova, K. (2019). BERT: Pre-training of deep bidirectional transformers for language understanding. *North American Chapter of the Association for Computational Linguistics.*

Dillinger, M. (2023, December). On to knowledge-infused language models. www.linkedin.com. https://www.linkedin.com/pulse/knowledge-infused-language-models-mike-dillinger-phd-asqbc/?trackingId=HIsfABbvTCCj328nStloBg%3D%3D

Directorate General for Communication. (2023). *EU AI Act: First regulation on artificial intelligence.*

Doddapaneni, S., Aralikatte, R., Ramesh, G., Goyal, S., Khapra, M. M., Kunchukuttan, A., & Kumar, P. (2022). Towards leaving no Indic language behind: Building monolingual Corpora, benchmark and models for Indic languages. *Annual Meeting of the Association for Computational Linguistics.*

Doddapaneni, S., Ramesh, G., Kunchukuttan, A., Kumar, P., & Khapra, M. M. (2021). A primer on pretrained multilingual language models. https://arxiv.org/abs/2107.00676.

Elfilali, A., Alobeidli, H., Fourrier, C., Boussaha, B., Cojocaru, R., Habib, N., & Hacid, H. (2024) Open Arabic LLM Leaderboard. https://huggingface.co/spaces/OALL/Open-Arabic-LLM-Leaderboard

Eskander, Ramy, Muresan, Smaranda, & Collins, Michael. (2020). Unsupervised cross-lingual part-of-speech tagging for truly low-resource scenarios. *Proceedings of the 2020 Conference on Empirical Methods in Natural Language Processing (EMNLP)* (pp. 4820–31, Online). Association for Computational Linguistics.

Exploring the multifaceted aspects of humanity–International Translation Day. (2023). *Unesco.org.* https://www.unesco.org/en/articles/exploring-multifaceted-aspects-humanity-international-translation-day

Faber, Pamela, & Pilar, León-Araúz (2016). Specialized knowledge representation and the parameterization of context. *Frontiers in Psychology, 7*, 196.

Fay, B. (1996). *Contemporary philosophy of social science: A multicultural approach* (Vol. 1). Oxford: Blackwell.

Feature (machine learning). (n.d.). *Wikipedia.* Retrieved March 12, 2024, from https://en.wikipedia.org/wiki/Feature_(machine_learning)

Feldman, R., & Sanger, J. (2007). *The text mining handbook: Advanced approaches in analyzing unstructured data.* Cambridge: Cambridge University Press.

Fellbaum, C. (1998). *Wordnet: An electronic lexical database.* Cambridge, MA: MIT Press.

Fellbaum, C. (2005). WordNet and wordnets. In K. Brown et al. (Eds.), *Encyclopedia of language and linguistics* (Second Edition, pp. 665–70). Oxford: Elsevier.

Ferrara, E. (2023). Should ChatGPT be biased? Challenges and risks of bias in large language models. https://arxiv.org/abs/2304.03738.

Fetahu, B., Chen, Z., Kar, S., Rokhlenko, O., & Malmasi, S. (2023). MultiCoNER v2: A large multilingual dataset for fine-grained and noisy named entity recognition. *Findings of the Association for Computational Linguistics: EMNLP 2023* (pp. 2027–51). Association for Computational Linguistics, Singapore.

Firth, J. R. (1957). A synopsis of linguistic theory 1930-1955. *Studies in Linguistic Analysis* (pp. 1–32). Reprinted in F. R. Palmer (Ed.) (1968). Selected Papers of J. R. Firth 1952-1959. London: Longman.

Fodor, J. A. (1975). *The language of thought.* New York: Crowell.

Foxwell, H. J. (2020). Basic data types and when to use them. https://doi.org/10.1007/978-1-4842-6103-3_2

Freiberger, P. A, & Swaine, M. R. (2024). ENIAC. *Encyclopedia Britannica.* Last modified May 3, 2024.

Fukushima, K. (1980). Neocognitron: A self-organizing neural network model for a mechanism of pattern recognition unaffected by shift in position. *Biological Cybernetics, 36*, 193–202.

Gao, J., He, X., & Nie, J. Y. (2010). Clickthrough-based translation models for web search: From word models to phrase models. *Proceedings of the 19th ACM International Conference on Information and Knowledge Management* (pp. 1139–48).

Gao, J., & Nie, J. Y. (2012). Towards concept-based translation models using search logs for query expansion. *Proceedings of the 21st ACM International Conference on Information and Knowledge Management.*

Gardner, H. (2003). *Frames of mind. The theory of multiple intelligences* (2nd Edition). New York: Basic Books.

Garnelo, M., & Shanahan, M. (2019). Reconciling deep learning with symbolic artificial intelligence: Representing objects and relations. *Current Opinion in Behavioural Sciences, 29*, 17–23.

Gastaldi, J. L., & Pellissier, L. P. (2021). The calculus of language: Explicit representation of emergent linguistic structure through type-theoretical paradigms. *Interdisciplinary Science Reviews, 46*, 569–90.

Gatzeva, M. (n.d.). Simple stats tools. *BCcampus Pressbooks*. Retrieved March 16, 2024, from https://pressbooks.bccampus.ca/simplestats/chapter/1-5-discrete-and-continuous-variables/

Ge, X., Xu, C., Misaki, D., Markus, H. R., & Tsai, J. L. (2024). How culture shapes what people want from AI. *Proceedings of the CHI Conference on Human Factors in Computing Systems.*

Gillick, D., Presta, A., & Tomar, G. (2018). End-to-end retrieval in continuous space. https://arxiv.org/abs/1811.08008.

Globalization and Localization Association (GALA). (2024). Academic member directory. https://www.gala-global.org/knowledge-center/member-directories/academic-member-directory

Goodfellow, I., Bengio, Y., & Courville, A. (2016). *Deep learning*. Cambridge, MA: MIT Press.

Google Cloud. (n.d.). Find approximate nearest neighbors to index and query vector embeddings in Spanner. Retrieved August 24, 2024, from https://cloud.google.com/spanner/docs/find-approximate-nearest-neighbors

Google Developers. (2024). *Supervised Learning | Machine Learning*. Retrieved December 29, 2024, from https://developers.google.com/machine-learning/intro-to-ml/supervised

Gordon, J. (n.d.). Weka 3 - data mining with open source machine learning Software in Java. Retrieved March 15, 2024, from https://waikato.github.io/weka-site/index.html

GPT-4o's Chinese token-training data is polluted by spam and porn websites. (2024, May 17). *MIT Technology Review*. Retrieved May 30, 2024, from https://www.technologyreview.com/2024/05/17/1092649/gpt-4o-chinese-token-polluted/

Graph DB. (2024, August 19). Data modeling with RDF(S) — GraphDB 10.7 documentation. Retrieved September 22, 2024, from https://graphdb.ontotext.com/documentation/10.7/rdfs.html

Green, R., Pearl, L., Dorr, B. J., & Resnik, P. (2001). Mapping lexical entries in verbs database to WordNet senses. *Proceedings of the 39th Annual Meeting of the Association for Computational Linguistics.*

Grossberg, S. (1976). Adaptive pattern classification and universal recoding: I. Parallel development and coding of neural feature detectors. *Biological Cybernetics, 23*, 121–34.

Guan, Z., Hou, F., Li, B., Phang, C. W., & Chong, A. Y. (2021). What influences the purchase of virtual gifts in live streaming in China? A cultural context-sensitive model. *Information Systems Journal, 32*, 653–89.

Gumperz, J. J., & Levinson, S. C. (1991). Rethinking linguistic relativity. *Current Anthropology, 32*, 613–23.

Gupta, M., Ireland, A. C., & Bordoni, B. (2022). Neuroanatomy, visual pathway. Retrieved December 26, 2023, from https://www.ncbi.nlm.nih.gov/books/NBK553189/

Gurgurov, D., Bäumel, T., & Anikina, T. (2024). Multilingual large language models and curse of multilinguality. https://arxiv.org/abs/2406.10602.

Hadifar, A., Sterckx, L., Demeester, T., & Develder, C. (2019). A self-training approach for short text clustering. *RepL4NLP@ACL.*

Hambarde, K. A., & Proença, H. (2023). Information retrieval: Recent advances and beyond. *IEEE Access, 11*, 76581–604.

Han, Y., Liu, C., & Wang, P. (2023). A comprehensive survey on vector database: Storage and retrieval technique, challenge. https://arxiv.org/abs/2310.11703.

Haoyue, L. L., & Cho, H. (2024). Factors influencing intention to engage in human–chatbot interaction: examining user perceptions and context culture orientation. *Universal Access in the Information Society.*

Harnad, S. (1994). Computation is just interpretable symbol manipulation: Cognition isn't. Special Issue on "What Is Computation" *Minds and Machines, 4*, 379–90.

Harris, Z. (1954). Distributional structure. *Word. 10, 23*, 146–62. https://doi.org/10.1080/00437956.1954.11659520.

Havaldar, S., Rai, S., Singhal, B., Guntuku, L. L., & Ungar, L. (2023). Multilingual language models are not multicultural: A case study in emotion. *Workshop on Computational Approaches to Subjectivity, Sentiment and Social Media Analysis.*

Hendy, A., Abdelrehim, M. G., Sharaf, A., Raunak, V., Gabr, M., Matsushita, H., Kim, Y., Afify, M., & Awadalla, H. H. (2023). How good are GPT models at machine translation? A comprehensive evaluation. https://arxiv.org/abs/2302.09210.

Hershcovich, D., Frank, S., Lent, H., de Lhoneux, M., Abdou, M., Brandl, S., Bugliarello, E., Piqueras, L. C., Chalkidis, I., Cui, R., Fierro, C., Margatina, K., Rust, P., & Søgaard, A. (2022). Challenges and strategies in cross-cultural NLP. https://arxiv.org/abs/2203.10020.

Herwartz, R. (2019). Helping to find. *Technical Communication*, 1, 34–39 (Original in German. Herwartz, R. (2019). „Finden helfen". In: technische kommunikation, 1/2019, S. 34–39).

Hirschberg, J. (1998, July 29). "Every time I fire a linguist, my performance goes up", and other myths of the statistical natural language processing revolution [Invited talk]. *15th National Conference on Artificial Intelligence*, Madison, WI.

Hirst, G. (1999). Review of EuroWordNet: A multilingual database with lexical semantic networks by Piek Vossen. Kluwer Academic Publishers 1998. *Computational Linguistics, 25,* 628–30.

Hofstede, G., Hofstede, G. J., & Minkov, M. (2010). *Cultures and organizations: Software of the mind* (Revised and expanded 3rd Edition). McGraw-Hill: New-York.

Hornyak, T. (2023). Why Japan is building its own version of ChatGPT. *Nature.* https://doi.org/10.1038/d41586-023-02868-z

Hu, J., Ruder, S., Siddhant, A., Neubig, G., Firat, O., & Johnson, M. (2020). XTREME: A massively multilingual multi-task benchmark for evaluating cross-lingual generalization. https://arxiv.org/abs/2003.11080.

Hu, S., Liu, Z., Lin, Y., & Sun, M. (2023). Word representation learning. In Z. Liu, Y. Lin, & M. Sun (Eds.), *Representation learning for natural language processing.* Singapore: Springer. https://doi.org/10.1007/978-981-99-1600-9_2

Hutchins, J. (1999). Warren weaver memorandum: 50th anniversary of machine translation. *MT News International, 22*(5–6), 15. https://aclanthology.org/1999.eamt-1.18.pdf

Hutchins, W. J. (2004). The Georgetown-IBM experiment demonstrated in January 1954. In R. E. Frederking & K. B. Taylor (Eds.), *Machine translation: From real users to research* (pp. 102–14). Springer. https://doi.org/10.1007/978-3-540-30194-3_12

IBM. (2023, December 5). What is self-supervised learning? Retrieved April 20, 2024, from https://www.ibm.com/topics/self-supervised-learning

Ji, S., Li, Z., Paul, I., Paaovala, J., Lin, P., Chen, P., O'Brien, D., Lou, H., Schütze, H., Tiedemann, J., & Haddon, B. (2024). *EMMA-500: Enhancing massively multilingual adaptation of large language models.* https://arxiv.org/abs/2409.17892.

Jiang, F., Drummond, T., & Cohn, T. (2024). Pre-training cross-lingual open domain question answering with large-scale synthetic supervision. *Conference on Empirical Methods in Natural Language Processing.*

Jiao, W., Wang, W., Huang, J., Wang, X., & Tu, Z. (2023a). Is ChatGPT a good translator? A preliminary study. https://arxiv.org/abs/2301.08745.

Jiao, W., Wang, W., Huang, J., Wang, X., & Tu, Z. (2023b). Is ChatGPT a good translator? Yes with GPT-4 as the engine. https://arxiv.org/abs/2301.08745v4

Johnson, R. L., Pistilli, G., Men'edez-Gonz'alez, N., Duran, L. D., Panai, E., Kalpokienė, J., & Bertulfo, D. J. (2022). The ghost in the machine has an American accent: Value conflict in GPT-3. https://arxiv.org/abs/2203.07785.

Johnson, M., Schuster, M., Le, Q. V., Krikun, M., Wu, Y., Chen, Z., Thorat, N., Viégas, F. B., Wattenberg, M., Corrado, G. S., Hughes, M., & Dean, J. (2017). Google's multilingual neural machine translation system: Enabling zero-shot translation. *Transactions of the Association for Computational Linguistics, 5,* 339–51.

Joseph, J. E. (2023). Ferdinand de Saussure. *Oxford Bibliographies Online.* https://www.oxford-bibliographies.com/display/document/obo-9780199772810/obo-9780199772810-0003.

xml#:~:text=Ferdinand%20de%20Saussure%20(b.,for%20structuralism%20and%20 post%2Dstructuralism.

Joshi, P. M., Santy, S., Budhiraja, A., Bali, K., & Choudhury, M. (2020). The state and fate of linguistic diversity and inclusion in the NLP world. *Annual Meeting of the Association for Computational Linguistics.*

Jurafsky, D., & Martin, J. (2020). *Speech and language processing: An introduction to natural language processing, computational linguistics, and speech recognition* (3rd Edition Draft). https:// web.stanford.edu/~jurafsky/slp3/ed3book.pdf

Kaasa, A., & Minkov, M. (2020). Are the world's national cultures becoming more similar? *Journal of Cross-Cultural Psychology, 51,* 531–50.

Kaplan, J., McCandlish, S., Henighan, T., Brown, T. B., Chess, B., Child, R., Gray, S., Radford, A., Wu, J., & Amodei, D. (2020). Scaling laws for neural language models. https://arxiv.org/ abs/2001.08361.

Karimzadehgan, M., & Zhai, C. (2010). Estimation of statistical translation models based on mutual information for ad hoc information retrieval. *Proceedings of the 33rd International ACM SIGIR Conference on Research and Development in Information Retrieval* (pp. 323–30). Geneva, Switzerland. https://dblp.org/rec/conf/sigir/KarimzadehganZ10.html

Karpukhin, V., Oğuz, B., Min, S., Lewis, P., Wu, L. Y., Edunov, S., Chen, D., & Yih, W. (2020). Dense passage retrieval for open-domain question answering. https://arxiv.org/abs/2004.04906.

Katzir, R. (2023). Why large language models are poor theories of human linguistic cognition: A reply to Piantadosi. *Biolinguistics, 17,* 1–12.

Kiefer, A. B. (2019). A defense of pure connectionism. *CUNY Academic Works.* https://academic-works.cuny.edu/gc_etds/3036

Kilgarriff, A., Jakubıcek, M., Kovar, V., Rychly, P., & Suchomel, V. (2014). *Proceedings of the Demonstrations at the 14th Conference of the European Chapter of the Association for Computational Linguistics.*

Kim, B., Kim, H., Lee, S., Lee, G., Kwak, D., Jeon, D.H., Park, S., Kim, S., Kim, S., Seo, D.H., Lee, H., Jeong, M., Lee, S., Kim, M., Ko, S., Kim, S., Park, T., Kim, J., Kang, S., Ryu, N., Yoo, K., Chang, M., Suh, S., In, S., Park, J., Kim, K., Kim, H., Jeong, J., Yeo, Y.G., Ham, D., Park, D., Lee, M.Y., Kang, J., Kang, I., Ha, J., Park, W.C., & Sung, N. (2021). What Changes Can Large-scale Language Models Bring? Intensive Study on HyperCLOVA: Billions-scale Korean Generative Pretrained Transformers. *Conference on Empirical Methods in Natural Language Processing.*

Kirk, H. R., Whitefield, A., Rottger, P., Bean, A. M., Margatina, K., Ciro, J., Mosquera, R., Bartolo, M., Williams, A., He, H., Vidgen, B., & Hale, S. A. (2024). The PRISM alignment project: What participatory, representative and individualised human feedback reveals about the subjective and multicultural alignment of large language models. https://arxiv.org/abs/2404.16019.

Ko, H. A., Yang, K., Ryu, M., Choi, T., Yang, S., Hyun, J., Park, S., & Park, K. (2023). A technical report for Polyglot-Ko: Open-source large-scale Korean language models. https://arxiv.org/ abs/2306.02254.

Kocmi, T., & Federmann, C. (2023). Large language models are state-of-the-art evaluators of translation quality. *European Association for Machine Translation Conferences/Workshops.*

Koehn, P. (2005). Europarl: A parallel corpus for statistical machine translation. *Machine Translation Summit.*

Lai, V. D., Ngo, N. T., Veyseh, A. P., Man, H., Dernoncourt, F., Bui, T., & Nguyen, T. H. (2023). ChatGPT beyond English: Towards a comprehensive evaluation of large language models in multilingual learning. https://arxiv.org/abs/2304.05613.

Lake, B. M., Ullman, T. D., Tenenbaum, J. B., & Gershman, S. J. (2017). Building machines that learn and think like people. *Behavioral and Brain Sciences, 40,* 253. https://doi.org/10.1017/ S0140525X16001837

Lample, G., & Conneau, A. (2019). Cross-lingual language model pretraining. https://arxiv.org/ abs/1901.07291.

Langer, S. K. (1951). *Philosophy in a new key: A study in the symbolism of reason, rite and art.* New York: Mentor Books.

Läubli, S., Fishel, M., Volk, M., & Weibel, M. (2013). Combining statistical machine translation and translation memories with domain adaptation. *Nordic Conference of Computational Linguistics.*

Laurence, A. (n.d.). AntConc. *Laurence Anthony's Website.* www.laurenceanthony.net/software/antconc/

Le, H., Vial, L., Frej, J., Segonne, V., Coavoux, M., Lecouteux, B., Allauzen, A., Crabb'e, B., Besacier, L., & Schwab, D. (2019). FlauBERT: Unsupervised language model pre-training for French. https://arxiv.org/abs/1912.05372.

LeCun, Y., Bengio, Y., & Hinton, G. (2015). Deep learning. *Nature, 521,* 436–44. https://doi.org/10.1038/nature14539.

Lewis, D. D. (1992). *Representation and learning in information retrieval,* Ph. D thesis, University of Massachusetts.

Li, C., Chen, M., Wang, J., Sitaram, S., & Xie, X. (2024). CultureLLM: Incorporating cultural differences into large language models. https://arxiv.org/abs/2402.10946.

Li, Y., Du, M., Song, R., Wang, X., & Wang, Y. (2023). A survey on fairness in large language models. https://arxiv.org/abs/2308.10149.

Liddy, E. D. (2001). Natural language processing. *SURFACE at Syracuse University.* Retrieved June 27, 2022, from https://surface.syr.edu/istpub/63/

Litschko, R., Glavas, G., Ponzetto, S. P., & Vulic, I. (2018). Unsupervised cross-lingual information retrieval using monolingual data only. *41st International ACM SIGIR Conference on Research & Development in Information Retrieval.*

Liu, C. C., Gurevych, I., & Korhonen, A. (2024). Culturally aware and adapted NLP: A taxonomy and a survey of the state of the art. https://arxiv.org/abs/2406.03930.

Łoboda, K., & Mastela, O. (2023). Machine translation and culture-bound texts in translator education: A pilot study. *The Interpreter and Translator Trainer, 17,* 503–25.

Lobur, J. (2018). *Essentials of computer organization and architecture.* Burlington, MA: Jones & Bartlett Learning.

Long, D., & Magerko, B. (2020, April). What is AI literacy? Competencies and design considerations. *Proceedings of the 2020 CHI Conference on Human Factors in Computing Systems* (pp. 1–16).

Lu, S., Bigoulaeva, I., Sachdeva, R., Madabushi, H. T., & Gurevych, I. (2023). Are emergent abilities in large language models just in-context learning? https://arxiv.org/abs/2309.01809.

Luccioni, A. S., Viguier, S., & Ligozat, A. (2022). Estimating the Carbon footprint of BLOOM, a 176B parameter language model. *Journal of Machine Learning Research, 24,* 1–15.

Lucky, R. W. (1967). Information theory and modern digital communication. *New Methods of Thought and Procedure: Contributions to the Symposium on Methodologies* (pp. 163–99). Springer, Berlin, Heidelberg. https://doi.org/10.1007/978-3-642-87617-2_10

Lyons, J. (1995). *Linguistic semantics: An introduction.* Cambridge: Cambridge University Press.

Lyu, C., Xu, J., Wang, L., & Wu, M. (2023). A paradigm shift: The future of machine translation lies with large language models. *International Conference on Language Resources and Evaluation.*

Ma, S., Dong, L., Huang, S., Zhang, D., Muzio, A., Singhal, S., Awadalla, H. H., Song, X., & Wei, F. (2021). DeltaLM: Encoder-decoder pre-training for language generation and translation by augmenting pretrained multilingual encoders. https://arxiv.org/abs/2106.13736.

MacKay, D. J. C. (2003). *Information theory, inference and learning algorithms.* Cambridge: Cambridge University Press.

Macken, L., Lefever, E., & Hoste, V. (2013). Texsis: Bilingual terminology extraction from parallel corpora using chunk-based alignment. *Terminology, 19*(1), 1–30.

Magueresse, A., Carles, V., & Heetderks, E. (2020). Low-resource languages: A review of past work and future challenges. https://arxiv.org/abs/2006.07264.

Makhoul, J. (1975). Linear prediction: A tutorial review. *Proceedings of the IEEE, 63,* 561–80.

Malmasi, S., Fang, A., Fetahu, B., Kar, S., & Rokhlenko, O. (2022). MultiCoNER: A large-scale multilingual dataset for complex named entity recognition. *International Conference on Computational Linguistics.*

Manning, C. D., Raghavan, P. & Schütze, H. (2008). *Introduction to information retrieval.* Cambridge: Cambridge University Press.

Manolescu, D. A. (1998). Feature extraction: A pattern for information retrieval. *The 1998 Pattern Languages of Programs Conference.*

Markowsky, G. (2024, May 24). Information theory | definition, history, examples, & facts. *Britannica.* Retrieved June 24, 2024, from https://www.britannica.com/science/information-theory

Martin, L., Muller, B., Ortiz Suarez, P., Dupont, Y., Romary, L., Villemonte de la Clergerie, E., Seddah, D., & Sagot, B. (2019). CamemBERT: A tasty French language model. *Annual Meeting of the Association for Computational Linguistics.*

Martins, P. H., Fernandes, P., Alves, J., Guerreiro, N. M., Rei, R., Alves, D. M., Pombal, J. P., Farajian, A., Faysse, M., Klimaszewski, M., Colombo, P., Haddow, B., Souza, J. G., Birch, A., & Martins, A. (2024). EuroLLM: Multilingual language models for Europe. https://arxiv.org/abs/2409.16235

Maruyama, Y. (2020). Symbolic and statistical theories of cognition: Towards integrated artificial intelligence. *IEEE International Conference on Software Engineering and Formal Methods.*

Marx, E., Leonhardt, T., & Bergner, N. (2023). Secondary school students' mental models and attitudes regarding artificial intelligence - A scoping review. *Computers and Education: Artificial Intelligence,* 100169.

Marzoev, A., Madden, S., Kaashoek, M. F., Cafarella, M. J., & Andreas, J. (2020). Unnatural language processing: Bridging the gap between synthetic and natural language data. https://arxiv.org/abs/2004.13645.

Math Insight. (n.d.). An introduction to vectors. Retrieved July 29, 2024, from https://mathinsight.org/vector_introduction

McCarthy, J. (2007). *What Is Artificial Intelligence?* https://www-formal.stanford.edu/jmc/whatisai/

McCarthy, J., Minsky, M. L., Rochester, N., & Shannon, C. E. (1955). A proposal for the dartmouth summer research project on artificial intelligence, August 31, 1955. *AI Magazine, 27*(4), 12. https://doi.org/10.1609/aimag.v27i4.1904

Meyer, I., Bowker, L., & Eck, K. (1992). Cogniterm: An experiment in building a knowledge-based term bank. *Proceedings of Euralex* 1992 (pp. 159–72). University of Ottawa, Canada.

Miceli Barone, A. V. (2016). Towards cross-lingual distributed representations without parallel text trained with adversarial autoencoders. *Rep4NLP@ACL.*

Mielke, S. J., Alyafeai, Z., Salesky, E., Raffel, C., Dey, M., Gallé, M., Raja, A., Si, C., Lee, W. Y., Sagot, B., & Tan, S. (2021). Between words and characters: A brief history of open-vocabulary modeling and Tokenization in NLP. https://arxiv.org/abs/2112.10508.

Mikolov, T., Chen, K., Corrado, G., & Dean, J. (2013a). Efficient estimation of word representations in vector space. https://arxiv.org/pdf/1301.3781.pdf

Mikolov, T., Yih, W., & Zweig, G. (2013b). Linguistic regularities in continuous space word representations. *Proceedings of the 2013 Conference of the North American Chapter of the Association for Computational Linguistics: Human Language Technologies* (pp. 746–51). Association for Computational Linguistics. https://aclanthology.org/N13-1090

Mikolov, T., Le, Q. V., & Sutskever, I. (2013c). Exploiting similarities among languages for machine translation. https://arxiv.org/abs/1309.4168.

Miller, George A. (1995). WordNet: A lexical database for English. *Communications ACM, 38,* 11. https://doi.org/10.1145/219717.219748

Minkov, M., & Hofstede, G. J. (2011). The evolution of Hofstede's doctrine. *Cross Cultural Management: An International Journal, 18,* 10–20.

Minkov, M., & Kaasa, A. (2021). A test of Hofstede's model of culture following his own approach. *Cross Cultural & Strategic Management, 28*(2), 384–406.

Minsky, M. L., & Papert, S. (1969). *Perceptrons.* Cambridge, MA: MIT Press.

Mitchell, M., & Krakauer, D. C. (2022). The debate over understanding in AI's large language models. *Proceedings of the National Academy of Sciences of the United States of America,* 120.

Morato, J., Marzal, M., Llorens, J., & Moreiro, J. (2004). WordNet applications. *Proceedings of the 2nd Global Wordnet Conference.* https://www.fi.muni.cz/gwc2004/proc/105.pdf

Moslem, Y., Haque, R., & Way, A. (2023). Adaptive machine translation with large language models. https://arxiv.org/abs/2301.13294.

Mozer, M. C. (2013). A focused backpropagation algorithm for temporal pattern recognition. *Backpropagation (eBook edition)* (pp. 137–69). Psychology Press.

Mueller, J. P., & Massaron, L. (2019). *Deep learning for dummies.* Hoboken, NJ: John Wiley & Sons.

MultiCoNER 2. (n.d.). Kaggle. Retrieved August 28, 2024, from https://www.kaggle.com/datasets/cryptexcode/multiconer-2/data

Murphy, K. P. (2012). *Machine learning: A probabilistic perspective.* Cambridge, MA: MIT Press.

Myung, J., Lee, N., Zhou, Y., Jin, J., Putri, R. A., Antypas, D., Borkakoty, H., Kim, E., Pérez-Almendros, C., Ayele, A. A., Guti'errez-Basulto, V., Ib'anez-Garc'ia, Y., Lee, H., Muhammad, S. H., Park, K., Rzayev, A., White, N., Yimam, S. M., Pilehvar, M. T., ... Oh, A. (2024). BLEnD: A benchmark for LLMs on everyday knowledge in diverse cultures and languages. https://arxiv.org/abs/2406.09948.

Nangia, N., & Bowman, S. R. (2019). Human vs. Muppet: A conservative estimate of human performance on the GLUE benchmark. https://arxiv.org/abs/1905.10425.

Naous, T., Ryan, M. J., & Xu, W. (2023). Having beer after prayer? Measuring cultural bias in large language models. https://arxiv.org/abs/2305.14456.

Neilson, L. (2019). Linguistic isolation: Ferdinand de Saussure's linguistic theory and the implications for historiography. *Armstrong Undergraduate Journal of History, 9*(1), Article 7. https://doi.10.20429/aujh.2019.090107 https://digitalcommons.georgiasouthern.edu/aujh/vol9/iss1/7

Nilson, N. (2009). *The quest for artificial intelligence.* Cambridge University Press. https://doi.org/10.1017/CBO9780511819346.001

NLTK. (n.d.). NLTK data. https://www.nltk.org/nltk_data/. Retrieved March 24, 2024, from https://www.nltk.org/nltk_data/

Norman, J. M. (n.d.). Warren weaver suggests applying cryptanalysis techniques to translation: History of information. https://www.historyofinformation.com/detail.php?id=2990 (accessed December 28, 2024).

OECD. AI (2024). Database of national AI policies. https://oecd.ai/dashboards.

Öner Bulut, S., & Alimen, N. (2023). Translator education as a collaborative quest for insights into the re-positioning of the human translator (educator) in the age of machine translation: The results of a learning experiment. *The Interpreter and Translator Trainer, 17,* 375–92.

Opitz, J., Wein, S., & Schneider, N. (2024). Natural language processing RELIES on linguistics. https://arxiv.org/abs/2405.05966.

Oracle. (2020, November 24). What is a database? Retrieved August 21, 2024, from https://www.oracle.com/ca-en/database/what-is-database/#relational

Osgood, C. E., Suci, G. J., & Tannenbaum, P. H. (1957). *The measurement of meaning.* Chicago: University of Illinois Press.

Ouyang, L., Wu, J., Jiang, X., Almeida, D., Wainwright, C. L., Mishkin, P., Zhang, C., Agarwal, S., Slama, K., Ray, A., Schulman, J., Hilton, J., Kelton, F., Miller, L. E., Simens, M., Askell, A., Welinder, P., Christiano, P. F., Leike, J., & Lowe, R. J. (2022). Training language models to follow instructions with human feedback. https://arxiv.org/abs/2203.02155

Papadimitriou, I., Lopez, K., & Jurafsky, D. (2022). Multilingual BERT has an accent: Evaluating English influences on fluency in multilingual models. https://arxiv.org/abs/2210.05619.

Papineni, K., Roukos, S., Ward, T., & Zhu, W. (2002). Bleu: A method for automatic evaluation of machine translation. *Annual Meeting of the Association for Computational Linguistics.*

Park, S., Moon, J., Kim, S., Cho, W., Han, J., Park, J., Song, C., Kim, J., Song, Y., Oh, T., Lee, J., Oh, J., Lyu, S., Jeong, Y., Lee, I. V., Seo, S., Lee, D., Kim, H., Lee, M., ... Cho, K. (2021). KLUE: Korean language understanding evaluation. https://arxiv.org/abs/2105.09680.

Peirce, C. S. (1931–1958). *Collected Papers (8 volumes).* Cambridge, MA: Harvard University Press.

Peng, K., Ding, L., Zhong, Q., Shen, L., Liu, X., Zhang, M., Ouyang, Y., & Tao, D. (2023). Towards making the most of ChatGPT for machine translation. *Conference on Empirical Methods in Natural Language Processing.*

Peters, M. E., Neumann, M., Iyyer, M., Gardner, M., Clark, C., Lee, K., & Zettlemoyer, L. (2018). Deep contextualized word representations. https://arxiv.org/abs/1802.05365.

Phuong, M., & Hutter, M. (2022). Formal algorithms for transformers. https://arxiv.org/abs/2207.09238.

Piantadosi, S. (2023). Modern language models refute Chomsky's approach to language. Lingbuzz Preprint, 7180.

Pieterse, J. N. (2003). *Globalization and culture: Global melange.* Lanham, MD: Rowman & Littlefield.

Piqueras, L. C., & Søgaard, A. (2022). Are pretrained multilingual models equally fair across languages? https://arxiv.org/abs/2210.05457.

Pires, T., Schlinger, E., & Garrette, D. (2019). How multilingual is multilingual BERT? https://arxiv.org/abs/1906.01502.

Poibeau, T. (2022). On "Human Parity" and "Super Human Performance" in machine translation evaluation. *International Conference on Language Resources and Evaluation*, Marseille, France.

Princeton. (n.d.). 2.1 wnstats(7WN) | WordNet. *WordNet.* Retrieved March 23, 2024, from https://wordnet.princeton.edu/documentation/21-wnstats7wn

Princeton. (n.d.). WordNet. Retrieved March 23, 2024, from https://wordnet.princeton.edu/

Prud'hommeaux, Eric, & Seaborne, Andy (2008, 15 January). SPARQL query language for RDF. World Wide Web Consortium.

Pustejovsky, J., & Stubbs, A. (2012). *Natural language annotation for machine learning.* Sebastopol, CA.

Qiu, Z., Ou, Z., Wu, B., Li, J., Liu, A., & King, I. (2024). Entropy-based decoding for retrieval-augmented large language models. https://arxiv.org/abs/2406.17519.

Radford, A., Narasimhan, K., Salimans, T., & Sutskever, I. (2018). Improving language understanding with unsupervised learning. Technical report, *OpenAI.*

Radford, A., Wu, J., Child, R., Luan, D., Amodei, D., & Sutskever, I. (2019). Language models are unsupervised multitask learners.

Rahman, C. M., Sohel, F., Naushad, P., & Kamruzzaman, S. M. (2010). Text classification using the concept of association rule of data mining. https://arxiv.org/abs/1009.4582.

Ralph, M. A. (1998). Distributed versus localist representations: evidence from a study of item consistency in a case of classical anomia. *Brain Lang, 64*(3), 339–60. https://doi.org/10.1006/brln.1998.1976. PMID: 9743547.

Rao, A., Yerukola, A., Shah, V., Reinecke, K., & Sap, M. (2024). NORMAD: A benchmark for measuring the cultural adaptability of large language models. https://arxiv.org/abs/2404.12464.

RapidMiner. (n.d.). RapidMiner documentation. Retrieved March 15, 2024, from https://docs.rapidminer.com/

Rei, R., Stewart, C. A., Farinha, A. C., & Lavie, A. (2020). COMET: A neural framework for MT evaluation. https://arxiv.org/abs/2009.09025.

Riezler, S., & Liu, Y. (2010). Query rewriting using monolingual statistical machine translation. *Computational Linguistics, 36,* 569–82.

Roberts, Siobhan (2016, April 30). The forgotten father of the information age. *The New Yorker.* Retrieved September 28, 2023.

Rodríguez-Cantelar, M., Estecha-Garitagoitia, M., D'Haro, L. F., Matía, F., & Córdoba, R. D. (2023). Automatic detection of inconsistencies and hierarchical topic classification for open-domain Chatbots. *Applied Sciences, 31,* 9095.

Rogers, A., Kovaleva, O., & Rumshisky, A. (2020). A primer in BERTology: What we know about how BERT works. *Transactions of the Association for Computational Linguistics, 8,* 842–66.

Rosenblatt, F. (1958). The perceptron: A probabilistic model for information storage and organization in the brain. *Psychological Review, 65,* 386–408.

Rumelhart, D. E., Hinton, G. E., & Williams, R. J. (1986). Learning representations by back-propagating errors. *Nature, 323,* 533–6.

Ruthrof, H. (2010). Linguistic arbitrariness and the 'Nebulous' world of Vorstellung in Saussure. Retrieved March 23, 2024, from https://core.ac.uk/download/pdf/11243213.pdf

Ryder, A. G., Alden, L. E., & Paulhus, D. L. (2000). Is acculturation unidimensional or bidimensional? A head-to-head comparison in the prediction of personality, self-identity, and adjustment. *Journal of Personality and Social Psychology, 79*(1), 49–65.

Sahlgren, M. (2006). The word-space model: Using distributional analysis to represent syntagmatic and paradigmatic relations between words in high-dimensional vector spaces (Doctoral dissertation, Institutionen för lingvistik). Retrieved from https://urn.kb.se/resolve?urn=urn:nbn:se:su:diva-1037

Salo-Pöntinen, H., & Saariluoma, P. (2022). Reflections on the human role in AI policy formulations: How do national AI strategies view people? *Discover Artificial Intelligence, 2.*

Salton, G., & Buckley, C. (1988). Term-weighting approaches in automatic text retrieval. *Information Processing and Management, 24,* 513–23.

Saphra, N., Fleisig, E., Cho, K., & Lopez, A. (2023). First tragedy, then parse: History repeats itself in the new era of large language models. https://arxiv.org/abs/2311.05020.

Satapathy, R., Cambria, E., & Hussain, A. (2017). *Sentiment analysis in the bio-medical* domain*: Techniques, tools, and applications.* Cham: Springer.

Scao, T. L., Fan, A., Akiki, C., Pavlick, E., Ili'c, S., Hesslow, D., Castagn'e, R., Luccioni, A. S., Yvon, F., Gallé, M., Tow, J., Rush, A. M., Biderman, S., Webson, A., Ammanamanchi, P. S., Wang, T., Sagot, B., Muennighoff, N., del Moral, A. V., … Wolf, T. (2022). BLOOM: A 176B-parameter open-access multilingual language model. https://arxiv.org/abs/2211.05100.

Scarton, C., Paetzold, G., & Specia, L. (2016). Quality estimation for language output applications. *Proceedings of COLING 2016, the 26th International Conference on Computational Linguistics: Tutorial Abstracts.*

Schank, R. C. (1972). Conceptual dependency: A theory of natural language understanding. *Cognitive Psychology, 3*(4), 532–631.

Schank, R. C., & Tesler, L. G. (1969). A conceptual parser for natural language. *International Joint Conference on Artificial Intelligence.*

Schmidhuber, J. (2015). Deep learning in neural networks: An overview. *Neural Networks, 61,* 85–117. https://doi.org/10.1016/j.neunet.2014.09.003

Schmidt, S., & Leoncio, P. (2023, July 12). What is a semantic knowledge graph? *metaphacts Blog.* Retrieved September 15, 2024, from https://blog.metaphacts.com/importance-of-semantic-knowledge-graph

Schmidt, T., & Wörner, K. (Eds.). (2012). *Multilingual corpora and multilingual corpus analysis* (Vol. 14). Amsterdam/Philadelphia: John Benjamins Publishing.

Schütze, H. (1992). Word space. *Neural Information Processing Systems.*

Searle, J. (1980). Minds, brains and programs. *The Behavioral and Brain Sciences, 3,* 417–57.

Sebastian-Coleman, L. (2013). *Measuring data quality for ongoing improvement: A data quality assessment framework.* Burlington, MA: Morgan Kaufmann.

Seelawi, H., Tuffaha, I., Gzawi, M., Farhan, W., Talafha, B., Badawi, R., Sober, Z., Al-Dweik, O., Freihat, A. A., & Al-Natsheh, H. T. (2021). ALUE: Arabic language understanding evaluation. In *Workshop on Arabic Natural Language Processing.*

Sennrich, R., & Volk, M. (2010). MT-based sentence alignment for OCR-generated parallel texts. *The Ninth Conference of the Association for Machine Translation in the Americas (AMTA 2010),* Denver, 31 October 2010–4 November 2010.

Shannon, C. E. (1948). A mathematical theory of communication. *Bell System Technical Journal, 27,* 379–423.

Shannon, C. E., & Weaver, W. W. (1963). *The mathematical theory of communications.* Urbana: University of Illinois Press.

Shavrina, T., Fenogenova, A., Emelyanov, A. A., Shevelev, D., Artemova, E., Malykh, V., Mikhailov, V., Tikhonova, M., Chertok, A., & Evlampiev, A. (2020). RussianSuperGLUE: A Russian language understanding evaluation benchmark. *Conference on Empirical Methods in Natural Language Processing.*

Shi, W., Li, R., Zhang, Y., Ziems, C., Yu, C., Horesh, R., Paula, R. A., & Yang, D. (2024). CultureBank: An online community-driven knowledge base towards culturally aware language technologies. *Conference on Empirical Methods in Natural Language Processing.*

Si, C., Zhang, Z., Chen, Y., Qi, F., Wang, X., Liu, Z., Wang, Y., Liu, Q., & Sun, M. (2023). Sub-character tokenization for Chinese pretrained language models. *Transactions of the Association for Computational Linguistics,* 11, 469–87. https://doi.org/10.1162/tacl_a_00560

Simon, H. A. (1995). Artificial intelligence: An empirical science. *Artificial Intelligence,* 77(1), 95–127.

Singh, S., Vargus, F., Dsouza, D., Karlsson, B. F., Mahendiran, A., Ko, W., Shandilya, H., Patel, J., Mataciunas, D., OMahony, L., Zhang, M., Hettiarachchi, R., Wilson, J., Machado, M., Moura, L. S., Krzemi'nski, D., Fadaei, H., Ergun, I., Okoh, I., ... Hooker, S. (2024). Aya dataset: An open-access collection for multilingual instruction tuning. https://arxiv.org/abs/2402.06619.

Sitaram, Sunayana, Choudhury, Monojit, Patra, Barun, Chaudhary, Vishrav, Ahuja, Kabir, & Bali, Kalika. (2023). Everything you need to know about Multilingual LLMs: Towards fair, performant and reliable models for languages of the world. *Proceedings of the 61st Annual Meeting of the Association for Computational Linguistics.*

Skadiņš, R., Tiedemann, J., Rozis, R., & Deksne, D. (2014). Billions of parallel words for free: Building and using the EU bookshop corpus. *Proceedings of the Ninth International Conference on Language Resources and Evaluation* (LREC'14).

Søgaard, A. (2022). Should we ban English NLP for a year? *Conference on Empirical Methods in Natural Language Processing.*

Son, G., Lee, H. A., Kim, S., Lee, J., Yeom, J. W., Jung, J., Kim, J. W., & Kim, S. (2023). HAE-RAE bench: Evaluation of Korean knowledge in language models. *International Conference on Language Resources and Evaluation.*

Sowa, J. F. (2000). *Knowledge Representation: Logical, Philosophical, and Computational Foundations.* Boston, MA: Brooks Cole.

Srivastava, A., Rastogi, A., Rao, A., Shoeb, A., Abid, A., Fisch, A., Brown, A. R., Santoro, A., Gupta, A., Garriga-Alonso, A., Kluska, A., Lewkowycz, A., Agarwal, A., Power, A., Ray, A., Warstadt, A., Kocurek, A. W., Safaya, A., Tazarv, A., ... Wu, Z. (2022). Beyond the imitation game: Quantifying and extrapolating the capabilities of language models. https://arxiv.org/abs/2206.04615.

Staar, P. W., Dolfi, M., & Auer, C. (2020). Corpus processing service: A knowledge graph platform to perform deep data exploration on corpora.

Stańczak, K., Ponti, E., Torroba Hennigen, L., Cotterell, R., & Augenstein, I. (2022). Same neurons, different languages: Probing morphosyntax in multilingual pre-trained models. *North American Chapter of the Association for Computational Linguistics.*

Stanford NLP Group. (n.d.). Dropping common terms: Stop words. Retrieved March 23, 2024, from https://nlp.stanford.edu/IR-book/html/htmledition/dropping-common-terms-stop-words-1.html

Statistics Canada. (2021, October 22). Data journey. Retrieved March 3, 2024, from https://www.statcan.gc.ca/en/wtc/data-literacy/journey

Studer, S., Bui, T. B., Drescher, C., Hanuschkin, A., Winkler, L., Peters, S., & Müller, K.-R. (2021). Towards CRISP-ML(Q): A machine learning process model with quality assurance methodology. *Machine Learning and Knowledge Extraction,* 3(2), 392–413. https://doi.org/10.3390/make3020020.

Sutcliffe, R. F. (1991). Distributed subsymbolic representations for natural language: How many features do you need? *AI and Cognitive Science'90: University of Ulster at Jordanstown*, 20–21 September 1990, 279. https://doi.org/10.1007/978-1-4471-3542-5_19

Sutton, R. (2019). The bitter lesson. *Incomplete Ideas (blog)*, *13*(1), 38.

Sutton, R. S., & Barto, A. G. (2014). Reinforcement learning: An introduction. Retrieved April 21, 2024, from https://web.stanford.edu/class/psych209/Readings/SuttonBartoIPRL-Book2ndEd.pdf

Synced. (2019a, February 22). Yann LeCun cake analogy 2.0. *Medium*. Retrieved May 18, 2024, from https://medium.com/syncedreview/yann-lecun-cake-analogy-2-0-a361da560dae

Synced. (2019b). *Yann LeCun Cake Analogy 2.0*. Retrieved April 21, 2024, from https://syncedreview.com/2019/02/22/yann-lecun-cake-analogy-2-0/

SYNTHETIC | English meaning - Cambridge Dictionary. (n.d.). Retrieved March 29, 2024, from https://dictionary.cambridge.org/dictionary/english/synthetic#google_vignette

Tao, Y., Viberg, O., Baker, R. S., & Kizilcec, R. F. (2023). Auditing and mitigating cultural bias in LLMs. https://arxiv.org/abs/2311.14096.

Tars, M., Purason, T., & Tättar, A. (2022). Teaching unseen low-resource languages to large translation models. *Conference on Machine Translation*.

The difference between adaptive ML and traditional ML. (2021, January 28). Retrieved March 9, 2024, from https://pandio.com/the-difference-between-adaptive-ml-and-traditional-ml/

Tiedemann, J. (2009). News from OPUS-A collection of multilingual parallel Corpora with tools and interfaces. *Recent Advances in Natural Language Processing* (pp. 237–48).

Touileb, S., & Nozza, D. (2022). Measuring harmful representations in scandinavian language models. https://arxiv.org/abs/2211.11678.

Touileb, S., Øvrelid, L., & Velldal, E. (2022). Occupational biases in Norwegian and multilingual language models. *Proceedings of the 4th Workshop on Gender Bias in Natural Language Processing (GeBNLP)*.

Translation Automation User Society/ TAUS (2024). *Annual Meeting*. https://www.taus.net/events/massively-multilingual-conference-albuquerque-2024

United Nations. (n.d.). Official document system. *Official Document System - Search*. Retrieved August 24, 2024, from https://documents.un.org/

Ustun, A., Aryabumi, V., Yong, Z., Ko, W., D'souza, D., Onilude, G., Bhandari, N., Singh, S., Ooi, H., Kayid, A., Vargus, F., Blunsom, P., Longpre, S., Muennighoff, N., Fadaee, M., Kreutzer, J., & Hooker, S. (2024). Aya model: An instruction finetuned open-access multilingual language model. https://arxiv.org/abs/2402.07827.

Vashee,K.(2023a).https://kv-emptypages.blogspot.com/2023/12/the-english-centric-bias-of-large.html

Vashee, K. (2023b). https://www.linkedin.com/feed/update/urn:li:activity:7139308081225633792

Vashee, K. (2024a). Comparing MT system performance. *ModernMT Blog*, 3 April 2024, blog. modernmt.com/comparing-mt-system-performance/.

Vashee, K. (2024b). The path to LLM-based machine translation. https://imminent.translated.com/llm-based-machine-translation

Vashee, K. (2024c). Personal communication.

Vashee, K. (2024d). The path to LLM-based machine translation. *Translated (Language Services Company)*. https://translated.com/LLM-for-translation-vs-neural-MT

Vaswani, A., Shazeer, N., Parmar, N., Uszkoreit, J., Jones, L., Gomez, A. N., Kaiser, Ł., & Polosukhin, I. (2017). Attention is all you need. https://arxiv.org/abs/1706.03762

Vauquois, B. (1968). A survey of formal grammars and algorithms for recognition and transformation in machine translation. *IFIP Congress-68 (No. 254-260)*.

Vechtomova, O. (2009). Query expansion for information retrieval. In Liu, L. & Özsu, M. T. (Eds.), *Encyclopedia of database systems*. Boston, MA: Springer. https://doi.org/10.1007/978-0-387-39940-9_947

Vector space–definition, axioms, properties and examples. (n.d.). Retrieved July 29, 2024, from https://byjus.com/maths/vector-space/

Velleman, P. F., & Wilkinson, L. (1993). Nominal, ordinal, interval, and ratio typologies are misleading. *The American Statistician, 47*(1), 65–72. https://doi.org/10.2307/2684788

Veres, C. (2021). Large language models are not models of natural language: They are Corpus models. *IEEE Access, 10*, 61970-61979.

Verhulst, F. (2012, September 3). Mathematics is the art of giving the same name to different things. Retrieved December 25, 2023, from https://www.nieuwarchief.nl/serie5/pdf/naw5-2012-13-3-154.pdf

Vidhyalakshmi, A. & Priya, C. (2020). Medical big data mining and processing in e-health care. In Emilia Balas, V., Solanki, V. K., & Kumar, R. (Eds.), *An industrial IoT approach for pharmaceutical industry growth: Volume 2* (pp. 1–30). Elsevier Science.

Vossen, P. (1998). Introduction to EuroWordNet. *Computers and the Humanities, 32*(2–3), 73–89.

Vries, W. D., van Cranenburgh, A., Bisazza, A., Caselli, T., Noord, G. V., & Nissim, M. (2019). BERTje: A Dutch BERT model. https://arxiv.org/abs/1912.09582.

Vuli´c, I. & Moens, M. F. (2015). Monolingual and cross-lingual information retrieval models based on (bilingual) word embeddings. *Proceedings of the 38th International ACM SIGIR Conference on Research and Development in Information Retrieval.*

Wang, P. (2019). A relevancy approach to cultural competence in translation curricula. In D. B. Sawyer, F. Austermühl, & V. E. Raído (Eds.), *The evolving curriculum in interpreter and translator education: Stakeholder perspectives and voices* (pp. 271–99). Amsterdam/Philadelphia: John Benjamins.

Wang, P. (2024, March 5). Interfacing with machine intelligence. Retrieved April 2024, from https://www.localizationinstitute.com/interfacing-with-machine-intelligence/

Wang, P., & Sawyer, D. B. (2023). *Machine Learning in Translation.* London, UK.

Wang, A., Pruksachatkun, Y., Nangia, N., Singh, A., Michael, J., Hill, F., Levy, O., & Bowman, S. R. (2019). SuperGLUE: A stickier benchmark for general-purpose language understanding systems. https://arxiv.org/abs/1905.00537.

Wang, A., Singh, A., Michael, J., Hill, F., Levy, O., & Bowman, S. R. (2018). GLUE: A multi-task benchmark and analysis platform for natural language understanding. *BlackboxNLP@EMNLP.*

Wang, X., Tsvetkov, Y., & Neubig, G. (2020). Balancing training for multilingual neural machine translation. https://arxiv.org/abs/2004.06748.

Weaver, W. W. (1949). Recent contributions to the mathematical theory of communication. In *The mathematical theory of communications* (pp. 1–28). https://courses.ischool.berkeley.edu/i218/s15/Weaver_Recent-Contributions.pdf

Weber, A. A., Thellmann, K., Ebert, J., Flores-Herr, N., Lehmann, J., Fromm, M., & Ali, M. (2024). Investigating multilingual instruction-tuning: Do Polyglot models demand for multilingual instructions? https://arxiv.org/abs/2402.13703.

Wendler, C., Veselovsky, V., Monea, G., & West, R. (2024). Do Llamas work in English? On the latent language of multilingual transformers. https://arxiv.org/abs/2402.10588.

Werner, C. (2015, January 1). Fire service technology. *Firehouse Magazine.* Retrieved March 8, 2024, from https://www.firehouse.com/tech-comm/cad-dispatch-systems/article/12024459/fire-service-technology

What is exploratory data analysis? (n.d.). *IBM.* Retrieved March 8, 2024, from https://www.ibm.com/topics/exploratory-data-analysis

What is feature extraction? Feature extraction techniques explained. (n.d.). *Domino Data Lab.* Retrieved March 12, 2024, from https://domino.ai/data-science-dictionary/feature-extraction

What is vector search? (2024, June 6). *IBM.* Retrieved August 24, 2024, from https://www.ibm.com/topics/vector-search

Wille, R. (1997). Conceptual graphs and formal concept analysis. *Proceedings of the Fifth International Conference on Conceptual Structures: Fulfilling Peirce's Dream* (pp. 290–303). Springer-Verlag, London.

Wooten, A. (2024). The vibrant and ever-changing landscape and possibilities for linguists in today's evolving language service careers. *Chartered Institute of Linguists Online Conference 2024*. https://www.youtube.com/watch?v=nGY2WMtHmXg

World Values Survey Association. (2024). WVS Database. www.worldvaluessurvey.org. https://www.worldvaluessurvey.org/wvs.jsp

Wu, S., & Dredze, M. (2020). Are all languages created equal in multilingual BERT? *Workshop on Representation Learning for NLP*.

Wu, Y., Schuster, M., Chen, Z., Le, Q. V., Norouzi, M., Macherey, W., Krikun, M., Cao, Y., Gao, Q., Macherey, K., Klingner, J., Shah, A., Johnson, M., Liu, X., Kaiser, L., Gouws, S., Kato, Y., Kudo, T., Kazawa, H., ... Dean, J. (2016). Google's neural machine translation system: Bridging the gap between human and machine translation. https://arxiv.org/abs/1609.08144.

Xiao, K. & Li, W. (2023). In the eye of the beholder: A sentiment analysis approach to readers' reception of translated metaphors in *Fortress Besieged*. In I. Lacruz (Ed.). *Translation in transition: Human and machine intelligence* (pp. 104–29). John Benjamins, Amsterdam, Netherlands.

Xu, Y., Hu, L., Zhao, J., Qiu, Z., Ye, Y., & Gu, H. (2024). A survey on multilingual large language models: Corpora, alignment, and bias. https://arxiv.org/abs/2404.00929.

Xu, L., Zhang, X., Li, L., Hu, H., Cao, C., Liu, W., Li, J., Li, Y., Sun, K., Xu, Y., Cui, Y., Yu, C., Dong, Q., Tian, Y., Yu, D., Shi, B., Zeng, J., Wang, R., Xie, W., ... Lan, Z. (2020). CLUE: A Chinese language understanding evaluation benchmark. *International Conference on Computational Linguistics*.

Yagnik, N., Jhaveri, J., Sharma, V., Pila, G., Ben, A., & Shang, J. (2024). MedLM: Exploring language models for medical question answering systems. https://arxiv.org/abs/2401.11389.

Yan, J., Yan, P., Chen, Y., Li, J., Zhu, X., & Zhang, Y. (2024). GPT-4 vs. human translators: A comprehensive evaluation of translation quality across languages, domains, and expertise levels. https://arxiv.org/abs/2407.03658.

Yang, E., Lawrie, D. J., & Mayfield, J. (2024). Distillation for multilingual information retrieval. https://arxiv.org/abs/2405.00977.

Yao, B., Jiang, M., Yang, D., & Hu, J. (2023). Benchmarking machine translation with cultural awareness. *Conference on Empirical Methods in Natural Language Processing*.

Yee, K., Dauphin, Y. N., & Auli, M. (2019). Simple and effective noisy channel modeling for neural machine translation. *Proceedings of the 2019 Conference on Empirical Methods in Natural Language Processing and the 9th International Joint Conference on Natural Language Processing*.

Yoo, K., Han, J., In, S., Jeon, H., Jeong, J., Kang, J., Kim, H., Kim, K., Kim, M., Kim, S., Kwak, D., Kwak, H., Kwon, S. J., Lee, B., Lee, D., Lee, G., Lee, J., Park, B., Shin, S., ... Sung, N. (2024). HyperCLOVA X technical report. https://arxiv.org/abs/2404.01954.

Yu, F., Peng, T., Peng, K., Tang, S. Y., Chen, C. S., Qian, X., Sun, P., Han, T., & Chai, F. (2016). Cultural value shifting in pronoun use. *Journal of Cross-Cultural Psychology, 47*, 310–16.

Zanettin, F. (2013). Corpus methods for descriptive translation studies. *Procedia – Social and Behavioral Sciences, 95*, 20–32. https://doi.org/10.1016/j.sbspro.2013.10.618

Zhang, M., Liu, Y., Luan, H., & Sun, M. (2017). Adversarial training for unsupervised bilingual lexicon induction. *Proceedings of the 55th Annual Meeting of the Association for Computational Linguistics*.

Zhao, H., Liu, Y., Tao, S., Meng, W., Chen, Y., Geng, X., Su, C., Zhang, M., & Yang, H. (2024). From handcrafted features to LLMs: A brief survey for machine translation quality estimation. https://arxiv.org/abs/2403.14118.

Zhu, H. (2014). Intercultural communication. In *The Routledge handbook of applied linguistics* (pp. 81–93).

Žižka, J., Dařena, F., & Svoboda, A. (2019). *Text mining with machine learning: Principles and techniques*. Boca Raton, FL: CRC Press.

INDEX

Note: **Bold** page numbers refer to tables; *italic* page numbers refer to figures and page numbers followed by "n" denote endnotes.